Taking Your
MEDICINE

Taking Your MEDICINE

*Drug Regulation
in the United States*

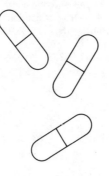

PETER TEMIN

HARVARD UNIVERSITY PRESS
Cambridge, Massachusetts, and London, England
1980

Library of Congress Cataloging in Publication Data

Temin, Peter.
    Taking your medicine.

    Bibliography: p.
    Includes index.
    1. Drugs—Law and legislation—United States.
2. Drugs—Law and legislation—Economic aspects—
United States.   3.   Drug trade—United States.
I. Title. [DNLM: 1. Drug industry—Economics—
United States.   2.   Drug industry—History—United
States.   3.   Drug and narcotic control—History—
United States.   4.   Drug utilization.
5. Legislation, Drug—History—United States.
QV11 AA1 T2t]
KF3885.T45   344.73′04233   80-16680
ISBN   0-674-86725-4

For Charlotte

ACKNOWLEDGMENTS

It is a great pleasure to acknowledge the various kinds of help I have received in the preparation of this book. The research was begun during a year's fellowship from the Charles Warren Center for the Study of American History at Harvard University. It was continued under a grant from the Sloan Foundation to the Economics Department at the Massachusetts Institute of Technology on the public control of economic activity. This grant also supported a seminar during which I had the opportunity to try out many of the ideas presented here and to get the reactions of both students and colleagues. My colleagues in this grant, Paul Joskow, Michael Piore, and William Wheaton, have been particularly helpful to me.

In the pages that follow, my discoveries and insights are mingled with those of other people who have heard or read various parts of the argument and shared their reactions with me. In addition to the MIT graduate students who have commented on various drafts and talks presented to the MIT Economics Department Sloan Seminar, the following people have read and commented on part or all of the manuscript: Douglas Cocks, Paul David, Peter Diamond, Jeffrey Harris, Peter Barton Hutt, Joseph Inglefinger, Paul Joskow, Louis Lasagna, Richard Merrill, Michael Piore, Richard Schmalensee, Robert Schwartz, Paul Starr, Steven Wiggins, and Joel Yellin. I am grateful to all of them for their cogent advice.

Research assistance was provided by Peter Berck, Steven Cecchetti, Michael Dreese, and Steven Epstein; secretarial assistance extraordinaire, by Maureen Ryan; and editorial assistance, by Harvard University Press's able Aida Donald. To all of them: thank you.

IMS, America, Ltd., kindly allowed me to use some of their copyrighted market data, which appear in tables 12–17 and 23. Also, the following organization and journals have allowed me to reproduce material published in their pages: American Enterprise Institute, *Bell Journal of Economics, Journal of Economic Behavior and Organization,* and *Journal of Law and Economics.*

Contents

TABLES

Taking Your
MEDICINE

ONE

Introduction

TAKING MEDICINAL DRUGS is a risky business. Even though medicines have become increasingly efficacious, there is always a chance that any given drug will fail to cure a condition or will induce an adverse reaction. As the chief justice of the California Supreme Court put it, "Ill health offers adventure; no one has a better chance to live dangerously than the ill who must take their medicine."[1]

Public policy toward medicinal drugs can be seen as an effort to minimize the extent of "living dangerously." In the baseball-oriented words of David Cavers, an author of the 1938 Federal Food, Drug, and Cosmetic Act: "Lives are at stake and . . . we are entitled to ask for something pretty close to errorless ball."[2] The analogy is unfortunate: the implicit assumptions that the risks from taking drugs come from human failings and that they can be eliminated entirely are both false. Reliance on these assumptions has distorted many observers' views of drug policy.

The Purposes of Drug Policy

In pursuit of "errorless ball," government policy toward medicinal drugs has progressively removed control over drug choices further and further from the consumer. In 1938 the federal Food and Drug Administration (FDA) extended its new legislative mandate to create a distinction between prescription and over-the-counter drugs. This regulation shaped the way an entirely new drug technology was introduced after World War

1

II, but delegating drug choices to doctors did not seem to be a sufficient response to the new technology. A 1968 government task force concluded that doctors could not be considered the consumer's "expert purchasing agent" for drugs. In the task force's harsh words, "A purchasing agent who purchased without consideration of both quality and price would be unworthy of trust."[3]

Congress responded to the thalidomide tragedy in the context of views like this—held both by regulators and by academic doctors—and superimposed another level of control over the doctors prescribing drugs. The Drug Amendments of 1962 strengthened the new-drug provisions of the 1938 law in ways that gave the FDA increasing control over which drugs a doctor could prescribe. Drug choice was doubly removed from the person actually ingesting the drug.

Yet criticism of the FDA and drug policy has increased rather than diminished. The uncertainty surrounding drugs has not been eliminated, and some critics demand to know why not. Meanwhile, an opposing group contends that efforts to banish drug risks have gone too far in the direction of transferring control to a government agency. Those who think or write about drugs therefore have to thread their way through a tangle of alternative criticisms from different and conflicting viewpoints.

Three distinct, albeit intertwined, risks in using medicinal drugs can be identified. There is the risk of overpaying for a drug, either because the price is high or the quality is low. There is also the risk of getting sick or dying as a result of taking a drug. In the language of the trade, this is the risk of an adverse drug reaction. And once sick, from whatever causes, there is the risk of not getting well. People can fail to recover because no suitable drug is available, because they take the wrong drug, or even because they take too much or too little of an appropriate drug.[4]

As might be expected, Congress, the courts, and the FDA have focused their attention on different risks at different times. Public policy toward medicines originated from a concern with the first, financial, risk in the early years of the twentieth century. This concern was displaced in part by attention to the second risk by midcentury, but the dominance of the first risk had already been built into the institutional structure of the FDA, where it still endures. Current medical critics of the FDA emphasize the third risk, that of not getting well, but this concern has not yet been embodied in public policy. The common failure to distinguish among these risks is illustrated in Senator Edward Kennedy's subcommittee hearings during 1973 and 1974. For the first ten days, witness after witness criticized the FDA for approving too many drugs and increasing the second risk, whereas in the last two days witnesses blamed the FDA for increasing the third risk by approving too few drugs.[5]

Greater clarity comes from recognizing that it is impossible to eliminate all risks from using medicines, though this has been a dominant aim of government policy. Because it is not possible, for reasons to be detailed in the pages to come, this goal has taken on aspects of the Holy Grail. Its pursuit has removed the consumer from control over the several aspects of drug use: when to take a drug, which drug to take, and how much of the drug to take. The drastic curtailment of consumers' control over their own progress in the interests of having the "best" drug chosen raises the question of how far the government should go to protect people from the possible consequences of their own risky choices.

This question is not unique to drugs. It applies as well to other facets of medical care and to the even broader area of consumer products. While there are many possible responses, the thrust of current government policy is to deal with risks by reserving decisions to experts, often those resident in government agencies. Drug policy is consistent—albeit further advanced—with policy in other areas. Examination of this question as it applies to medicines therefore provides an opportunity to raise questions of more general import as well.

The trend toward reliance on experts can be observed in the common distinction between prescription and over-the-counter drugs. The latter, of course, can be bought without a doctor's prescription, whereas the former cannot. This distinction is relatively new to the industry, since all nonnarcotic drugs were available without a prescription until just before World War II.[6]

A parallel, but older, distinction is between ethical and proprietary drugs. Ethical drugs are those advertised only to doctors, and the curious nomenclature refers to the original 1847 code of ethics of the American Medical Association (AMA), which excluded advertising to the public from ethical medical practice.[7] Proprietary medicines are those advertised directly to the public, including the so-called patent medicines. This term signified that the ingredients of the medicines were secret, not that they were patented. While many ethical drugs on the market today are patented, they are not patent medicines.

The growing role of prescriptions in the drug industry is shown in table 1. Less than one-third of all medicines bought in 1929 were prescribed by doctors. The drugs bought this way may not have been different from the drugs bought without prescriptions; the first row of the table distinguishes

Table 1. Consumer expenditures for prescription drugs and all medicines, selected years (dollars in millions).

Year	Prescription drugs	Drugs and drug sundries	Prescription drugs as a percentage of all medicines
1929	190	600	32
1949	940	1640[a]	57
1969	5395	6480	83

Sources: C. Rufus Rorem and Robert P. Fischelis, *The Costs of Medicines,* pub. no. 14 of the Committee on the Cost of Medical Care (Chicago: University of Chicago Press, 1932), p. 18; *Prescription Drug Industry Fact Book* (Washington, D.C.: Pharmaceutical Manufacturers' Association, 1977), p. 68; Nancy L. Worthington, "National Health Expenditures, 1929–1974," *Social Security Bulletin,* 38 (February 1975): 13. The estimate of total drug expenditures in 1929 used here is Worthington's. If Rorem and Fischelis's estimate of this item and of prescription drug expenditures for that year were used, the latter's share would be only 27 percent.
   a. 1950.

the way drugs were bought, not necessarily which drugs were bought. This proportion had risen to over half of all medicines just after World War II, when certain drugs could no longer be legally purchased without a prescription. As this category expanded in response to the wave of drug introductions in the 1950s, the proportion of medicines prescribed by doctors rose to over four-fifths of the total in 1969.

Federal drug regulation originated in the early twentieth century during the Progressive period, when most drugs were chosen personally by consumers. The government undertook to aid consumers by providing them with information and by driving drugs with false or misleading labels off the market. Since there were few effective drugs and since most people taking medicines were, consequently, reasonably healthy, drug regulation was seen in the context of food regulation rather than of medical care. The predominant aim of policy was to ensure that fair value was received for money spent.

The FDA tried to extend its legislative mandate during the early New Deal period, but not until a drug company had unwittingly produced a toxic preparation that killed over a hundred people did Congress respond with a new law—the 1938 Federal Food, Drug, and Cosmetic Act. This legislation added a concern for drug safety to the FDA's mission, and it provided the occasion for the agency to issue a regulation distinguishing over-the-counter from prescription drugs.

While the FDA controlled directly which drugs could be on the market and how they could be sold, this regulation gave doctors the right to control any individual's access to these drugs. The FDA seems to have decided that people were no longer competent to administer some medicines to themselves and thus made doctors their expert agents. It is not obvious why this marketing procedure for drugs was introduced in 1938, but this particular resolution of the question of who—consumers, pharmacists, doctors, or the FDA—should choose which medicine people take has had enormous impact.

After World War II the number of drugs available, the range of diseases and conditions amenable to drug therapy, and the power of drugs all increased dramatically. Enthusiasm about the power of the new "wonder drugs" was high in the late 1940s and has scarcely diminished since, but it should not blind us to their limitations. While most of the decline in mortality over the past century and a half was due to a decline in infectious diseases (those potentially treatable by antibiotics), almost all the decline preceded the discovery of the antibiotics. And, comments a noted medical historian, "even since 1935 they have not been the only or, probably, the main influence."[8]

A new drug industry emerged in the context of the FDA's prescription-only regulation. Characterized by large firms selling new, patented drugs, the industry earned high profits and extensive legislative attention. Congressional concern, as reflected in hearings on the drug industry, focused initially on financial issues. A series of hearings entitled "Administered Prices" and "Competitive Problems in the Drug Industry" stretched through the 1960s and beyond. Despite the revelations of these voluminous proceedings, Congress as a whole refused to follow the lead of the investigating subcommittees. Senator Estes Kefauver's efforts to lower drug prices became—with the aid of the thalidomide tragedy—the 1962 Drug Amendments that did not mention prices or competition.[9]

At almost the precise time these amendments were passed, the postwar rate of new drug introductions fell off sharply, from an average of fifty per year in the 1950s to an annual average of twenty in the 1960s (see table 2). As a result of the Kefauver hearings and these coincident events, a number of economists investigated the drug industry with emphasis on two questions: Is the drug industry competitive? And, what determines the rate at which new drugs are introduced? The first question is designed to shed light on the financial risk of buying drugs, since in the economists' model a competitive industry charges the lowest maintainable prices. The second question bears on a different risk, that of not having a needed drug, and, more precisely, on the effects of the 1962 Drug Amendments

Table 2. Number of new single drugs introduced in the United States, 1941-1979.[a]

Year	New drugs	Year	New drugs
1941	20	1961	48
1942	14	1962	29
1943	10	1963	16
1944	14	1964	18
1945	14	1965	23
1946	20	1966	12
1947	24	1967	25
1948	27	1968	11
1949	42	1969	9
1950	33	1970	16
1951	39	1971	14
1952	40	1972	11
1953	54	1973	19
1954	43	1974	18
1955	40	1975	16
1956	47	1976	15
1957	54	1977	18
1958	49	1978	23
1959	66	1979	16
1960	51		

Source: *Nonproprietary Name Index* (New York: Paul de Haen, 1974); *New Product Survey* (New York: Paul de Haen, 1977–1979).

a. Although the primary source for all estimates of the rate of introduction of new drugs seems to be Paul de Haen, a variety of series exists. Different volumes of the *Nonproprietary Name Index* itself have different data. For example, the data used by Peltzman in his influential study, also from de Haen, are somewhat lower for the 1950s. Sam Peltzman, "An Evaluation of Consumer Protection Legislation: The 1962 Drug Amendments," *Journal of Political Economy,* 81 (September 1973). All the series show the same trends, but caution is needed in interpreting any single entry.

on the availability of drugs today. By and large, the economic literature is sharply critical of the 1962 Drug Amendments and of the FDA, reaching conclusions that have been echoed and elaborated in a series of books by congressional staff members and journalists.[10]

The pressure from congressional hearings and the subsequent critical literature has affected the FDA's performance. J. Richard Crout, director of the FDA's Bureau of Drugs, described conditions in the FDA when he arrived there in 1972: "There was open drunkenness by several employees, which went on for months. There was intimidation internally ... People—I'm talking about division directors and their staffs—would engage in a kind of behavior that invited insubordination. People tittering in corners, throwing spitballs—I'm describing physicians ... [It was] a kind of behavior I have not seen in any other institution as a grown man." The *New York Times* called the FDA "the Federal Government's most criticized, demoralized and fractionalized agency" in 1977.[11]

It is not my goal to add to the critical chorus; neither is it to echo the conclusions of citizen advisory panels that have reported on the FDA in recent decades—in 1955, 1968, and 1977—and recommended that its budget be increased.[12] The aim of this inquiry is to clarify the goals of public policy toward medicinal drugs. The first step, already begun in these introductory pages, is to describe the nature of drug risks. The second step is to understand the evolution of our current drug policy. The final step is to draw back from the details of medicinal drugs, analyze behavior in uncertain situations, and draw conclusions from the narrative and the analysis about the most beneficial direction for drug policy to take. Before these substantive chapters begin, however, it will be useful to note some of the distinguishing features of the market for medicinal drugs and a few terms used to describe individual modes of behavior and institutional structures.

The Medicinal Drug Market

One of the problems a doctor—or anyone else, for that matter—faces in choosing drugs today can be seen in the price data for a few drugs. Consider ampicillin and tetracycline, two of the potent antibiotics introduced in the 1950s and 1960s. Their patents have expired, and they are now produced by many firms. They have been for several years two of the drugs most often prescribed by generic—as opposed to brand—name.[13] On the basis of the frequent assertion from the FDA and others that chemically equivalent drugs are in fact identical, any economist would expect the prices of these drugs from different suppliers to be roughly the same.[14] The case for chemical identity is particularly strong for ampicillin and tetracycline, since the FDA certifies the chemical purity of every batch of antibiotics produced. The case for price identity is strong because drugs are easily transported, are sold in a national market, and have their prices published in a single source.[15]

Despite all this, there is a wide distribution of wholesale prices for both ampicillin and tetracycline. Over a dozen firms sold ampicillin in 1979 for under $6.00, while almost that many sold it for over $12.00. Over thirty

Table 3. Number of companies selling ampicillin and tetracycline at various prices, 1979.

Wholesale price per 100 capsules, 250 mg (dollars)	Ampicillin			Tetracycline		
	Without brand name	With brand name[a]	Total	Without brand name	With brand name[a]	Total
1.00–1.99	0	0	0	6	0	6
2.00–2.99	0	0	0	29	3(1)	32
3.00–3.99	0	0	0	7	4(1)	11
4.00–4.99	5	0	5	0	14(4)	14
5.00–5.99	11	1(1)	12	0	5(1)	5
6.00–6.99	12	0	12	0	0	0
7.00–7.99	7	1	8	0	0	0
8.00–8.99	3	3(2)	6	0	2	2
9.00–9.99	1	2(1)	3	0	1	1
10.00–10.99	0	0	0	0	0	0
11.00–11.99	0	3(1)	3	0	1	1
12.00 and over	4	7(5)	11	0	2(2)	2

Source: *Drug Topics Red Book* (Oradell, N.J.: Medical Economics Co., 1979); brand names taken from IMS America, National Prescription Audit, *Generic Market Reports, 1979: Ampicillin, Tetracycline* (Ambler, Pa.: IMS America, 1980).

a. Numbers in parentheses refer to trade-name firms. See table 23 for identification and sales of these firms.

firms sold tetracycline for under $3.00, while almost that many charged more than $4.00 and six firms charged more than $8.00 for the "identical" product (see table 3). The higher priced tetracyclines are all brand-name drugs, as opposed to the generic product, but not all brand-name tetracycline is sold for a high price.[16] How can these price spreads exist?

One key to this disparity must be the difficulty of knowing when different brands of a single drug are identical or which brand of a drug is best in any specific case. This is not to say that one cannot choose rationally between an antibiotic and an analgesic, but rather that choices within small classes of similar drug products pose questions without definitive answers. There frequently is no single "best" drug, and typically it is impossible to know whether such a drug exists; these factors affect the demand for drugs in very important ways. The regulation of drugs follows ultimately from this uncertainty and lack of information.

The simplest type of drug information is cost. How hard would it be for doctors and consumers to learn about drug prices? Sixty companies sell ampicillin and seventy-five sell tetracycline under many different names. Few other drugs are sold by as many suppliers, but there are approximately 1,000 different chemical entities sold either singly or in combination. The *Physicians' Desk Reference (PDR)*, a standard reference for doctors, lists approximately 2,500 drug products made up from these 1,000 chemical entities; the *Drug Topics Red Book,* a product and price reference for pharmacists, contains 170,000 entries.

This voluminous listing, however, contains very little information on the costs of different drugs that is usable by the consumer or doctor. The *Red Book* gives wholesale prices but not retail prices. The link between the two is loose because the retail price of a drug within any locality varies both among pharmacies and over time in any one pharmacy.[17] In addition, the *Red Book* does not identify the chemical composition of brand-name drugs. The *PDR* identifies drugs by both brand name and chemical composition, but it lists only a small fraction of the products in the *Red Book* and it lacks prices. Neither volume, in any case, is easily available to the general public, and the latter is not easily available to doctors. The only source of systematic price data that doctors might see is a pocket book giving an irreverent summary of the therapeutic information in the *PDR* and other compendia for common drugs and approximate prices for these drugs by brand.[18]

Nevertheless, cost information is easier to find than information on drug benefits. Data on efficacy are scattered through a wide variety of medical journals that are not available in general libraries and are not easily understood without medical and statistical training. The extant data are, in addition, woefully incomplete, so that even the trained investigator with access to a good medical library will find the pursuit of information on the comparative effectiveness of similar drugs or different brands of the same drug to be peculiarly frustrating.

There are several reasons why more information on the comparative effectiveness of drugs does not exist. First, the concept of effectiveness is itself vague. While it clearly must relate in some way to the ability of a drug to correct some undesirable condition, it can relate to many other drug characteristics as well. The method of administration—oral, injectible, topical—and the dosage required both can be considered. Speed of action and durability of action are also important. In addition to a drug's effectiveness against any specific disease, the breadth of conditions it treats may be relevant if tests to identify particular problems are difficult. The myriad possible adverse drug reactions are relevant as well. Drugs without adverse side effects are preferable to those with unwanted results, but adverse reactions vary among themselves approximately as much as the beneficial effects and are therefore as difficult to classify and evaluate.

The multidimensional nature of drug effectiveness does not mean that knowledge is absent. It means rather that knowledge is costly to acquire and that different investigators will concentrate on different dimensions. Information is likely to be incomplete, confusing, and sometimes contradictory.

A second reason why there is not more information on comparative drug effectiveness follows from the nature of physicians' activities. Practicing doctors are engaged in treating patients. They vary treatment according to the patient's condition, using the therapy they consider most appropriate. However, since the effects of drugs vary from person to person, it would be necessary to observe a sample of patients to get information that could be applied outside the original clinical situation. Further, to connect the observed effects with the drugs taken—as opposed to some other cause—the patients have to be chosen randomly to receive or not receive the drugs. In other words, the research doctor has to vary his treatment of patients for reasons other than clinical ones, reasons uncorrelated with patients' clinical problems.

Clinical medicine and drug research are separate activities. Doctors treating patients are in no position to construct random samples of patients or to observe the effect of different therapies. It would violate their professional relations with their patients, and it would raise ethical questions about the role of doctors.[19] They must rely on research physicians and statisticians for careful and statistically valid information on drug effectiveness.

A third reason for the scarcity of comparative drug information relates to the second. The need for statistical procedures in the analysis of drug therapy, which results in conflicts between clinical practice and medical research, also demands of doctors technical skills that they do not normally possess. Epidemiological research, to use the medical term for statistical investigations, is needed because the effects of drugs and diseases vary among individuals. However dramatic the case of one person may be, there is no way to determine how much—if any—of this single story can be extrapolated to other contexts. Norman Cousins checked out of the hospital while suffering from a serious disease and proceeded to recover. Does that mean that we should check out only if we have the same disease as Cousins? That we should only check out of the same hospital as Cousins? Or that God watches out for children, drunks, and well-known editors? The remarkable story of Norman Cousins does not suggest an answer.[20]

To find out, one must analyze the experiences of a variety of people in slightly different circumstances. Samples of subjects must be drawn from the populations that the results will be applied to, where the populations are defined according to some relevant characteristics: age, location, symptoms, diseases, and so on. And it is necessary to analyze the results by formal statistical techniques to find out if the observed variation was due to chance or to some identifiable cause, if the sample was large enough to contain the desired information, or which of two plausible explanations is preferable.

Statistics, however, is not popular among doctors. As with the concept of random samples, it cuts against the grain of medical training and practice. Doctors treat individual patients and write clinical reports; statistical analysis of large populations is a distinct activity. Doctors generally are not well-qualified to do epidemiological research or to evaluate epidemiological reports in the literature, and medical journals contain almost no reports of randomized clinical trials.[21]

Finally, even if these conceptual and professional difficulties were absent, many of the experiments needed to discriminate between drugs are expensive and difficult. Small differences cannot be isolated without large samples. Comparative efficacy in a variety of clinical situations, however defined, also may not be clear without large-scale experiments. The payoff from these experiments may not be large: the best and second-best drugs may be almost equivalent. And because current drug regulations do not involve *comparative* effectiveness, they have not generated research on this question. Whether or not society would benefit from more experiments of this kind, the paucity of them at the moment means that doctors and consumers have to make many decisions without experimental evidence on the comparative effect of alternative choices. In addition to the uncertainty that would exist in the treatment of any individual patient even with the best information possible, there is an additional uncertainty stemming from the lack of information.

Sociological research in the drug market has centered on these very factors of uncertainty and ignorance. Both academic sociologists and commercial market analysts have investigated the influence of different sources of information and the effect of risk on prescribing habits. Starting in the early 1950s, a host of investigators interrogated doctors on their responses to the advertising campaigns of the emerging integrated drug firms. The doctors replied that they relied heavily, but not exclusively, on the promotional activities of the drug firms: detail men, direct mail advertisements, and journal advertisements.[22]

These sociological drug studies share a common methodology. They asked physicians how they had decided to try a new product and which influences had been most important. The answers differed depending on the sample and the particular questions posed, and there is good reason to doubt that the answers contain much information. The investigators asked doctors to recall and express verbally the process by which they had made complex decisions, but a substantial body of research has accumulated that demonstrates that people cannot accurately describe their own thought processes in making decisions. They can inform a questioner about their mood or about their past actions, but not about the impact of various factors on decision making. According to a recent summary and synthesis of research about self-reporting: "The evidence indicates it may be quite misleading for social scientists to ask their subjects about the influences on their evaluations, choices or behavior."[23]

In short, the present state of knowledge allows neither for the selection of a unique "best" drug in general nor for a cogent description of doctors' reactions to the uncertainty surrounding their behavior. To evaluate current policy, a more intensive look at decision making under uncertainty is needed.

Modes of Behavior

In the presence of uncertainty, people act differently depending both on who they are and on what situation they face. The different types of behavior can be grouped into three distinct "modes" or ideal types without implying that anyone follows any single mode all the time. On the contrary, most people switch from one mode to another as conditions vary or as they are called upon to play different roles (doctor, lawyer, patient) in society.

The first mode may be characterized as *instrumental.* This is the type of behavior economists assume prevails in market settings. It is represented most often by the abstraction of the *homo economicus* or the profit-maximizing firm, ceaselessly striving to attain a unitary goal against the constraints imposed by the actions of similarly minded individuals or firms. Since people or firms in the instrumental mode act consistently, in the sense that no sequence of their actions leads to an outcome in conflict with an outcome reached by a different chain, consistent behavior is also often called rational, indicating that it does not lead to internal contradictions.

Economists assume almost automatically that people engaged in market behavior act instrumentally or rationally. Other social scientists almost automatically assume that they do not. The necessity to choose between the polar alternatives has isolated economics within the social sciences, although there are occasional signs of rapprochement. Instead of choosing sides, however, I propose a middle ground which asserts that people act this way part of the time. The question is not whether people act this way, but when they act this way.

The second ideal type of behavior is *customary* or traditional behavior. People acting in the customary mode do today more or less what they did yesterday. I say "more or less" because it often appears to them that they are repeating their previous pattern when they are in fact deviating from it. This can happen because of faulty memories, because the context in which the actions take place has changed so that familiar actions no longer seem familiar, or because a variation introduced by someone else has become incorporated into the tradition. It can happen because customs or habits are not hard and fast, not explicit or published in a code of regulations. They are implicit in people's actions.

Customary behavior is all around us. It is the object of anthropological, sociological, and psychological studies. To choose a historical example, it is the core of Marc Bloch's study of feudalism, in which he shows that customs "known" from time immemorial and sancified by God changed radically from generation to generation. Alternatively, it is the result of what Max Weber called "the routinization of charisma."[24]

A contemporary example is provided by the organizational theory of the firm, which holds that industrial firms are repositories of customary behavior. They operate by rules of thumb that are honored as long as their results provide a minimum level of organizational well-being. When the rules of thumb fail to achieve this minimum level, they are replaced temporarily by a search for better rules, that is, by instrumental behavior.[25]

The third ideal type of behavior is *command* behavior. This mode is the product of a context in which one person can order another to perform or refrain from performing a specific action and can impose penalties for noncompliance. In some contexts, these sanctions may be legal. In others, they may consist of excluding the noncomplier from the context of the order, as in firing a recalcitrant employee. In still others, the sanctions may be various forms of physical violence.

There are two striking differences between customary and command behavior. Change comes about in the former without the consciousness of the people involved; it appears in the latter as a result of the decisions of identifiable individuals. And while customary behavior constrains all actors more or less equally, command behavior recognizes a hierarchy in which only some people have the ability to direct behavior and make the changes just alluded to. It will be shown that doctors follow custom in choosing drugs and issue commands in prescribing them.[26]

These modes of behavior have been apparent to other observers of modern medicine. For example, three "models" of behavior in medicine have been identified by sociologist Eliot Freidson. His bureaucratic model corresponds to command behavior and describes behavior in hierarchical situations where the chain of command is clear. The professional model corresponds to customary behavior; it describes behavior among communities of peers where the peer group controls—or fails to control, as Freidson discovered in his study of a medical clinic—the behavior of its members. Finally, the market model corresponds to instrumental behavior as it describes the behavior of merchants and other people acting in competitive situations. Two attributes of the professional model or customary mode are of interest here. First, there has been little analytic study of this model; second, the model allowed a wide range of behavior to persist in the medical context examined.[27]

The form of personal interaction differs among the modes. The characteristic means of communication in instrumental behavior is explicit exchange. People barter or pay money for goods or services they want; they can balance the benefit to them of having these goods or services against the cost. The characteristic means of interaction in command behavior, clearly, is a command or order—or a prescription. In the customary mode, the typical means of personal interaction is reciprocity, with the affect that goes along with it. As befits the nature of this mode, reciprocity is informal and nonquantitative. Reciprocity cannot be added up like a price, nor can it be formally itemized like an order. Yet we all experience reciprocity in our daily lives, and only the most callous would deny its importance.[28]

This discussion of communication can be stood on its head to suggest a way of telling which mode of behavior is being observed. Since each mode has its characteristic form of communication, the mode of behavior in use can be inferred from the type of communication observed. Unfortunately, this test, though unobjectionable on logical grounds, often is hard to apply. Reciprocity and affect can be implicit in a relationship and difficult to observe. Their qualitative nature eludes quantification, giving rise to possible conflicts of interpretation. And, while they are always present in customary relationships, they may also appear in the context of other modes of behavior. This test therefore needs to be supplemented with another.

Just such a second test emerges naturally from the description of the three modes of behavior. People acting in the instrumental mode evaluate actions by their results: they comare the *output* of their activities against some explicit or implicit standard. People acting in the customary mode ignore the results of their actions; they concentrate on the actions themselves, on the *inputs* to a set of activities. They compare the actions they perform with a set of loosely defined—if explicitly defined at all—norms. This test shows that doctors are following custom in choosing drugs, not maximizing some objective function by evaluating the effects of alternative choices.[29]

Command behavior differs from both instrumental and customary behavior on these dimensions. In contrast to the former, people acting in the command mode evaluate actions by examining the actions themselves; in contrast to the latter, they evaluate these actions by references to an explicitly formulated set of directions emanating from an identifiable source. A prescription is a command, and the acts of writing and filling it are examples of command behavior.

Consumers clearly employ customary behavior as they choose among over-the-counter medicines. They have even less access to knowledge of the results of their actions than doctors, and they get their guidance through informal channels different from but similar to those used by doctors. Consumers may also employ customary behavior when choosing a pharmacy. They may establish a personal relationship with a pharmacist which dominates their choice of where to buy drugs and which may affect as well their choice of over-the-counter drugs. But consumers also may act instrumentally to minimize the time spent or the effort expended in filling a prescription. They may do this as a matter of course, or they may opt out of their customary behavior from time to time under special conditions.

Pharmacists similarly act instrumentally and customarily by turns. Since drug prices are neither easily observed nor an important factor in the choice of pharmacies, druggists by and large set drug prices in a customary fashion. They have little concern with or understanding of the effects of their price-setting actions, and they concentrate on the price-setting rules themselves. If a pharmacist has an ongoing relationship with a drug wholesaler, this interaction may affect the retail prices as much as anything else the pharmacist does, by affecting the composition of the store's stock and the source of its drugs. By contrast, druggists may spend considerable time making reasoned, instrumental choices about the extent of the product line they will carry, about the layout of the store, and about other commercial aspects of the business. Drug chains have begun to make an effort to introduce instrumental pricing procedures into the retail drug market as well.

Institutional arrangements or structures can be grouped into three types, parallel with the three modes of behavior. Customary behavior thrives in what we may call community settings, where informal interactions and continuing relationships are the norm. The existence of a community allows the informal reciprocity characteristic of customary behavior to take place, and the continuity of a community encourages the growth of affect that accompanies the reciprocal actions. Instrumental behavior can be used to its best advantage in market settings, where the explicit exchanges needed to pursue a unified set of goals are facilitated by the institutional surrounding. Command behavior needs hierarchical institutions, whether formal or informal, for its operation.

This threefold classification scheme of institutions follows from the division of behavior into three modes. As with the modes, this list of institutions consists of ideal types, and any particular institution may evince qualities of more than one type. For the purposes of this argument, all that is needed is that actual institutions may be grouped easily and consistently into these three categories and that transitions between institutional forms can be identified and distinguished from the ongoing operation of continuing institutions.

Transitions, of course, are critical. Each type of institution is linked to a mode of behavior, and each mode of behavior, similarly, is linked to a different class of institutions. This correspondence between modes of behavior and institutional types implies that there is some relationship between changes of behavior and changes in institutions. The nature of this relationship will be developed explicitly later, but two preliminary hypotheses should be mentioned now. First, the link between behavior and institutions is not in general very strong. In other words, while there is a tendency for behavior and institutions to come together according to the correspondence between them, this tendency may be worked out over a long period of time—or not at all if conditions change in the interim. Second, changes in behavior have stronger effects on the structure of institutions than changes in institutions have on the mode of behavior. Alternatively, a change in the mode of behavior is more likely to lead to an institutional change than an institutional change is to produce a change in the mode of behavior.[30]

The various dimensions of current government drug policy assume that consumers cannot choose drugs for themselves. In fact, the policy of restricting the marketability of some drugs assumes that doctors cannot choose drugs alone either; government aid is needed. The central question of this study is whether these paternalistic assumptions are justified and whether their current manifestations can be defended.

TWO

Drug Regulation
in the Progressive Era

MODERN DRUG REGULATION in the United States
dates from the Progressive period. Even though the story of this chapter
begins before the decades usually cited as the Progressive era and continues up to the eve of the Great Depression, the spirit that underlies the
measures adopted is that of Progressivism. Looked at from this angle,
therefore, the story concerns the implementation of general ideas about
the proper role of government in a specific area.

From another point of view, the story reveals also the beginning of a
new view of medical care and of the government's role in controlling it.
The government intervened to control the delivery of health care in several apparently disconnected ways during the Progressive period. These
isolated strands—not all of which appear in conventional histories of
drug regulation—were not woven into a fabric until a later time. The
story resembles one of those novels where a variety of characters are
shown living their separate lives while the reader waits for the incident
where their lives intersect.

Progressive thought was a reaction to changes in the American economy that decisively moved it away from the constructs of classical economics. Although this transformation had little effect on the economists
themselves—of which more later—it dominated most of what can be
characterized as "social thought."[1]

The Drug Industry before World War I

Starting roughly in the 1880s, modern business organizations came to
dominate economic life.[2] Managers coordinated the activities of a firm's

different operating units and controlled the flow of resources among them. A major part of the economy's resources, in other words, was not allocated by the interactions of many people in an impersonal market, but was sent to one or another destination by the decisions of identifiable persons.

This shift from the invisible hand to the "visible hand"—to use Alfred Chandler's phrase—was occasioned by the increased volume and speed of flows in the late nineteenth-century economy. As machines became more sophisticated, they produced more products in a given time. The inventories of these products had to be coordinated with the inventories of other products and with the provision of customer services. And the cash flow returning from the customer to the manufacturer also needed to be controlled. As the speed with which products and cash were transported and transmitted back and forth increased, the control over timing became more important. In a business in which a high volume of outstanding bills was financed by an equally high volume of cash receipts sent in from distant branches, a temporary diminution of the cash flow could mean disaster. Similarly, the ability to get the products to the retail outlets in the right quantities and at the right times could mean the difference between success and failure.[3]

The rise of the modern business firm and of the associated managerial class engendered the perception that the traditional "island community" of the average American and the opportunity for individual advancement were being destroyed. The changes in the economy became visible to all Americans as the large firms extended their activities into retail distribution and as the railroads introduced their products into small towns. The increasingly efficient distribution network came at the expense of many middleman jobs and, perhaps more importantly, at the expense of local control over the last few steps of the distribution process.[4]

Even though American consumers had long been part of a national and even international economic order, their connections with the larger economy had been mediated by a local social network. Their food may have been grown far away; their clothing may have been put together from raw cotton in several stages at different places. Nevertheless, the final sale and possibly also the final steps of production generally involved the local community. The members of this community could therefore see themselves as part of a local social order, one in which local custom and tradition played an important role. As national corporations intruded into this setting, the role of local custom diminished, and people felt themselves cut loose from familiar relationships and traditions. In the language of chapter 1, they were forced out of a community into a market. On the assumption that people acted in their community setting largely along customary lines, that is, that the preexisting match between behavior and institution had been stable, this move then created a tension between the existing customary mode of behavior and the new market institutions.

Professional people, who had seen themselves as the leaders of their communities, were subject to the greatest tension. In addition to finding themselves in a new and less comfortable institutional structure, they also found themselves less powerful than the managers of the new corporations. Their wealth was less than the wealth of the new capitalists, and their economic power was small compared with the emerging power of the middle and top managers. The result of this shift, according to Richard Hofstadter, was that "conditions varied from profession to profession, but all groups with claims to learning and skill shared a common sense of humiliation and common grievances against the plutocracy."[5]

In this context, a debate arose over the proper role of government. Most people, including most professionals, felt the tension between their unchanging mode of behavior and the changing institutional framework. But some people, whose behavior changed, welcomed the new institution. The new setting had not come about by natural forces; it had been the work of men who had adopted an instrumental mode of behavior and changed the institutions in which they operated in pursuit of their goals. They were the owners and managers of the new business organizations; they also were the people whose behavior was in harmony with the new—not the old—institutions.

The proponents of change used the theories of Social Darwinism and classical economics to justify a minimal role for government. Their opponents relied on a hodgepodge of theories—the social gospel, historical economics, sociology, pragmatism—which had as their common element the idea of an ongoing community. They supported an active interventionist role for the government as the protector of communities against the inroads of markets. Even though they never succeeded in formulating a simple creed analogous to the models of classical economics, they carried the day in the arena of politics. The government, at all levels, actively involved itself in the operation of the economy.[6]

There were many facets of this activity, but two of them affected the delivery of medicinal drugs most directly. More precisely, two of them created the foundations for later control over the sale of medicinal drugs. These two were licensing laws and pure food and drug legislation.

We can distinguish hostile and friendly licensing in this period. Hostile licensing, an older pattern that had fallen into neglect during the nineteenth century, is imposed on the licensed group by outsiders. Friendly licensing is controlled by the licensees themselves; it was a novel phenomenon of the Progressive period. The changes in transportation and communication that fostered the growth of the modern corporation also permitted the establishment of national associations of independent professionals, craftsmen, and merchants. These associations had as their goal the preservation of their members' relative economic and social position in their communities. They seized on licensing as a way of creating an occupational monopoly to oppose the threatening monopoly power of the large corporations. In contrast to the nascent antitrust movement, which attempted to restore competition where it had been stifled by the new large firms, the licensing movement attempted to contain the market power of corporations by creating new market power in the hands of opposing groups. Instead of trying to lower corporate prices, a variety of occupational groups enlisted government aid in raising theirs. Instead of opposing the rise of large business organizations, they tried to maintain their positions relative to them.

This view is too simplistic, for licensing was not successful where the market power of independent craftsmen directly opposed the market power of large firms. Quite the contrary, licensing succeeded where there was no organized body of opposition. Self-employed professions or crafts could be licensed because there was no employer to be hurt by higher wages. And people who sold their services directly to the public could be licensed because the purchasers who would pay higher prices did not constitute a political force in their own right. It is more accurate, therefore, to say that the growth of friendly licensing was a reaction to the growth of corporate power than to say that it opposed it directly. To the extent that licensed groups could raise their prices, they offset the effects of monopoly corporate prices, but they did not confront the corporations in any specific market.

The absence of organized opposition was necessary for friendly occupational licensing, but not sufficient. The potential licensees had to convince the legislatures and the courts that licensing them was a valid exercise of the state's police power. The precise limits of this power were never specified, and states differed among themselves in their willingness to license occupations. Doctors, plumbers, barbers, funeral directors, nurses, electricians, horseshoers, dentists, and others tried to get licensed. The United States Supreme Court upheld the licensing of doctors in 1888, and the others who could show a link—however tenuous—with health or safety also achieved their goal. Barbers succeeded in demonstrating such a link, as did plumbers in most states, but horseshoers could not.[7]

Doctors had been licensed by many states in the early nineteenth century, but almost all states repealed penalties on unlicensed practitioners before midcentury. Before the germ theory of Pasteur, it was impossible to maintain a "scientific" standard for medical therapy. The conceptual basis for such a science simply did not exist, and the doctors themselves expressed this lack by dividing into mutually antagonistic factions. The orthodox doctors, who relied on massive medication and bleeding to cure their patients, were opposed by homeopaths and eclectics, both of whom opposed the harsh therapy of the orthodoxy. After the development of the germ theory in 1870, but owing more to the changes in the economy just described than to the increase in scientific knowledge, the various factions of doctors came together to advocate licensing laws.

State licensing of doctors was universal by the turn of the century, and the state licensing boards were sufficiently organized to form the National Conference of State Medical Examining and Licensing Boards in 1891. The typical board had a majority of orthodox doctors with minority representation from the two dissident sects. Doctors were licensed by other doctors.[8]

Pharmacists also sought and obtained licenses in this period. The American Pharmaceutical Association discussed a model licensing bill in 1869, but refrained from endorsing it. The association was bold enough to send the bill around to state governments in 1872, and it adopted and circulated a revised model bill in 1900. Both model bills proposed the establishment of a licensing board appointed from a list supplied by pharmaceutical colleges and societies. Between the promulgation of the two model bills, almost all states adopted licensing laws for pharmacists, with the rise in states requiring licenses following the rise in states with state pharmaceutical associations by five years or less.[9]

What did all this mean for the consumer trying to buy drugs? There were three ways to get drugs around the turn of the century. The first way, and the most obvious from a late twentieth-century perspective, was to go to a doctor and get a prescription for a pharmacist to fill. Despite the apparent familiarity of this process, it is important to realize that a prescription did not play the same role then that it plays today. In one respect, of course, it did. Prescriptions were orders from a physician to a pharmacist to give a patient a specific drug or combination of drugs. But there the similarity ended. Any drug that could be obtained with a prescription could also be obtained without one.[10] Moreover, a prescription, once issued, could be used as many different times for as many different people as desired. Presciptions, in other words, were a convenience to be used or not as the situation indicated.

The implications of this system were spelled out by a doctor writing in 1901:

Physicians do not, and, as a rule, would not, even if it could conveniently be done, copyright their prescriptions. Consequently, the druggist has a legal right to use the formula as often as he pleases, provided there is no intoxicant or other poison therein contained, which requires a physician's order for dispensation . . .

The druggist copies prescriptions, refills prescriptions, prescribes across the counter in a vaguely empirical, enthusiastically panacea-like way . . . If a physician's prescription falls into his hands, and he thinks it suitable, he does not hesitate to put it up on a large scale, advertise it as a cure-all, and sell it by the dozen as "Dr. So-and-So's prescription for this, that, and the other."[11]

As this passage makes clear, the relationship between doctors and patients at the turn of the century was far different from that today. Patients did not need to go to a doctor to get a drug; nor were they bound by the doctor's selection if they did. They were free to purchase the drugs of their choice.

The second way to get drugs, therefore, was for consumers to simply go to their local drug store and buy whatever they wanted. To be sure, medical licensing laws prohibited nondoctors from "practising medicine," including prescribing drugs. This restriction may have barred a pharmacist from recommending a drug that he did not sell, but it did not seem to have any effect on his freedom to promote the sales of his own wares. The distinction between doctor and druggist was not a clear one for many purposes.

This overlap of function went the other way, too: drugs could be obtained directly from doctors. Most doctors, in fact, dispensed drugs rather than writing prescriptions for others to fill.[12] Medicine was not yet the elite profession it was to become, and we may presume that doctors were eager to get the extra activity and income from selling drugs.[13]

The licensing laws did not have any effect on this system in their initial years. With their pervasive grandfather clauses, the new laws did not put any existing doctor or tradesman out of business. And they did not restrict the availability of particular drugs by requiring a prescription or other certification. Over time the laws operated to limit the number of doctors and pharmacists, which—we may infer—raised the price of their services. But this development did not restrict the availability of any drugs; nor—since it affected only the retail end of the drug industry and because the drug industry itself changed drastically in the middle third of the twentieth century—did it have a large effect on drug prices.

The importance of licensing laws, therefore, was in their potential for interaction with other laws, which would only be realized after 1938. Taken by themselves, they are more interesting for their underlying assumptions. The laws represent a rejection of competition by independent professionals and tradesmen. These groups felt that the communities within which they had maintained their relative incomes and status were being undermined and that they could not rely on the growing market institutions to guarantee them the income they thought their skills should provide. Therefore, they turned to the government to protect their positions.

An alternative legislative thrust attempted to restrict or eliminate the adulteration and misbranding of drugs. This approach appears from a modern perspective to strike more directly at the public policy problems inherent in the manufacture and sale of drugs, but it, too, had little impact on the provision of drugs in this early period. Nevertheless, the pure food and drug legislation of the Progressive period is interesting both for the groundwork it laid for the future and for what it reveals about the attitudes of policymakers toward competition.

Two classes of drugs can be distinguished in the late nineteenth century. The first were those whose composition and technique of manufacture were listed in the *United States Pharmacopoeia* and the *National Formulary,* known today by the initials *USP* and *NF* that appear on bottles of aspirin and vitamins. The first edition of the *USP* was published by doctors in 1820 as a standard list of pharmaceutical preparations. It was revised periodically with the increasing help of pharmacists. The *NF*, written by pharmacists from the start, was first issued in 1888 as a supplement to the *USP*. It contained drugs not in the *USP* or too new to be included in the *USP*.[14]

The selection criteria for the *USP* were kept secret, and the *NF* was even less exclusive than its older cousin.[15] Of the many drugs included in these compendia, fewer than a dozen are still considered today to be "reliable and effective pharmaceutical preparations." They include digitalis, morphine, quinine, diphtheria antitoxin, aspirin, and ether. The two hundred or so other drugs were either useless or of only "minor" benefit.[16] Nevertheless, these drugs constituted the respectable nonsurgical therapeutic arsenal of doctors at the time. There was no indication at the time that the few drugs listed here were in some way different from the others in the compendia, and there was no anticipation of radical changes in the list of available drugs. Even when doctors perceived that a drug was effective, they had no way to discover the limits of its effectiveness. Consequently, those doctors who discovered that these few drugs "worked" tended to prescribe them for everything, appropriately (by modern standards) or not. In the words of one author: "The great lesson . . . of medical history is that the placebo has always been the norm of medical practice."[17]

The formulary drugs can be contrasted with patent or proprietary medicines, which were made by secret processes from unknown ingredients and sold under trademarked names. These medicines, or at least those of them that were later analyzed, appear to have been composed largely of either water or alcohol. Radam's Microbe Killer and Liquozone, for example, were basically colored water, while Hostetter's Bitters and Peruna could easily have been classified as liquor. Lydia Pinkham's Vegetable Compound was 18 percent alcohol—more than most wines. These patent medicines were no more useful in the treatment of disease than the typical formulary drug, although they were not markedly harmful either. Patent medicines containing opium constitute a more difficult problem. They were even more effective than those containing alcohol at relieving the symptoms of users, but they were also more addictive. Most modern writers attach little importance to the former effect and thus regard these patent medicines as dangerous. But in an age when neither respectable medicine nor the advice of a doctor was likely to effect a cure, the relief of symptoms may have been a worthy achievement.[18]

In fact, if we allow for this difference in expected benefit from drugs, consumers may not have been much worse at choosing drugs in the late nineteenth century than doctors are today. If we assume that they were interested only in the relief of symptoms, then they had information available to them that allowed choices to be related in a rough way to drugs' effects. But they did not have either the therapeutic or the statistical knowledge needed to make a reasoned choice between alternative drugs, and their drug choices were based on customary patterns. They were influenced by a variety of factors unrelated to drug effectiveness, and advertising was a potent means of influencing customs and expanding drug sales.

Patent medicines were advertised widely, both to the public and to doctors. Advertising to the public was concentrated in newspapers, with whom the makers of patent drugs had a symbiotic relationship. The advertising revenues supported the newspapers at the same time as the ads themselves helped to sell the medicines. These ads often conflicted with stories in the papers and with informed opinion about the contents of the patent medicines or the dangers of taking some of them, in the same way cigarette and liquor ads today often carry a different message from news stories about the effects of smoking and drinking. But far from banning patent medicine advertisements from their pages—as some advertising media have done today with cigarette and liquor ads—newspapers generally opposed legislation restricting them. Legal restrictions would have diminished an important source of newspaper advertising revenue.[19]

Although most patent medicine advertising was directed at consumers, the manufacturers did not neglect doctors. For example, a medical professor reported receiving 424 circulars about medicines in 1899. Only 54 cited trials by physicians that had been reported in medical journals. The others contained spurious endorsements from a variety of disreputable sources. Nevertheless, the advertisements were effective enough to stimulate a doctor to explain to colleagues in the *Yale Medical Journal* how they could dispense patent medicines without revealing that they were doing so. His secret was to repackage the patent medicine: "Dispense [it] in a plain bottle, avoiding in this way original packages." He urged doctors to write the name of the drug in Latin, with the maker's name in parentheses if he needed it, so that he could retain the trade of the customer who might otherwise buy the medicine without visiting a doctor again.[20] The makers of patent medicines tried to convince doctors to prescribe their products, but patent medicines bought without the aid of a doctor represented a commercial threat to the medical profession.

The patent medicine business was not a particularly profitable one. There were a few spectacular successes, but many failures. No one has collected data on the average profitability of the manufacturers, but the ease with which someone could introduce a new patent medicine restricted the profits that any seller could make. Even if sales were high, the advertising expenses necessary to retain the market restricted profitability. Patent medicines by and large were made by small, marginal firms. The scientific discoveries of the late nineteenth century increased the sales of patent medicines by seeming to provide an assurance of effectiveness, but the growth reflected the entry of new small firms rather than expansion of the existing ones.[21]

These firms, with their allied newspapers, constituted one interest group. They were organized into the Proprietary Medicine Manufacturers and Dealers Association, formed in 1881. Opposed to them—or, more accurately, in competition with them—were the doctors and the "respectable" drug houses that made the ingredients of the preparations listed in the *USP* and *NF*. It should be emphasized that these respectable firms, even those that bear the names of drug firms existing today, did not resemble today's drug manufacturers. They were small, they did not undertake any serious research, and the cost of their raw materials was the largest single component of the price of their products. They typically did not sell their products under brand names, and—unlike the makers of patent medicines—they advertised exclusively to doctors.[22]

The legislative conflicts over labeling and adulteration laws found the Proprietary Association on one side, but the doctors largely absent from the other. There were many reasons for the lack of direct opposition, but the most important was that the legislative discussion of pure drugs took place in the context of discussions of pure food. The 1906 law was known universally—even in the margins of the United States *Statutes at Large*—as the Pure Food Act, although its full title was "An Act for preventing the manufacture, sale, or transportation of adulterated or misbranded or poisonous or deleterious foods, drugs, medicines, and liquors, for regulating traffic therein, and for other purposes."[23] The supporters of this act were not primarily concerned with medical care, but rather with the food supply.

The Pure Food Act of 1906

The campaign for pure food laws started first in the states, and almost every state had passed laws regulating some aspects of the food supply by the turn of the century.[24] The concern moved onto the national stage in the 1890s, where it was supported actively by Harvey W. Wiley, chief of the Division of Chemistry in the Department of Agriculture. The Division of Chemistry was based on a discipline, not a problem, and its organizational survival depended on finding problems to solve. Wiley, who became division chief in 1883, saw that food adulteration was a good problem for this purpose. He was an active missionary with a flair for publicity. He maintained links with all the many groups interested in pure food legislation and acted as a spokesman and coordinator for them. His concerns, as well as the more general Progressive malaise, can be seen in this passage from his biographer:

To maintain the integrity of the food supply, an ancient problem, had become more difficult ... As processing shifted from home to factory, competition intensified, and manufacturers, their ethical standards dulled by the impersonality of their function, debased their goods in the struggle to survive. To reduce costs, some added chicory to coffee, mixed inert matter with ground pepper, or sold a mixture of glucose, flavoring, and hayseed, appropriately colored to conceal the fraud, for raspberry jam. Such practices, though they scarcely undermined the public health, shocked Wiley.[25]

The Progressive vision of a vanished, noncommercial past still lives in this statement from the 1950s; the references to dulled ethical standards and intensified competition reproduce the rhetoric of the earlier period. Wiley was opposed to the replacement of community institutions by market institutions. The strains in the economy cited as examples of Wiley's concerns are noteworthy for their triviality, and their very triviality is evidence that the underlying issue was the pervasive institutional change, not the isolated changes in the supply of food. Wiley's concern was with petty fraud permitted by the absence of community, not with any danger to the well-being of the public, and this focus on the marginal producer of shady goods pervades the entire early history of federal food and drug regulation.

Pure food bills were submitted to Congress more or less continually throughout the 1890s and early 1900s. They all died, although they occasionally passed one or the other house. And while they typically included sections on drugs, they differed in their definitions of drugs. Some restricted the drugs that would be covered by the law to those listed in the two formularies; others cast a wider net.[26]

Despite the long legislative history, there is no evidence of public concern or involvement before the turn of the century. Then Wiley organized his famous and dramatic "Poison Squad" in 1902. He had a dozen volunteers restrict themselves to specified diets that included a variety of food additives for the six months from December 1902 to June 1903. He found that food additives like boric acid, salicylic acid, benzoate of soda, and formaldehyde were all harmful to the volunteers' metabolism, digestion, or health. But the findings were less important than the well-publicized test itself, whose popular name reveals the attitude of its sponsors.[27]

The muckrakers joined the debate with a series of articles by Samuel Hopkins Adams in *Collier's* in 1905 and 1906. Upton Sinclair's *The Jungle* appeared in February 1906, containing the graphic image of Durham's Pure Leaf Lard made out of the remains of workmen who had fallen into the cooking vats. President Theodore Roosevelt supported pure food legislation in his annual message to Congress in December 1905, partly in response to this publicity. The Pure Food Act passed Congress and was signed by the president in June 1906.[28]

To the extent that the Pure Food Act was passed in response to *The*

Jungle, the law missed its mark. Sinclair was attacking the practices of large meat packers; the Pure Food Act aimed at small, marginal suppliers of food. To make the point dramatically, a bill signed on the same day as the Pure Food Act gave the Department of Agriculture direct authority to inspect animals used in meat-packing plants.[29] Public outrage over *The Jungle* was used by advocates of general legislation on adulteration to secure passage of their act, even though it did not refer to and was separate from a bill on the inspection of meat packing.

This legislative pattern was repeated in 1938 and again in 1962. In each case, food and drug legislation was passed in response to public outcry over an existing hazard. But in each case also, the law passed by Congress either did not deal with the danger at all—as in the 1906 response to *The Jungle*—or dealt with it only in passing while adding major new provisions on unrelated topics. Consequently, interpreting food and drug legislation as responses to the public's desires misses a critical part of the story. Public pressure led to some kind of new law, but other forces determined the kind of law it would be. These other forces in 1906 consisted mainly of pressure from interested businesses and the organizational needs of Wiley's Division of Chemistry.

The American Medical Association was largely invisible during these proceedings. The association began a crusade against "nostrums" in 1900, but a reorganization in the following year absorbed any energy that might have gone into this effort. Even *The Journal of the American Medical Association* (*JAMA*), which had promised in 1900 to purge its pages of patent medicine advertisements, defaulted on its pledge. The AMA began its crusade again in 1905. It organized its Council of Pharmacy and Chemistry, resolved again to eliminate nostrum ads from *JAMA,* and urged passage of pure food legislation. However, the new campaign was dropped in March 1906 as a result of internal dissension, and the AMA remained inactive thereafter. A *JAMA* editorial in March 1906 claimed that no bill at all was preferable to one without a board of experts to evaluate the regulated products, but its impact was offset by AMA telegrams to Congress supporting the Pure Food Act the following June and the association's welcome of the law after it was passed.[30] If doctors benefited from the passage of this legislation, it was a benefit that owed nothing to their organized activity.

The business community did not take a unified position on the proposed legislation. The Proprietary Association, as might be expected, opposed any regulation of drug sales. Food manufacturers divided according to whether they would be helped or hurt by the bill. The most famous example of competition through legislation was the successful efforts of the dairy industry to ban or restrict the sales of oleomargarine. But the ramifications of the legislation spread into smaller areas as well. The American Baking Powder Association consisted of those firms making baking powder from alum, as opposed to the cream of tartar used by the Royal Baking Powder Company. They were opposed to labeling requirements that would force them to reveal that they were using alum, presumably out of fear that consumers would not buy baking powder so labeled even though it could compete successfully with baking powder made from cream of tartar in the absence of raw-material labels. The association's attitude toward the proposed legislation fluctuated according to whether its scope extended to baking powder,[31] and the provisions of the Pure Food Act reflected in part the outcome of many struggles among competing business groups. Since all the firms involved were small, there is no suggestion that the political contest was between big and small businesses. Any bias toward large firms came from a general theoretical outlook, not from specific political pressure.

The law that emerged from this welter of competing influences defined drugs quite broadly. It covered the drugs in the two national formularies and, in addition, "any substance or mixture of substances intended to be used for the cure, mitigation, or prevention of disease of either man or other animals." A drug was deemed to be adulterated if it deviated from the standards of the formularies without admitting as much on the container or "if its strength or purity fall below the professed standard or quality under which it is sold." A drug was considered misbranded if it was sold under a false name, if it was sold in the package of another drug, or if it failed to identify and quantify the presence of a short list of addicting substances, including alcohol, morphine, opium, cocaine, and heroin. The term *misbranded* in general referred to "any statement . . . which shall be false or misleading in any particular." Adulterated or misbranded articles could be seized by the government and their manufacturers prosecuted, but no dealer could be prosecuted if he had a guarantee from his supplier of compliance with the law.[32]

The law, in short, made misrepresentation illegal. It did not force the manufacturer to disclose the contents of his preparations, but if he chose to do so, the government would monitor his accuracy. The producer was obligated to inform the consumer about narcotic content, and he was required to adhere to common standards if he chose to employ a common name for his product. In addition, no statement could "be false or misleading in any particular"—a high standard. But if the producer wanted to avoid the scope of the law entirely, he could produce a nonnarcotic preparation, give it a novel name, and say little definite about it.

The largely passive stance of the law exposes a particular view of competition. Unlike the licensing laws, the Pure Food Act of 1906 did not reject competition as a way of allocating resources. It provided an aid to competition. Consumers could use instrumental behavior to choose among competing products only if they knew what the differences among them were. Labels could be an aid to consumers, informing them of the contents of a package without forcing them to test the ingredients personally. But if consumers used labels as substitutes for analysis, producers had every incentive to label their products as something better than they were. Each consumer could not maintain a chemical laboratory to check the labels on drugs; it was logical to delegate this function to a specialized agency. And since the information about a package's contents was the same for any potential purchaser, it was logical to delegate this function to the government. The choices of what drugs should be produced and what drugs should be bought were left entirely in the hands of private producers and consumers.

The new law therefore encouraged people to modify their behavior. By making instrumental behavior easier and more rewarding, that is, by making information about drugs more readily available and more reliable, it made the switch from customary to instrumental behavior in drug purchasing more attractive. The conflict between customary behavior and market institutions therefore was to be resolved—if the law was to be successful—by changing behavior to accord with the changed institutional framework. As noted in chapter 1, this path to stability is taken less often than the alternative of changing the institution to conform to the dominant mode of behavior.

The law had two immediate effects. The first was to transform the *USP* and *NF* from private publications into official standards for drug manufacture. According to one contemporary author, this change would obviate the almost universal practice of specifying Squibb when prescribing chloroform. But a more skeptical observer claimed that "until recently, the *National Formulary* was a modest, unobtrusive, harmless and really useful little book ... in which the tottering great-grandmothers of the materia medica were resurrected from their well-earned sleep in the therapeutic graveyard to join in a merry dance with the lusty and vociferous youngsters of the modern therapeutic yellow press." Setting the *NF* up as an official standard of the federal government was an unnecessary rejuvenation of these "tottering great-grandmothers."[33]

The second immediate effect was to enlarge the role of the Agriculture Department's Division of Chemistry, renamed the Bureau of Chemistry, which was to administer the new law. The bureau's appropriation rose by a factor of five and its employees by a factor of four between 1906 and 1908. In organizational terms, the law was a great success for Harvey W. Wiley.[34]

Nevertheless, Wiley himself was never satisfied with the way the law was enforced. His missionary zeal outran the enthusiasm of his superiors in the Department of Agriculture and probably the limits of the law as well. Samuel Hopkins Adams wrote to Wiley on March 26, 1907, "I find a general disposition to obey the law in the letter, though to evade it as far as possible in the spirit." Wiley replied on April 1, "Our experience is in accord with yours."[35] Limited by his superiors and evaded by producers, Wiley resigned in 1912 to become a private advocate of more stringent reform.

Despite his complaints that the law was not being applied as effectively as possible, Wiley himself neglected drugs. Only 135 of the first 1,000 judgments obtained under the 1906 law concerned drugs.[36] The criminal proceedings concentrated on small-scale producers, in accord with Wiley's view of where the dangers of competition lay. The one achievement of the law as it applied to drugs was to lower the narcotic content of patent medicines. Hostetter's Bitters went from 39 percent alcohol to 25 percent, for example, even though demand fell off. But part of the credit for this change belongs to the Internal Revenue Service, which taxed medicines designed to provide alcohol in "dry" regions, and part to the Harrison Anti-Narcotics Law of 1914, which separated the control of narcotics from the general concern with food and drugs.[37] The achievement this separation represents, while not to be slighted, therefore lies outside the mainstream of the story of medicinal drugs.

Even if Wiley had been more zealous about drugs, it is not clear that he could have done any more. The Bureau of Chemistry issued regulations on the accuracy of therapeutic claims, basing them on the law's requirement that labels not be "false or misleading in any particular." The regulations then were used to indict the shipper of a presumed cancer remedy for claiming or implying on the label that the contents were effective in curing cancer. The case was contested and reached the Supreme Court in 1911, where Justice Oliver Wendell Holmes spoke for the majority.

Holmes based the decision on a detailed grammatical analysis of the law's wording. Starting from the assumption that the therapeutic claims were false—an assumption made only for the purpose of his argument—

Holmes said, "What we have to decide is whether such misleading statements are aimed at and hit by the words of the act." His answer was no. A very close reading of the paragraph containing the injunction that labels not be "false or misleading in any particular" led Holmes to the conclusion that "the phrase is aimed not at all possible false statements, but only at such as determine the identity of the article, possibly including its strength, quality, and purity." The 1906 law intended, in other words, to assure the customer of the identity of the article purchased, not of its usefulness. The government could not prosecute drug manufacturers for false or misleading therapeutic claims.

This is the main thrust of the opinion, but in the final paragraph, Holmes went on to add "but a word as to what Congress was likely to attempt." Why, Holmes speculated, did Congress limit the scope of its act in this way? He replied, "It was much more likely to regulate commerce in food and drugs with reference to plain matter of fact, so that food and drugs should be what they professed to be, when the kind was stated, than to distort the uses of its constitutional power to establishing criteria in regions where opinions are far apart." In support of his contention that opinions on therapeutic effects differ, he cited a 1902 decision of the Supreme Court denying the right of the Post Office to withhold delivery of articles with false therapeutic claims. The claims were stated to be opinions, which were not capable of being proven right or wrong and which therefore—I infer from Holmes's reference to the Constitution—were protected by the constitutional guarantees of freedom of speech. A dissenting opinion, written by Justice Charles Evans Hughes, contested Holmes's construction of the law, but agreed with him on the limitation of congressional power in the realm of uncertain knowledge.[38]

Holmes's afterword turned out to be more important than the body of the opinion. Congress could rewrite the law to enlarge its scope, but it could not cross the boundary between fact and opinion that Holmes had mapped. The Sherley Amendment to the Pure Food Act, passed in the following year, was the result. It added to the existing law the requirement that labels should not contain "any statement . . . regarding the curative or therapeutic effect . . . which is false and fraudulent."[39] The last two words show the Supreme Court's influence. Without Holmes's final word, the amendment would have stopped before them, but the Supreme Court had served notice that the Bureau of Chemistry could not prosecute people simply for false therapeutic claims because therapeutic claims in general could not be proven true or false. The government was obligated to prove fraud, that is, it had to show that the producer knew that his therapeutic claims were wrong. This turned out to be difficult, for the simple reason that the producer could always claim ignorance. The 1906 law, which did not extend to advertising in any case, did not provide much scope for the regulation of drugs, and the state of medical knowledge at the time did not allow its extension.

A later commissioner of food and drugs who joined the Bureau of Chemistry in 1907 looked back on this period as a bleak one. In his words: "The drug work of the Bureau got off to a bad start. It never seemed to interest Dr. Wiley as the food work did. It suffered, too, from less-than-competent technical directions. The Johnson decision created a severe handicap, not entirely overcome by the Shirley [sic] amendment."[40]

This poor record did not make everyone unhappy. The Proprietary Association, which had opposed the Pure Food Act with all its strength, discovered that it could live quite happily with the new law. The Bureau of Chemistry eliminated marginal producers who were giving the business a bad name and created conditions suitable for the growth of the larger firms. The Sherley Amendment forced producers to be vague in their therapeutic claims, but did not otherwise trouble them. The production of the Proprietary Assocation's members rose by 60 percent from 1902 to 1912; instead of eliminating patent medicines, the law favored the larger producers at the expense of the smaller.[41]

Similar frustrations surrounded the attempts of other government agencies to control the distribution of patent medicines. Starting around the turn of the century, the Post Office refused to deliver fraudulently labeled patent medicines and devices, giving rise to the case Holmes later cited. The Supreme Court ruled in 1902 that therapeutic claims were not matters of fact; they were opinions and subject to the protection of the law. This decision hobbled the Post Office's effort at regulation.[42]

The Federal Trade Commission (FTC), set up to restrain the growth of monopoly in 1915, included drug advertising within its scope. It saw its role through the 1920s as working with the business community to police competitive conditions, a policy which meant working with large firms to contain marginal firms. By eliminating potential competition at the fringes, the FTC was acting in concert with the other government agencies that promoted the growth of the larger drug firms. But the range of the FTC, like that of the Bureau of Chemistry, was restricted by the Supreme Court. The FTC was not designed to protect the consumers directly, the Supreme Court said in 1931. It could do so only indirectly by promoting competition. To prosecute, the court said, the FTC had to show injury to a competitor, not to customers.[43] The FTC was not to undermine the market institution; it was to maintain it. Consumers would be protected by the operations of the market, not by direct government action.

Among private groups, the AMA stood out as the leader in the crusade against ineffective medicines, even though its activities were confined largely to the publication of several books. The AMA had established its Council on Pharmacy and Chemistry in 1905 and its own chemical laboratory in 1906. It publicized their findings in a variety of books with titles like *Nostrums and Quackery* and *The Propaganda for Reform in Proprietary Medicines*. The AMA reprinted Samuel Hopkins Adams's *Collier's* articles in *The Great American Fraud*, which it sold below cost. It simultaneously opposed the publication in medical journals of "nostrum" ads and tried to find acceptable ads for these same journals. And it attempted to inform doctors about useful drug therapy in volumes like *New and Non-official Drugs*, which described drugs that were not yet in one of the now-official formularies.[44]

By the time the economy began its greatest depression in 1929, there was a variety of noncommercial activity in the drug field. The regulatory part of the Bureau of Chemistry became the Food, Drug, and Insecticide Administration in 1927 and the Food and Drug Administration in 1931. It had a budget of $1.6 million and over five hundred employees at the time of its final name change, twice the budget and slightly more employees than the whole Bureau of Chemistry in 1908. At the same time, the AMA and other groups publicized the evils of nostrums and ineffective medicines. But the FDA was mainly concerned with the food supply— despite the generality of its title—and the AMA's publicity appeared to have little impact. Very few new medicinal drugs had appeared since the turn of the century, and very little could be accomplished with drug therapy. The legislation and publicity forced patent medicine makers to be more circumspect in their advertising, but it did not discourage consumers from buying all sorts of potions.[45]

Drug regulation before the Depression thus had the following characteristics. First, its thrust was to consolidate the shift from community to market in the late nineteenth century. People had been acting comfortably in the customary mode within local communities during most of that century. Communities were not isolated, but people made many economic decisions in terms of the local community nonetheless. We may hazard the guess that medical decisions were even more customary and community-oriented than most others. As the economy changed at the end of the century, people found that they were acting more and more within market institutions rather than communities. This created a tension between their customary mode of behavior and the institutional setting. Drug policy in the early years attempted to deal with this tension by encouraging people to utilize instrumental behavior, that is, to alter their behavior to accord with market institutions. It operated by requiring drug manufacturers to furnish information about their products, assuring purchasers of the veracity of that information—at least as it extended to the drug's composition—and eliminating obvious frauds from the market. The FDA, FTC, and AMA all saw the provision of accurate information as their primary function, although the FDA was the most influential of the three.

This policy did not fit well with the other line of policy in the medical area, the licensing laws for doctors and pharmacists. Licensing laws attempted to create new institutions that could insulate people from the effects of the market—new communities to replace the old, extending along professional rather than geographic lines. Since these two lines of policies were not coordinated, it was not clear before the Depression whether drug policy would move toward the extension or the restriction of the market in medicinal drugs.

The second characteristic of drug policy before the Depression was that it was not notably effective. Medical technology was still relatively primitive; there were few effective drugs and even fewer ways of identifying them. Most drugs were traditional ones limited in their function to the immediate relief of common symptoms. People had some rough idea of which drugs worked, both from their own limited experience and from the traditions of their local community. The information affected by the public policy had little to do with these beliefs, and we may presume that this policy had little effect on people's decisions.

Third, drug policy had one effect on the supply of drugs that was noticeable even before the Depression. The FDA was successful in its efforts to get a variety of products off the market. These products were those disallowed by the 1906 law either because they were sold under misinformation about their contents or because of obvious fraud in the description of effects. These products typically were made by small firms, and the administration of the law operated to put more pressure on small firms than on large. Since no drug firms were very large at this time, this bias was not very important. But it is the beginning of a trend that continues through all subsequent public policy toward drugs.

Finally, the limits of public policy toward drugs were set outside the agencies making and administering that policy. In particular, the FDA wanted to extend its control over the sale of drugs further than it was permitted to do by the Supreme Court. Conditions in 1929, consequently, were doubly unstable. Not only had the tension between most people's mode of behavior and the institutional setting been approached in an unpromising way, but the FDA saw itself as constrained by outside forces in the exercise of its perceived duty.

THREE

The Legacy
of the New Deal

THE DRUG INDUSTRY'S SALES increased greatly between the passage of the Pure Food Act of 1906 and the Great Depression, growing by a factor of six in the twenty years or so that separated them. Druggists' preparations—the material out of which pharmacists and, to a lesser extent, doctors made medicines consumed by the public—accounted for only two-fifths of the total throughout the period. The remainder consisted mostly of patent medicines, accompanied by some proprietary medicines advertised to doctors. At the retail level, patent medicines still accounted for half of all drug sales in 1929. Drug regulation under the 1906 act had not succeeded in directing consumer expenditures away from patent medicines by the start of the Depression.[1]

The Federal Food, Drug, and Cosmetic Act of 1938

This "failure" may have created a desire for more legislation in the minds of people both within and outside the government, but it did not lead directly to new laws. The initial impetus for a revision of the Pure Food Act came in the early days of the New Deal, even though the Federal Food, Drug, and Cosmetic Act, the result of this impetus, did not pass Congress until 1938 and came out of quite different concerns. The Food and Drug Administration was still part of the Agriculture Department, and the idea of rewriting the food and drug law came from an interchange in the spring of 1933 between W. G. Campbell, the chief of the

FDA, and Rexford G. Tugwell, the newly appointed assistant secretary of agriculture.

The precipitating factor was a routine letter from the Department of Agriculture, written by the FDA and sent to Tugwell for his signature. The letter explained the FDA's policy toward spray insecticides, which was a compromise between the FDA's opposition to their use and support for the farmers coming from the rest of the Department of Agriculture. The letter said the FDA was acting "in the interest of public health and the welfare of the fruit and vegetable industry." Tugwell turned the letter back to the FDA, asking why the insecticide in question was not simply banned as a poison. After an initial burst of irritation that Tugwell would ask them why they had not done something they had been trying to do for years, the leadership of the FDA realized that he was attempting to support them, not to attack them. Campbell explained the situation to Tugwell and then took the opportunity to recommend amending the Pure Food Act. Tugwell said he would discuss this idea with the president and called Campbell back the same day to report White House approval. Paul Dunbar, Campbell's assistant and successor as chief of the FDA as well as the author of an account of this interchange, reacted by saying, "Why not write an entirely new law?"[2]

The new law, however, was to be written by old people. Reform was coming from within the FDA and therefore could be expected to strengthen the agency, rather than to change the administration of the law. Even though the impetus for revision came from a question about the FDA's relationship to its institutional home, the Department of Agriculture, this was not the subject of the proposed reform. The impulse for reform, such as it was, was unrelated to the content of reform that emerged.

In fact, the committee that drafted the new law was instructed to propose revisions that did not affect the administrative framework through which it was to be enforced. The alternative, as the committee envisaged it, was to strengthen the law by creating a more powerful agency that could license producers and enforce its own decisions without operating through the Department of Justice. Other alternatives might have occurred in a looser discussion, such as product liability legislation on the model of more recent laws or greater separation between the control of food and drugs. But one member of the committee reflected after the act's passage that the difficulty of getting the bill that was actually written through Congress shows that the committee could not successfully have proposed more radical reform.[3]

The FDA was the successor to Harvey W. Wiley's Bureau of Chemistry. The 1906 act said that the regulations necessary for its enforcement should be made by the secretaries of the treasury, agriculture, and commerce and labor, while examinations of specimens should be done in the Bureau of Chemistry or under its direction. The secretary of agriculture was charged with the responsibility of following up any suspected violations of the act found by the bureau.[4] Given Wiley's proselytizing energy and his role in securing passage of the act, these provisions came to mean that the Bureau of Chemistry administered the act, subject to the constraints imposed by having to work through the secretary of agriculture and the Department of Justice for prosecutions.

The bureau's regulatory functions were separated from its myriad other functions in 1927. The regulators went into the newly formed Food, Drug, and Insecticide Administration, renamed the Food and Drug Administration in 1931, while the remainder of the bureau joined the old Bureau of Soils to make a new Bureau of Chemistry and Soils. The personnel of the FDA was the same as in the old Bureau of Chemistry, and its leadership was drawn almost exclusively from the bureau. At the beginning of 1937, the chief (Campbell), assistant chief (Dunbar), five division chiefs, and nine field chiefs had all begun work in the Bureau of Chemistry before the start of 1908.[5] It is only logical to assume that their views of food and drug regulation had been formed within the context of the 1906 law.

The new bill was introduced in Congress in 1933, but failed to pass in that session. Neither congressional nor presidential support was strong, and Franklin Roosevelt assented when Congress wanted to adjourn its special session without action on this bill. The bill stayed before Congress for five years before it was finally passed in 1938. In Tugwell's words: "The legislation existed in a kind of limbo from 1933 to 1938, periodically being used as an illustration of the New Deal's socialistic tendencies but actually never being pushed by any political sponsor."[6] The bill finally passed on the heels of a drug disaster, much as the 1906 act was passed in the wake of *The Jungle*'s appearance.

The bill that passed was neither a simple response to the drug tragedy nor the same bill that had been introduced in 1933. It had been watered down during its long legislative history, but the drug incident resulted in adding new provisions rather than restoring previous ones. Tugwell's opinion was that "The Food, Drug, and Cosmetic Bill as it passed in 1938 was a discredit to everyone concerned with it. What had started out in 1933 on a tide of consumer approval to be a new charter of honesty and fair dealing in the manufacture and sale of products in everyday use had ended up as a renewed permission to exploit the public . . . Consumers, so far as could be seen, had no votes. At least they had no voices."[7]

The legislative history of the 1938 act has many similarities to that of the 1906 act. The congressional debate lasted several years before leading to passage. The president—Roosevelt in both cases—sent a message to Congress supporting the bill, but does not seem to have worked actively on its behalf.[8] And the law finally passed in response to a burst of publicity about a health hazard.

The American Medical Association was more clearly in favor of new legislation in the 1930s than before 1906, but hardly more active. The association testified in favor of strong legislation in 1935, but did not show much interest before or after. As in 1906, passage of the law was largely unrelated to the activities of the AMA.[9]

As in the early 1900s, the main support of the Depression bill came from within the government itself. The FDA organized a "Chamber of Horrors" in 1933 to garner support for the new bill, but this imitation of Wiley's Poison Squad failed to arouse much enthusiasm. The founders of Consumers Union wrote two books on patent medicines, *Your Money's Worth* and *100,000,000 Guinea Pigs,* but also failed to initiate much discussion. Tugwell knew the authors, and he may have been responding as much to their views as to the organizational problems of the FDA in his support of new legislation, but there is little evidence of broad-based support for the new law.[10]

If popular support for drug legislation in the Depression seems scant, there is also little evidence of public opposition. According to one of the bill's authors, the proprietary drug industry could not oppose the bill openly because they would destroy public confidence in their products by suggesting that regulation would interfere with sales. The manufacturers therefore worked behind the scenes to water down the bill. In addition, the press did not support food and drug legislation. Even more than in 1906, the new law was seen as a threat to advertising and therefore to the press. Tugwell's link to the bill made it symbolic of a challenge to business in general as well.[11]

It is hard to evaluate reasons given for silence or indifference, but the argument that it was concern about advertising revenues that dominated the press gets considerable support from the fate of advertising in the final legislation. The Federal Food, Drug, and Cosmetic Act of 1938, like its predecessor, did not extend to advertising. The advertising provisions in the bill were removed in its final legislative days, and this surgery may have been as important as anything else in securing final passage.

Control over advertising was left with the Federal Trade Commission, which was given new powers in 1938 by the Wheeler-Lea Amendment to the Federal Trade Commission Act. Despite the amendment, however, the FTC had far less power over questionable advertising than the FDA had over problematic labeling. The new legislation removed the necessity of proving injury to a competitor; the FTC could protest injuries to consumers and false advertising directly. But the definition of falsity in the Wheeler-Lea Amendment fell short of the one in the FDA's enabling legislation. The Pure Food Act, it will be recalled, prohibited labels that were "false or misleading in any particular." Wheeler-Lea prohibited advertising that was "false in a material respect." In addition, the FTC lacked the FDA's power of seizure, and it could prosecute only if it could show "intent to defraud or mislead." Finally, the FTC worked even more closely with the business community than did the FDA.[12]

Control over advertising remained far less strict than control over labeling as a result. The Wheeler-Lea Amendment had little force for the same reason that the Sherley Amendment was a dead letter. A law that required proof of fraud for successful prosecution could reach only a few blatant practices. Anyone operating in a gray area of medical knowledge or who could make a case for purity of motives was beyond the reach of such a law. It took the FTC sixteen years to get the word *liver* removed from Carter's Little Liver Pills.[13]

If separating control over advertising from control over labeling was one factor leading to passage of the Federal Food, Drug, and Cosmetic Act, the Elixir Sulfanilamide disaster was the other. The Massengill Company, a respected drug firm since 1897, wanted to sell a liquid form of sulfanilamide, the first of the new sulfa drugs, which it already sold in tablets and capsules. The company found that sulfanilamide would dissolve in diethylene glycol and that the resultant solution had a reasonable appearance and taste. This solution, labeled Elixir Sulfanilamide, went on the market in September 1937.

Alas, the Massengill Company had not tested diethylene glycol for toxicity, and it turned out to be toxic indeed. Just over a hundred people died a painful death from taking Elixir Sulfanilamide. The FDA seized as much of the preparation as it could find once it was alerted to the situation, retrieving all but 6 of the 240 gallons made. But the FDA could not prosecute Massengill for causing the deaths of a hundred people; under the 1906 law it could only prosecute the company for mislabeling its product. *Elixir* is a term used to describe an alcohol solution, and it was misapplied to diethylene glycol. Massengill paid a fine of $26,100. It was the largest fine ever paid for mislabeling, but it is small when measured against so many deaths.[14]

The Elixir Sulfanilamide incident led to the introduction in the House of a bill banning interstate commerce in harmful substances. It was included in the committee version of the Food, Drug, and Cosmetic Act, where it formed the new-drug approval part of the law.[15] The momentum given to the whole bill by this addition was enough to carry all the other provisions except those on advertising through Congress. As with *The Jungle* in 1906, public concern over a particular health problem dragged a substantial amount of only tangentially related legislation through Congress in its wake.

The Federal Food, Drug, and Cosmetic Act of 1938 needs to be described in some detail, both because it is the law—as amended—that prevails today and because a number of its provisions have had a curious history. It differed from the 1906 law in being far longer and organized by regulated commodity (food, drugs, and so on) rather than by type of violation (adulteration, misbranding). It also defined drugs to include products affecting bodily structure or function in the absence of disease and for the first time included medical "devices."

The chapter on drugs and devices consisted of five sections. The first two sections, on adulteration and misbranding, were much more detailed than the comparable sections of the old law. Adulteration was defined in greater detail, and the label—which still could not be "false or misleading in any particular"—had to contain much more information than before. All ingredients and the quantity of each had to be identified. Directions for the use of the drug and warnings about its dangers had to be included also. This entirely new labeling requirement, one of the most important parts of the law, is worth quoting:

Sec. 502. A drug or device shall be deemed to be misbranded ... (f) unless its labelling bears (1) adequate directions for use; and (2) such adequate warnings against use in those pathological conditions or by children where its use may be dangerous to health, or against unsafe dosage or methods or duration of administration or application, in such manner and form, as are necessary for the protection of users: *Provided,* that where any requirement of clause (1) of this paragraph, as applied to any drug or device, is not necessary for the protection of the public health, the Secretary shall promulgate regulations exempting such drug or device from such requirement.

Finally, a drug was deemed mislabeled if it was dangerous to health when used in the dosage recommended in the label as required by section 502 (f).

The third section of the chapter on drugs and devices listed exemptions to the labeling requirements of the previous section. A drug or device did not have to be labeled in accordance with the law if it was to be repackaged or reprocessed before being sold to consumers, and it was exempt from some labeling requirements if it was to be dispensed on the written prescription of a licensed physician, dentist, or veterinarian. It was *not* automatically exempted from section 502 (f) if it was sold by prescription.

The fourth section dealt with certification of coal tar colors for drugs, and the fifth was the bill on new drugs introduced in response to the Elixir Sulfanilamide disaster. New drugs could not be delivered for interstate shipment unless an effective application had been filed with the secretary of agriculture. The application had to describe the contents, manufacture, and uses of the drug and to demonstrate that it was safe for use under the recommended conditions. It became effective sixty days after filing unless the secretary objected. The secretary could object, among other reasons, if the application did not show that the drug was "safe for use under the conditions prescribed, recommended, or suggested in the proposed labeling thereof" or if it did not contain adequate tests of the drug's safety. The secretary could suspend the effectiveness of an application for due cause and could grant exemptions to the requirement of having one for "drugs intended solely for investigational use by experts qualified by scientific training and experience to investigate the safety of drugs."[16]

This final section created a new class of drugs. There had never before been a distinction between new and old drugs, and never before had a producer needed to get governmental permission to start marketing a drug. In one sense, he still did not. He needed to file an application, but the government did not have to respond. Silence by the government left the producer free to act. Nevertheless, the requirement of filing a new drug application represents a chipping away at the ideal of competition. In some cases *not* involving fraud or misrepresentation, the government—not the market—would decide what would be sold.

In a state of open competition, all drugs would be introduced to the market, and only those that were safe for use would survive the competitive struggle. In response to the Elixir Sulfanilamide episode, Congress backed away from this position. Only some products could be allowed into the competitive arena. The government would not assure consumers of finding the best product, but it would assure them that they would not be physically harmed by searching on their own. The 1906 act had outlawed fraud in the interest of preventing financial loss to the consumers. The 1938 act also outlawed unsafe products in the interest of protecting the physical well-being of consumers. Government regulation was coming to be seen as providing more protection to the consumer than the competitive process. As Tugwell said, the 1938 law was "strictly in the line of the new philosophy—to regulate industry, but not to require of it planning or performance. If manufacturers were to be required to conform to wage-and-hours requirements and to treat each other fairly [by the National Industrial Recovery Act of 1933], they ought also to be asked to treat their consumers fairly."[17]

The old law assumed that people could use instrumental behavior to choose drugs if they had correct information on the drugs' composition. The new law retreated from this assumption. Since people could not be trusted to draw the proper implications from a listing of ingredients—however detailed and accurate it might be—the government imposed two new requirements on drug manufacturers. They had to provide instructions for use of the drug, and they could not market "unsafe" drugs at all. The 1906 law tried to change behavior to fit comfortably into a market setting; the 1938 law abandoned the market setting for direct commands in specified circumstances. Significantly, the institutional change was directed at the point where change was most rapid, the introduction of new drugs.

Even though the 1938 law restricted the range of drugs that could be offered on the market and mandated that information about them be supplied to the consumer, it appeared to leave the eventual choice of drugs—among those available, to be sure—to the consumer himself. This was stated publicly to be the aim of the FDA in proposing and supporting the legislation. Self-medication was to be improved and facilitated, not hampered. Campbell, the chief of the FDA, said forcefully in Senate hearings at the start of the legislative process: "There is no issue, as I have told you previously, from the standpoint of the enforcement of the Food and Drugs Act about self-medication. This bill does not contemplate its prevention at all. If it did a single short section in the measure could have been drawn up to that effect. But what is desired . . . is to make self-medication safe."[18] He reemphasized the point in the same forum in the following year: "All of the provisions dealing with drugs . . . are directed toward safeguarding the consumer who is attempting to administer to himself."[19] The *House Report* on the bill that eventually became law explicitly adopted Campbell's point of view: "The bill is not intended to restrict in any way the availability of drugs for self-medication. On the contrary, it is intended to make self-medication safer and more effective."[20]

Despite these assurances from the chief of the FDA, the agency moved within six months of the bill's passage to curtail self-medication sharply and thereafter used a substantial and increasing proportion of its drug resources to enforce its imposed limitations.

The Prescription-Only Regulation

Most drugs, it is well to remember, were sold without the intervention of a doctor before the Great Depression. The distinction between doctors and pharmacists was virtually complete by 1929; consumers got less than 5 percent of their drugs directly from doctors. But pharmacists still operated independently of doctors at the end of the 1920s. Even though most drugs ordered by prescription—like most other drugs—were purchased from drugstores, prescriptions were not needed to buy any non-narcotic drug. Only about one-quarter of the drug sales from drugstores were ordered by prescription. Pharmacies sold many more patent medicines and approximately as many home remedies as drugs ordered by prescription. At the same time, less than 5 percent of drug advertising was directed at doctors, a reflection of pharmacists' independence from the control of physicians—and a sharp contrast with conditions today. Almost all drug advertising at the end of the 1920s consisted of newspaper and magazine ads directed at the public.[21]

The Federal Food, Drug, and Cosmetic Act was signed by the president in June 1938, and the FDA promulgated regulations to enforce it before the end of that year. Among these regulations were those making clear the scope of the exemption from labeling requirements set forth in section 502 (f), which were that a drug's label had to include directions for use and warnings about possible dangers arising from use. The exemption was:

if the label of such drug or device bears the statement *"Caution: To be used only by or on the prescription of a _____"* (the blank to be filled in by the word *"Physician," "Dentist,"* or *"Veterinarian,"* or any combination of such words), and all representations or suggestions contained in the labeling thereof with respect to the conditions for which such drug or device is to be used appear only in such medical terms as are not likely to be understood by the ordinary individual, and if such shipment or delivery is made for use exclusively by, or on the prescription of, physicians, dentists, or veterinarians licensed by law to administer or apply such drug or device; but such exemption shall expire when such shipment or delivery, or any part thereof is offered or otherwise disposed of for any use other than by or on the prescription of such a physician, dentist, or veterinarian.[22]

It seems simple enough. The law said that the FDA could exempt drugs or devices from the requirement to include recommended usages and the dangers of misuse when these regulations were "not necessary for the protection of the public health." The FDA interpreted this to mean that—among other conditions—the usage and dangers labels were not needed for drugs sold by prescription. To ensure that drugs without these labels would in fact be sold by prescription, the FDA required that they have a warning on the label, that they be shipped for this exclusive purpose, and that any instructions be unintelligible to the layman. The FDA said further that the exemption expired if the drug or device was sold without a prescription, making the seller immediately guilty of misbranding the product in question. It all seems simple and logical—until its implications are understood.

The act said elsewhere (section 503) that drugs sold by prescription were exempt from some labeling requirements, but it did not say which drugs were to be sold by prescription or that some drugs could not be sold without one. This regulation is different. It says that drugs with certain kinds of labels—"Caution . . ."—can only be sold by prescription. It allows the drug companies to create a class of drugs that cannot legally be sold without a prescription by putting the appropriate label on them.

This is a stunning change in the way drugs were to be sold. Before this regulation took effect, consumers could simply buy any nonnarcotic drug they desired. They could of course consult a doctor and get a prescription, but they were under no obligation to do so. Under the new regulation, certain drugs were now beyond the consumer's reach. The drug companies would decide which, although the FDA could sue them for mislabeling if it disagreed with their choices.

Far from encouraging self-medication, as the FDA's chief had said the 1938 act would do, this provision sharply curtailed it. Drug manufacturers and the FDA would now decide which drugs consumers could select from; consumers were no longer considered capable of selecting drugs on their own. Their inadequacy was to be emphasized and increased by writing the labels for prescription drugs "in such medical terms as are not likely to be understood by the ordinary individual." The FDA had appointed doctors as the consumers' purchasing agents.

The 1938 law reduced the scope of competition by making it harder to introduce new drugs into the market. The government rather than the market was to protect consumers. The FDA went further along this road in its administrative regulation. Even though the government undertook to guarantee the safety of all available drugs, consumers were not to be allowed to choose freely among them. Some—to be selected by an unspecified process—were obtainable only under professional guidance. Congress assumed that people could not understand the implications of a list of ingredients; the FDA assumed that they could not or would not understand and follow directions for use.

Going further than the law, although in the same direction, the FDA changed the institutional setting in which some drugs were to be sold from a market to a hierarchical arrangement in which consumers would be directed—ordered—to purchase drugs chosen by people above them in the hierarchy. The FDA in essence had abandoned the aim of the 1906 law, to make the market work by encouraging instrumental behavior. It had instead joined the other strand of public policy toward medicine, the campaign to supplant the market with hierarchical arrangements, which had found expression in state licensing of doctors. The 1938 FDA regulation on prescriptions placed the choice of some drugs—the number to be determined later—in the hands of these licensed doctors. Drug purchasing was imbedded into an existing medical hierarchy, and the interaction between the two requirements—for doctors to be licensed and for consumers to get prescriptions for drugs—strengthened the apparent need for both. The two strands of Progressive drug policy came together in 1938.

This confluence was the result of a change in the direction of FDA policy. Instead of trying to encourage instrumental behavior, the FDA had decided that people would not switch from the customary mode and that hierarchical structures consequently were preferable to markets. And the agency wrote the regulation in such a way as to validate this new attitude. By specifying that any suggestions for the use of prescribed drugs "appear only in such medical terms as are not likely to be understood by the ordinary individual," the FDA ensured that "ordinary individuals"would not be able to act instrumentally toward those drugs.

The FDA's assumptions were new to the drug market in 1938. Had they arisen from a change in the technology of producing drugs, from the availability of many new and complex drugs? The answer, as will be shown later, is no. The drug revolution came after 1938. The discovery of the first sulfa drugs, Prontosil and sulfanilamide, had been announced in 1935, but little occurred in the next few years to suggest that this was not simply the isolated identification of another therapeutic agent, like Salversan or insulin. The regulation grew out of conditions that predated the revolution in drug therapy produced by the wonder drugs of the 1940s. The dangerous component of Elixir Sulfanilamide was the solvent, not the sulfa drug.

What else, other than a change in drug technology, could have altered the FDA's assumptions? We do not know with any certainty, but there are one or two clues. The agency's *Annual Report* for 1939 identified the regulation as the result of "an administrative conclusion of some moment." The conclusion resulted from a conflict the FDA saw within the new law. The act said that all drugs must be labeled adequately, adding that any drug that was dangerous to health when used as the label suggested was automatically misbranded. But the report asserted, "Many drugs of great value to the physician are dangerous in the hands of those unskilled in the uses of drugs. The statute obviously was not intended to deprive the medical profession of potent but valuable medicants."[23]

The conflict was created by the assumption underlying the first of the two sentences quoted. The FDA assumed that adequate directions for self-medication could not be written for some drugs. The reasons for this assumption are not given. There were no new drugs with complicated modes of administration that only a doctor could understand, and there was very little knowledge of drug interactions even among professionals. Insulin, which had been commercially available for well over a decade, was surely as dangerous and as complex to administer as any other drug, but there is no mention of it. Instead, aminopyrine, cinchophen, neocinchophen, and sulfanilamide were listed as dangerous. Is the danger that a drug's full therapeutic potential will not be realized by consumers acting alone? Is it that drugs will be used indiscriminately? The phrase "potent but valuable" in the FDA's *Annual Report* suggests a perceived problem along these lines, but the detailed reasoning behind this critical regulation is not known.[24]

If we assume a modicum of consistency in the FDA's actions, then the administration of this regulation provides evidence of the motive in formulating it. The FDA began to prosecute pharmacists for violations of the regulation with a lag due, presumably, to the war. The enforcement of the distinction between prescription and over-the-counter drugs was at the expense of pharmacists, not manufacturers, Action against one pharmacist was completed in 1943, against two more in 1945, and against more in subsequent years. Although the actions involved several drugs, two classses appear over and over again: sulfa drugs (chiefly sulfathiazole) and barbiturates (Nembutal and Seconal).[25] The problems with these two classes appear to be mirror images of each other: people used too little of the sulfa drugs and too much of the barbiturates according to the FDA. They did not use large enough dosages of sulfa drugs to cure the infections they had, and they did not use small enough dosages of the barbiturates to avoid addiction. In neither case is the danger hard to explain or understand. The problem does not seem to be that people would not understand the directions for use, but rather that they would not choose to follow them.

The FDA's concentration on a few drugs suggests also that the agency did not see the prescription-only category as a large one; they saw it as an intermediate step between being safe enough to sell and dangerous enough to be banned. Drugs on the borderline, "potent but valuable," could be put into this intermediate class and the necessity for making a black-and-white decision avoided. If this suggestion is accurate, it explains the lack of contemporary discussion. At the time the regulation was issued, it was of only limited interest. The therapeutic revolution immediately after World War II then transformed this comparatively minor rule into a central feature of drug regulation.

One spurious justification for the regulation must be noted, partly because it appears to embody a common misconception and partly because it was given by an authority in the field of drug regulation. The regulation was justified in a law review article by reference to the wording of the law which allowed exemptions to the labeling requirements when they were "not necessary for the protection of the public health." If a drug was sold by prescription, the argument ran, then the full directions and warning required by law were not necessary for the protection of the public health.[26] This argument is reasonable, but it misses the point. The regulation does not articulate the conditions of prescription sales; it requires prescription sales. It does not give the implications of a consumer's choice; it eliminates that choice.

This argument is taken from an academic account some years later. The regulation did not arouse much discussion at the time, and its effect on the function of prescriptions was never tested in the courts. The case usually cited as its court test, *U.S.* v. *Sullivan,* was concerned with other aspects of the law, and the distinction between prescription and over-the-counter drugs simply was accepted. Sullivan's Pharmacy in Columbus, Georgia, had received sulfathiazole tablets in bottles of 1,000 with adequate labels of the "Caution . . ." variety. On two separate occasions, the pharmacy removed a dozen tablets from the bottles, put them into pill boxes, and sold them without the warning labels. They were also sold without prescriptions, as the district court record makes clear. The FDA's case against Sullivan was taken up through the courts until it was decided by the Supreme Court in 1948.

The issues before the court, as expressed in the opinions, were two. First, did the act cover the resale of a drug within a state after the drug had passed through interstate commerce? The majority argued that it did, and the dissent was silent. This aspect of the decision was written into the law in the Miller Amendment of 1948.[27] Second, was repackaging of drugs included in the proscribed activities listed in the law? Alteration, mutilation, destruction, obliteration, and removal of labels was prohibited, as well as any other act that resulted in a drug's being misbranded. The majority of the court argued that the prohibition included repackaging drugs without recopying the label: Justice Felix Frankfurter argued from the vagueness of the prohibition that it did not.

There is no mention in the Supreme Court's opinion whether the drugs were sold by prescription. Even though the record of the lower court was clear on this question, it was not an issue in the final decision. The legal distinction between prescription and over-the-counter sales introduced by the regulation was not controversial. The intervention of the government into a local drug sale was.[28]

The Humphrey-Durham Amendment, 1951

By the end of 1948, the extension of the law to cover the final sale of drugs and the ability of the FDA to sustain its prosecutions were clear, but the legality of requiring prescriptions was still unsettled. The FDA had been moved from the Department of Agriculture to the Federal Security Agency (FSA) in 1940, and the head of that agency described the situation clearly to Congress in 1951: "While some lawyers have disagreed, I believe that authority for our present regulation and for its proposed revision is found in the present statute—though it is contained in one four-line proviso. At least in its general pattern, the regulation was held valid by the Supreme Court of the United States in *United States* vs. *Sullivan.*"[29] The "four-line proviso" is the last part of section 502 (f) quoted above. The FSA administrator acknowledged that the decision in *U.S.* v. *Sullivan* was not as explicit as he would have liked.

He was testifying because Congress was considering an amendment to the Federal Food, Drug, and Cosmetic Act that would clarify the legal status of prescriptions. The discussion of the amendment centered on how to draw the line between prescription and over-the-counter drugs, but the amendment itself also clarified other ambiguous areas. Telephone prescriptions and prescription refills, not recognized in the law, were included in the amendment's restatement of the rules on prescriptions. The amendment had been proposed to clarify a variety of these controversial or ambiguous FDA rules on prescriptions.[30]

The House considered the amendment first. The committee report noted that the existing law allowed the manufacturer to decide whether a drug was to be sold by prescription only or over the counter. The result was that "lack of uniformity . . . has led to great confusion." The same drug could be classified as a prescription drug by one manufacturer and as an over-the-counter drug by another. It could even be labeled differently in separate shipments by the same manufacturer. Druggists who sold a prescription drug over the counter could be prosecuted for misbranding, but if the FSA, the FDA's parent agency, disagreed with the manufacturer's designation of a drug, it had to sue the manufacturer. Given the relative size of drugstores and drug manufacturing firms around 1950, it was far easier to enforce adherence to the drug companies' labeling than to affect the labeling itself.

The House committee consequently recommended that the responsibility for designating whether a drug was to be sold by prescription only or over the counter be given to the FSA. The House bill reworded the FDA's regulation to require a prescription for a drug if "its toxicity or other potentiality for harmful effect . . . has been determined by the [Federal Security] Administrator, on the basis of opinions generally held among experts, . . . to be safe and efficacious for use only after professional diagnosis." The FDA's regulation had acquired a paragraph explaining why certain drugs needed prescriptions, and the House's references to "toxicity or other potentiality for harmful effect" and to drugs that were "safe and efficacious for use" were taken from the regulation. The House kept the FDA's reference to efficacy and added the requirement that the FSA decide which drugs were to be sold by prescription.

The National Association of Retail Druggists favored giving the FSA this power; the Association of Pharmaceutical Manufacturers, the American Drug Manufacturers' Association, the American Pharmaceutical Association, and the Proprietary Association opposed it. A minority report joined the drug manufacturers in opposing this grant of power. The report said, ironically in view of its acceptance of the distinction between prescription and over-the-counter drugs, that "the bill as reported jeopardizes the traditional right of self-medication and choice of remedies." (It in fact jeopardizes the rights of manufacturers, not consumers.) "The bill," the minority continued, "could very well become a handmaiden of socialized medicine." It would raise the costs of drugs and increase agitation for government relief.[31]

The Senate committee reported the controversy over the House proposal to grant new power to the FSA. It reported further that the FDA and FSA had agreed to remove this provision from the amendment and that the manufacturers' associations had been satisfied with this concession. It concluded that "the subcommittee was assured by the FDA and FSA that the bill, while not in their view the best solution, would be workable in the form proposed under the agreement." The drug manufacturers had enough muscle to prevent the FDA from interfering with their right to designate the terms of sale of their drugs. Instead of making an administrative decision, which the drug companies could appeal, the FDA would have to sue the companies for misbranding if it disliked their decisions.

The Senate committee said that its definition of dangerous drugs, that is, drugs requiring prescriptions, was "substantially the same" as the one in the FDA regulation. But a careful look at the Senate version of the bill, which became the Humphrey-Durham Amendment, shows that the reference to "efficacy" had been removed. The law was to deal only with safety under the new amendment, as it did under the 1938 provisions for new drugs.[32]

Several aspects of the story about the origin and passage of the Humphrey-Durham Amendment are relevant here, some because they were not controversial and some because they were. In the first group, the most important paradox of the discussion was the apparent absence of controversy over the heart of the matter: the FDA's division of medicinal drugs into two categories. The FDA had assumed that adequate directions for laymen could not be written for some drugs. It followed that any directions written for laymen were misleading and that any such drug labeled for laymen was misbranded. The only way to label the drug properly was for prescription only. Instructions should be available, but not on the label—according to this argument.[33]

Before 1938 the function of drug legislation was to prevent fraud—to ensure that the labels informing consumers about the chemical and known therapeutic properties of drugs were adequate and correct. The government did not undertake to limit consumers' drug choices, other than for narcotics, an exception that shows by its restricted scope how broad the domain of consumer choice was to be. The 1938 act added the function of assuring safety—of assuring the public that any drug on the market could be taken in reasonable quantities without harm. The government thereby restricted choice by excluding harmful substances from the market, but it left laymen free to choose among all nonharmful, nonnarcotic drugs.

By the end of 1938, the FDA had announced that the government would sharply curtail this freedom of choice. Consumers, the FDA said, were not competent to make their own drug choices. The manufacturers would decide by their labeling practices which drugs were safe for consumers and which were not, and licensed physicians and dentists would select from among those drugs that the manufacturers thought were dangerous the ones that the consumer could use. The government had delegated the consumer's choice to manufacturers and doctors. And nobody commented.

Almost nobody. A law review article in 1947 argued that the Congress had not intended the labeling rules of the 1938 law to be used to restrict sales of some drugs to prescription. The author reviewed the history just presented and argued that the clear legislative intent of Congress was to aid self-medication, not to restrict it. He questioned the legality of the FDA rule, but predicted that the courts would uphold it. He expected that the courts would not examine the rule carefully, but instead would presume that the FDA was expert and informed in its special area.[34] His predictions were confirmed the following year by the decision and opinions in *U.S.* v. *Sullivan*.

This change in the underlying assumptions of drug legislation came about through internal FDA processes. The shift from assuming a capable consumer to assuming an incompetent one occurred in the FDA within six months of the Federal Food, Drug, and Cosmetic Act's passage. Not only was the shift in assumptions not controversial, but the method by which it was accomplished also occasioned no comment. The decisions of Harvey W. Wiley's organization were ratified by the courts and enacted into statute by Congress. Neither branch of the government undertook to question the FDA's assumptions.

The FDA had decided that the encouragement of instrumental behavior in the 1906 law had not been sufficient to induce many people to switch from the customary mode. Had this change in assumptions occurred in the 1950s, it might have been explained by the wider range of drugs available, but this was the 1930s. Most drugs existing before World War II—with a few prominent exceptions—had as their goal the relief of symptoms. Consumers experiencing these symptoms could perceive the extent to which different drugs relieved them and could, as a result, make reasonable choices among nonaddicting drugs. They still retained this capacity in 1938.

The change came from outside the market for drugs. It was the government's perception that altered, not individuals' behavior. As a result of the Depression, policymakers in the federal government lost faith in the ability of the market economy to protect people from a variety of economic and noneconomic ills, and the New Deal moved in to substitute regulatory protection. The FDA's regulation, like the Federal Food, Drug, and Cosmetic Act itself, was simply a logical extension of this view. The attitude toward drug purchases could be justified after the fact by the changes taking place at the time of the postwar Humphrey-Durham Amendment, but it had been imposed on the drug market from outside well before then.

The 1906 law was passed at a time when many people thought in terms of reforming markets to eliminate problems while retaining the benefits of competition. These benefits were not as apparent in the 1930s as they had been earlier, and government bureaucrats were willing to forgo them in favor of administered behavior. The change from a market structure to a hierarchical structure in the distribution of medicinal drugs therefore derived partly from influences other than the mode of individual behavior. Independently of how people were acting, many policymakers had lost faith in the ability of markets to ensure a satisfactory use of resources. Market institutions consequently were abandoned for two reasons: some people shifted away from instrumental behavior, while other people lost faith in the market institutions themselves.

One effect of this change in underlying assumptions was to benefit doctors. By curbing self-medication, the government channeled business to the doctors and increased the value of their licenses. Remarkably, the government took this action without any strong urging by doctors. The AMA testified in favor of the 1906 and 1938 laws, but it was largely absent from the legislative discussions. Either the doctors had some subtle form of influence, or they did not understand what was happening, or they realized that no effort on their part was needed to propel the public into their offices.

In sharp contrast to the doctors, the manufacturers had to fight for their gains. To curb the FDA's power to classify drugs, the manufacturers' associations had to enter into explicit negotiations. Their success in these negotiations is hardly surprising. The surprising element is that the FDA was increasing its power over manufactuers in other ways that were not controversial at all. Different aspects of the government's surveillance of the drug industry do not seem to have been related to one another.[35]

Insulin had been discovered by F. G. Banting at the University of Toronto in the early 1920s and was produced under his patents during the interwar years. The University of Toronto imposed strict control over the manufacture of insulin to assure uniformity of dosage. Each diabetic needs a constant amount of insulin to function effectively, and either too much or too little can have debilitating effects leading to death. Since the desired dosage of insulin, once determined, does not change frequently, diabetics typically purchased and administered insulin to themselves without recourse to doctors after the initial determination. It was important to assure them that the preparation they purchased did in fact contain the quantity of insulin they needed.

The Insulin Committee of the University of Toronto set quality standards for insulin produced under its patent and operated a testing laboratory to ensure that every new lot produced by its licensees met its standards. This procedure worked well during the interwar years, but could not continue beyond December 23, 1941, when one of the important insulin patents used to enforce it was due to expire. The Insulin Committee, the AMA, and the governing board of the *United States Pharmacopoeia* recommended to Congress that the government take over the quality-control function. The proposed amendment to the Food, Drug, and Cosmetic Act was passed within three days of its introduction. It was signed and became law three days after that on December 22, 1941—one day before the patent expired. The insulin manufacturers collaborated in drafting the regulations, and there is no record of opposition to the FDA's assumption of the Insulin Committee's power.[36]

Penicillin began to be produced on a large scale during World War II. Quality control over its manufacture was imposed by military purchasing specifications. As the war drew to a close and the production capacity of penicillin manufacturers began to outrun the military demand, the possibility of producing the drug for civilian use became a reality. With the example of insulin firmly in mind, the FDA consulted with the pencillin producers and agreed on a system of quality control. The FDA would examine and certify each batch of penicillin produced. An amendment to the Federal Food, Drug, and Cosmetic Act creating this system passed Congress without objection in July 1945. The law was amended to include streptomycin in this certification system in 1947 and to include chlortetracycline, bacitracin, and chloramphenicol in 1949. It was extended later to include all other antibiotic drugs as well.[37]

It is curious that the model of insulin was applied to antibiotics without controversy. Unlike insulin, the precise dosage of antibiotics is not of great importance. They are sufficiently nontoxic that the patient can be given a large "excess" amount without harm. The certification of every batch of antibiotics was justified by the instability and impurity of antibiotics and by the lack of knowledge that surrounded their manufacture, but these arguments only highlight the problem.[38] The arguments for control in the two cases were completely different, but the pattern of government action dominated the differences in therapeutic context. Batch certification had become a customary response to a wide range of stimuli.

The drug manufacturers did not object to governmental control over the quality of antibiotic drugs, but they did object to the idea that the government should decide which drugs needed to be sold only by prescription. They did not record their motives in these two decisions, but it is possible that the companies thought they stood to suffer more from losing the right to designate which drugs needed prescriptions than from losing control over antibiotic quality. The need for prescriptions to buy antibiotics turned out to be critically important for the postwar growth of the drug industry. It is probable that most prescription drugs would have been so designated in any case, but the drug companies may not have known that in 1951. Quality control, by contrast, may have increased the costs of new and small firms more than those of established manufacturers and functioned as a partial barrier to entry. It is hard to know.

Finally, of all interesting aspects of the Humphrey-Durham Amendment, the use of the word *efficacy* is most notable. The Federal Food, Drug, and Cosmetic Act said that new drugs needed only to be examined by the FDA with an eye toward their safety, whereas the FDA regulations on prescriptions in 1951 spoke of "safety and efficacy." The revised House bill referred to "opinions held among experts qualified by scientific training and experience to evaluate the safety and efficacy of such drugs" in determining whether a drug was "safe and efficacious for use only after professional diagnosis," but these references to efficacy were cut out in the Senate version which was enacted into law.[39] The Senate committee noted, however, that safety was to be considered in context, implying that efficacy was at issue whether listed in the law or not.

FOUR

The Therapeutic Revolution

THIS DISCOVERY of sulfanilamide and penicillin initiated a revolution in the production and distribution of medical drugs. It is natural to see the legal changes just chronicled and the changes in assumptions that underlay them as the result of this revolution. But this is not how it happened. The decisive changes in assumptions and in the legal rules took place in 1938, on the eve of the therapeutic revolution, but clearly anterior to it.

It follows that the present drug market is not simply a product of technical progress in the last generation. In fact, the opposite is more nearly true: many characteristics of the drug industry are products of our view of drugs and of the regulations imposed on their use which reflect and enforce this view. The legal framework within which the drug industry transformed itself had implications both for what would be sold and for who would profit by the sale. These implications were not foreseen before World War II, but they existed nonetheless.

The Drug Industry between the Wars

Drug companies in the 1930s were far different from the drug firms of today. They did not advertise to doctors because any non-narcotic drug could be purchased without a prescription, and they did not engage in large-scale research because drug technology was essentially fixed. Research was not a separately budgeted item in annual reports; the drug industry was a straightforward manufacturing industry.

The range of products sold in the 1930s was described recently by the president of Merck, who joined one of the present firm's parent companies in 1937:

> You could count the basic medicines on the fingers of your two hands. Morphine, quinine, digitalis, insulin, codeine, aspirin, arsenicals, nitroglycerin, mercurials, and a few biologicals. Our own Sharp and Dohme catalog did not carry a single exclusive prescription medicine. We had a broad range of fluids, ointments, and extracts, as did other firms, but we placed heavy emphasis on biological medicines as well. Most of our products were sold without a prescription. And 43 percent of the prescription medicines were compounded by the pharmacist, as compared with 1.2 percent today.[1]

Digitalis and nitroglycerin were used for heart disease, the arsenicals and mercurials were primitive anti-infective agents, and the biologicals were vaccines and antitoxins through which the body averted or cured itself of certain bacterial diseases. "Exclusive prescription medicines" were nonexistent before the postwar drug revolution. All ethical drugs were produced freely by more than one firm, and most were sold without prescription. Finally, none of the drugs the speaker mentioned resulted from research done by the drug industry.

An exhaustive study of the cost of medicines in the early 1930s found an absence of controversy over prices. One explanation offered was that "medicines are relied upon by the public to cure or relieve conditions which do not interrupt the day's routine," and each patient "feels he can choose without disadvantage from among several brands of prepared medicines." These factors apparently freed the sellers of drugs from the onus of charging too much because the consumer who did not like the price of any one medicine could buy another or do without. The price of drugs, the authors concluded, was no different from the prices of automobiles, oranges, or theater tickets.[2]

The assumption in the study was that consumers were capable of making reasonable choices between competing drugs in the interwar years. If they acted in the instrumental mode, they made the best choices possible at the prevailing prices. If they acted customarily, they could not go too far wrong owing to both the rapid feedback on the alleviation of symptoms and the small risk of harm from drugs. Because consumers were active in choosing among reasonable alternatives—one of which was to do without—they had no complaints.

Despite the absence of research for new products and of controversy over the price of drugs, there was still a distinction between what we now call brand-name and generic products. The American Medical Association exhibited a poster at its annual meetings during the 1920s showing that twelve common drugs cost approximately four times more under brand names than the same products sold generically. Companies justified brand-name products—then as now—on the basis of their convenience in prescribing and their excellent quality. The quality claims were made in the face of presumed universal compliance with *United States Pharmacopoeia* and *National Formulary* standards and without any arguments to support them. The AMA opposed brand-name products on the grounds that their existence led to duplication of pharmacy stocks, raised prices, and encouraged self-medication.[3] The context is different from today's, but the arguments are familiar.

Just as there were very few effective drugs in the early 1930s, there were still very few diseases they could cure. A 1931 symposium on fighting diseases with drugs listed only seven diseases that drugs could control and another seven that were considered partially controllable. Others were stated to have as yet only inadequate preventives and cures.[4] Of the first seven diseases, five (diphtheria, smallpox, typhoid, rabies, and tetanus) were controlled by either vaccines or antitoxins. The others were controlled by man-made drugs: syphilis by Salversan and hookworm disease by derivatives of carbon tetrachloride. The distinction between vaccines and antitoxins on the one hand and synthetic drugs on the other corresponds to Paul Ehrlich's distinction between passive and active therapy, which can be used to organize the description of drug research before the discovery of sulfanilamide.[5]

Some bacterial diseases are the result of toxins produced by the bacteria, which can be isolated and separated from the organism that makes them. The body opposes them by manufacturing antitoxins. A vaccine is a small amount of a toxin that induces the body to make antitoxins which then render it immune to larger incursions of the toxins should they occur. The vaccine itself does not fight the disease. An antitoxin serum adds to the body's supplies of antitoxin to facilitate the victory of antitoxin over toxin. It is obtained by injecting a toxin into animals—vaccinating them—and recovering and concentrating the antitoxin that the animals produce.

Ehrlich, regarded today as the father of modern chemotherapy, classified the use of vaccines and antitoxins as passive therapy, because the chemist was the body's second in the duel with disease, not a principal. As he put it, "The antibodies are magic bullets which find their targets by themselves."[6] Ehrlich dedicated himself to the search for artificial "magic bullets" that would actively fight specific diseases within the body. His pursuit of active therapeutic agents was very important for the development of the theory of chemotherapy, but it yielded only one new drug.

In April 1910 Ehrlich announced the discovery of a new cure for syphilis. This disease, though seldom serious in our era of effective antibiotics, was a major scourge of late nineteenth-century Europe. Ehrlich's discovery therefore had an immediate and large impact on the nature of hospital therapy and on the composition of hospital populations. Nevertheless, the dramatic effects of the discovery did not encourage others to follow Ehrlich's research plans. First of all, even with the most careful screening then available, there was no guarantee that valuable drugs would be identified. Salversan had been found and patented in 1907, but its therapeutic effect had been missed. Second, Ehrlich had published in 1906 a discouraging account of his unsuccessful efforts. The discovery had to be seen in light of the extended and apparently hopeless search. As if to emphasize this point, the drug was named originally by its number in the sequence of arsenic-containing compounds that Ehrlich had tested. The number, 606, was not inviting. And finally, other investigators did not have similar successes. Ehrlich himself found an improvement for number 606 in the 914th arsenical tested. He named it Neosalversan to differentiate it from the original Salversan, and it replaced the original in therapy because of its greater solubility and ease in use. But neither he nor others found other magic bullets. The goal did not seem attainable or even approachable for a quarter of a century.[7]

Instead, drug therapy made progress in other areas. Nutrition and the role of vitamins became better understood, although there was a persistent tendency to regard each new discovery as a panacea for all mankind's ills. Given the limits of known testing procedures and the optimism of the 1920s, it could hardly have been otherwise. And more and more biologicals, therapeutic products of man himself or of animals metabolically close to man, were found. The most dramatic of these was insulin.

Looking back from the perspective of forty years and the drug revolution of the 1940s, a clinical doctor could still say that "there has been nothing ever again as thrilling as the discovery of insulin. It came, as it were, out of a clear sky, and not only the event itself, but also the timing of it, was perfect . . . We had just made the world safe for democracy . . . All we needed was to cure disease."[8] The 1922 announcement by Banting, Best, and Macleod of Toronto was as overwhelming for the treatment of diabetes as Ehrlich's had been for syphilis. The emotional impact may have been even stronger, since hospitals contained many diabetic children who previously had no chance of survival. But as the passage just quoted suggests, the discovery of insulin was not seen as the continuation of Ehrlich's search. The chemical basis of insulin bore no relation to that of Salversan. The drug's method of operation was no closer: insulin provided a hormone missing in the diabetic patient; it did not attack or stimulate the attack of an invading organism. And the method used to manufacture insulin was closer to the methods used to produce diphtheria antitoxin than to those used to make Salversan. The Hygienic Laboratory of the United States Public Health Service had supervised the manufacture and distribution of biologicals since the start of the century; the Insulin Committee of the University of Toronto supervised the production and sale of insulin in similar fashion.[9] Salversan and insulin were important, but isolated, steps in the development of medicinal drugs.

On the eve of what we now call the therapeutic revolution, progress thus appeared to be coming mostly from the realm of biological products. New man-made drugs derived from plants appeared from time to time, but systematic progress was being made only in isolating and producing toxins, antitoxins, and antibacterial serums. The future of drug research seemed to lie with Ehrlich's passive immunization. Thirty-two separate serums were developed for the thirty-two known strains of pneumonia, and the immunization idea was transferred to ailments that did not involve infectious diseases. The treatment for hay fever was to inject the patient with an extract from the pollen of the offending plant. Sulfa drugs, antibiotics, and antihistamines were not just unknown; they were unanticipated.[10]

"The age of miracle drugs began with the announcement in 1935 that the first effective cure had been found for a number of bacterial diseases,"[11] but the age began slowly. As with any dramatic change, it took a while for observers and participants to realize the magnitude of the revolution. The Federal Food, Drug, and Cosmetic Act was introduced into Congress in 1933, before the 1935 announcement, and the announcement's implications were not appreciated until after 1938, when the act passed.

There were in fact two announcements in 1935. In the first, Gerhard Domagk, a pharmacologist testing the antimicrobial properties of dyestuffs at I. G. Farbenindustrie, announced the discovery of a new anti-infective called Prontosil. In the second, it was announced that Prontosil was decomposed by the body into two components and that one of them, sulfanilamide, was the active ingredient. The first announcement, therefore, reported a success in the tradition of Ehrlich. Extensive screening of chemical compounds had yielded another magic bullet that would destroy disease-causing microorganisms without attacking the host. The second announcement rendered the patent on the new drug worthless by showing its active ingredient to be a substance that was first obtained in 1908 and allowed since then to go into the public domain. Anyone was free to manufacture the new drug.

Many firms began to manufacture sulfanilamide, and—as Ehrlich had done with Salversan—they set about to find improved forms of it. Sulfanilamide M&B 693, effective against bacterial pneumonia and a replacement for the thirty-two specific sera, was announced in 1938. Sulfapyridine, a safer form of sulfanilamide, become available in the same year. It was replaced by sulfathiazole in 1939, which was superceded by sulfadiazine in 1940.[12] The sulfa drugs, or sulfanilamides, were more numerous than the derivatives of Salversan by 1940, but there was still no hint that further modification of the sulfanilamide molecule would yield drugs with effects qualitatively different from those of the parent compound.

There are several reasons why the discovery of sulfanilamide did not immediately revolutionize the drug industry. It took time to learn about the effects of this new drug and its derivatives and to discover which derivatives had what effects. Investigators in the 1930s had the example of Salversan and its tiny crop of derivative compounds before them; their expectations of further discoveries were not high. In addition, sulfanilamide was not produced under patent protection, and its production consequently did not generate enough profits to finance a major program of chemical research. Even if it had, it is not clear that such a program would have been undertaken in such an apparently unpromising direction in the midst of the Great Depression. And finally, when World War II brought prosperity to the drug industry, the sulfa drugs were partly superseded by penicillin and antibiotics in general as a focus for research. With the benefit of hindsight and with knowledge of the drugs developed from the sulfa drugs in the 1950s, we can identify 1935 as the beginning of the age of miracle drugs, but only a seer could have said the same in 1935.

A history of pharmacy published in 1937 consequently could fail to mention sulfanilamide entirely, and a history of medicine published in 1945 could refer to "chemotherapeutic agents such as neosalversan, sulfanilamide and its related compounds, and penicillin," without distinguishing among them. But not everyone was blind. A history of medicine published in 1940 by a distinguished medical observer saw the sulfa drugs as revolutionary and caught a glimpse of their role in drug research. The revolutionary aspect of sulfa drugs, according to this study, was their mode of action. Instead of killing microorganisms directly, that is, instead of being germicides, they impeded the microorganisms' metabolism. They starved the germs to death. Ehrlich's problem was that he looked for toxic substances—heavy metals, mercury, arsenic—which harmed both microorganisms and their hosts; the sulfa drugs, by contrast, were not directly toxic to either germ or host. Instead, they imposed a selective "economic boycott." Their low toxicity provided room for experimentation which would generate many new drugs in the decade or so after 1940. But only the possibility of variation, not the actuality of new drugs, could be seen or guessed at in 1940.[13]

To the extent that the Federal Food, Drug, and Cosmetic Act was passed in response to the Elixir Sulfanilamide tragedy, it appears as a legislative response to the new age. But this appearance is deceptive. The legislation was first introduced well before the disaster. The section dealing with new drugs was added afterward, but even this was not a response to the new age. The toxicity problem was in the solvent, not in the sulfa drug: diethylene glycol was not a new substance. The law consequently did not refer exclusively to newly produced chemical compounds; it referred to all substances newly introduced into use as drugs. The 1938 law was the product of regulatory experience under the old, pre-anti-infective technology, not a response to the new.

It follows that the administrative regulations promulgated to enforce the new law in 1938 were also designed within the framework of the old technology. The assumption that consumers were no longer able to choose their own drugs owed something to Domagk's discovery, if the importance of sulfa drugs in the early application of the regulation is an indication of the FDA's motives in issuing it. But the FDA's change owed less to the particular experiences of the drug industry than to general perceptions of the economy in the Depression. After all, experience with the new sulfa drugs was still quite limited and restricted in its applicability to other drugs. The existence of a distinction between prescription and over-the-counter drugs was not a by-product of the new age of miracle drugs; it antedated the introduction of virtually all of these drugs.[14]

Discovery of the Antibiotics

Of all the new drugs, penicillin was the most important. Curing substantially the same infections as the sulfa drugs and then more, penicillin captured the limelight from its predecessor drug. Yet it is possible that penicillin might never have been developed but for the sulfa drugs; their existence gave a major stimulus to penicillin research in the early 1940s.

The antibacterial action of penicillium mold—as the precursors of penicillin were known—was observed several times in the late nineteenth century. The research extended up to animal trials that demonstrated the therapeutic usefulness of the primitive penicillin, but the implications of these trials were not realized until after the efficacy of penicillin had been demonstrated independently of them. The development of penicillin dates instead from Alexander Fleming's 1929 paper on the use of penicillium in laboratory investigations. While Fleming appreciated the germicidal properties of his mold, even he was not sanguine about the possibility of developing it for therapeutic use. In 1929 Domagk had not yet broken the ice and made the realization of Ehrlich's dream seem possible.[15]

The medical history of penicillin began during World War II when British scientists at Oxford undertook the study and development of penicillin as a germ killer. The context in which research on penicillin took place had changed because of the war, which increased the demand for anti-infective agents, and because of the discovery of sulfa drugs, which increased the perceived possibility of finding such agents. The Oxford team announced its first results in 1940 and detailed them the following year. Having demonstrated the therapeutic properties of penicillin, they then joined in a cooperative venture with the American military establishment to develop production techniques. New methods of culturing penicillin molds, new strains of penicillium, and selective breeding all contributed to enlarging the output of the drug. The first successful human use of penicillin was in 1941. Only about a hundred cases could be treated in 1942, but enough penicillin was being produced by the end of 1943 to satisfy the military demand. Prior to that time, as all viewers of old World War II movies know, sulfa drugs had been the standard wartime therapy.[16]

As the war continued, the factors that had minimized the impact of the sulfanilamide discovery on people's expectations were systematically altered. Investigators began to accumulate knowledge about the therapeutic properties, the modes of activity, and the ease of manipulation of both sulfa drugs and penicillin. The discouraging specter of Ehrlich's long and largely fruitless investigations was replaced by the more promising experiences of Domagk, Fleming, and the Oxford team. Penicillin was no more patentable than sulfanilamide, since it was a known substance before its therapeutic properties were appreciated, but we may presume that the manufacture of scarce anti-infectives was nevertheless a profitable activity in wartime. The government spent almost $3 million subsidizing penicillin research, sold its penicillin plants after the war to private manufacturers at half their cost, and allowed accelerated amortization on private construction.[17] In addition, the profitability of sulfa drug and penicillin production was reinforced by the change in business climate around 1940; any investment with government blessing looked better during the war than before. And, while the discovery of penicillin distracted attention from research on the sulfa drugs, it also showed that there was more than one route to the discovery of new and important drugs.

The result was a great mushrooming of drug research. The faint, tentative stirrings of the late 1930s were encouraged and enlarged.[18] The drug industry began to transform itself from a fairly typical manufacturing industry to one based on the continual progress of technical knowledge. This transformation involved the development of a new technology, the growth of a new industry structure, and the marked intensification of certain older marketing practices. The new technology grew from the exploration of the research opportunities opened up by the possibility of finding new sulfa drugs and new antibiotics. It would be hard to say which line has been more productive, but the latter is more amply documented. The antibiotics are not completely typical of the drug industry, but the wealth of material published about them allows us to see clearly the changes taking place within the industry.[19]

Penicillin was produced by nineteen different American companies in 1944, but the largest five accounted for 88 percent of the total. Only one firm, Squibb, was vertically integrated; that is, Squibb was the only firm that manufactured the drug, packaged it, and sold it directly to pharmacies and hospitals. The largest firm, Pfizer Laboratories, which was not integrated forward, made almost twice as much penicillin as Squibb. Thus, the industry was not dominated by integrated drug companies in the mid-1940s, although they did exist.

The share of penicillin produced by the top five penicillin producers in 1944 fell to 43 percent in 1950, and the price of penicillin dropped from $3,955 a pound in 1945 to $282 in 1950. Entry into the manufacture and packaging of penicillin was sufficiently easy to make its production highly competitive.[20]

Three developments of the immediate postwar years combined to change the context within which new antibiotic drugs were introduced. First, Selman Waksman at Rutgers University discovered a technique of screening soil samples to find new antibiotics. Since harmful microorganisms do not survive in the ground, it was reasonable to assume that the soil contained a variety of germicidal substances and that careful search of soil samples would expose them. Waksman demonstrated his method's effectiveness by discovering streptomycin, the first new antibiotic since penicillin. Unlike Salversan, penicillin was not to be an isolated phenomenon.[21]

Second, it emerged that the new drugs were patentable. They would not be patentable if they were simply natural substances, but the natural materials found by Waksman's method were not in suitable form to be used medically. The Patent Office ruled that the chemical modifications made to streptomycin to enable it to be purified created a new product and that both this new product and the process by which it was made were patentable. Streptomycin was introduced commercially in 1946, and Merck obtained a patent on this "new composition of matter" in 1948. In the words of the patent: "For the first time streptomycin is available in a form which not only has valuable therapeutic properties but also can be produced, distributed, and administered in a practicable way."[22]

It is worth noting that the streptomycin patent, and later drug patents as well, were on specific drugs. The drug industry was transformed by a research technology, rather than a production technology. This method of doing research could not be patented since it was an approach—a series of questions—rather than a specific procedure, and it produced a variety of outcomes, not a single product. A patent only protects a single product; it cannot protect its owner against competition from a close substitute. Patents, therefore, were important for the development of the drug industry both for what could be patented (after streptomycin) and for what could not.

While Merck's patent was important for the development of the industry, it did not change the way drugs were marketed. Worried about possible criticism for using public facilities at the university and a valuable public health discovery for private gain, Waksman convinced Merck to license streptomycin production on an unrestricted basis. Merck consequently assigned its patents to the Rutgers Research Foundation. Merck was not an integrated firm; it made streptomycin and sold it to packagers and distributors in competition with other firms. Streptomycin consequently appeared on the market in the same way as penicillin, produced by many firms and sold under its generic name. The price of streptomycin followed the price of penicillin as competition among its producers forced it down during the 1950s.[23]

The third development was operational. Instead of licensing other firms to use their patents, innovating firms began to use their patent rights to retain a monopoly over the production of their new drugs. In doing so, they acquired control over the quantity produced, which enabled them to restrict output to obtain monopoly profits. Output was restricted by announcing a high price for the new drugs and then only producing the amount that could be sold at that price. Despite the impact of the new drugs on society, their high prices still need to be seen as a way of reducing the quantity sold.

The firms could have accomplished the same end by licensing other producers. Royalty payments are a cost to the licensee; they raise the price at which a competitive producer can sell above the competitive price without the license. High enough royalty payments can cause even competitive licensees to duplicate the monopoly price and therefore to cause only the monopoly output to be sold. The problem is that the required royalty is very high indeed when demand is inelastic at the competitive price. If the elasticity of demand is one and a quarter at the monopoly price, then this price is five times the competitive price (for constant costs) and the required royalty is 80 percent of sales. The Food and Drug Administration's regulation introducing a class of prescription drugs allowed the manufacturer to classify its new drugs, and most of the drugs discovered after World War II were classified as prescription drugs. As such, they were ordered (prescribed) by doctors who did not pay for them and often did not know their price. In light of this fact and of the newness and effectiveness of the "wonder drugs," the elasticity of demand might well have been less than one and a quarter, and the profit-maximizing royalty could have been even higher than 80 percent of sales.

This is an order of magnitude higher than any previous patent royalties in the drug industry. Royalties under the streptomycin patent were set at 2.5 percent of sales, which was typical of the industry at the time.[24] Profit-maximizing behavior in the postwar context hence required behavior dramatically at variance with the existing industry standards. The successful firms would be those who could make this break with the past.

Following the behavioral theory of the firm, we can see the drug firms as being pushed outside the acceptable domain of actions by a change in the external environment.[25] They were jolted by the change into searching for a more appropriate pattern of action, and either of two might have sufficed. They might have raised their royalty rates by an order of magnitude, or they might have refrained altogether from giving licenses. It may be accidental that they chose the latter, and a theory that explains their choice may explain too much. Nevertheless, there are several reasons why termination of unrestricted license might have been preferred to continuing them at the dramatically higher price.

It may not have occurred to the firms to simply raise the price of licenses. When searching for a radical change, one that breaks with recent practice may be easier to perceive than one that is closer. In addition, royalties of 80 percent or more of sales might have been hard to enforce. The incentives for cheating would have been strong, and the political pressure against them could have been devastating. Exclusive production was an established pattern in other fields, and it masked the changes taking place. Finally, exclusive production was more compatible with the forms of advertising made possible by the FDA's 1938 regulation than licensed production, even at high rates. In particular, sales agents (detail men) could represent a single supplier more easily than a group of licensees.

The change from nonexclusive licensing to restricted production can be seen most clearly in what came to be called broad-spectrum antibiotics. Lederle Laboratories introduced Aureomycin (chlortetracycline) in 1948, Parke-Davis introduced Chloromycetin (chloramphenicol) in 1949, and Pfizer Laboratories introduced Terramycin (oxytetracycline) in 1950. All these drugs were presented similarly and as superior to penicillin. Their chemical structures were unknown; their generic names were not introduced until later. The chemical similarity of Aureomycin and Terramycin was only worked out in 1952, when their generic names were coined, and the harmful side effects of Chloromycetin only became apparent in the same year.[26] Up to then, the drugs were for all practical purposes identical.

Each drug was produced only by the firm that held the patent. In addition, Lederle and Parke-Davis were already integrated firms, but Pfizer was not. It had been the largest producer in penicillin in 1944 and seen its position eroded by Squibb. Then the introduction of new drugs had reduced the position of penicillin in the antibiotic market, diminishing Pfizer's share of the market for antibiotics even further. Pfizer consequently decided to integrate forward to exploit its own drug and regain its competitive position.

By not licensing their patents, these firms were able to restrict production of their own drugs, but the simultaneous discovery of three similar drugs limited each producer's market power. The producers attempted to regain market power by differentiating their products along the lines that any other consumer good is differentiated. Since the therapeutic effects of the drugs appeared to be identical, other, more familiar quality dimensions had to be emphasized: the firms intensified their advertising, their detailing, and their reliance on company identities. The postwar pattern of integrated drug companies competing by introducing and marketing new drugs was beginning to take shape.[27]

The pattern was not yet stabilized by the beginning of the 1950s, however. Despite the presence of patented monopoly positions and integrated marketing organizations, the price of Aureomycin fell by two-thirds in its first few years on the market. The prices of the new drugs stayed close together, and the prices of other drugs experienced smaller declines as they joined the slide along the way. Clearly, competition among similar drugs was a good substitute for competition among the suppliers of a single drug. The Waksman technique apparently made introduction of a competing drug almost as easy for an integrated firm as initiating production of an existing one. A patent monopoly and a marketing organization may have been necessary for the creation of market power; they were not sufficient.

The introduction of tetracycline, an event notable for its complexity and controversy, provided the occasion for the final steps toward the current industry structure. Litigation over the tetracycline patent and over the price behavior of the patent holders has continued for over two decades, exposing to public view much that would otherwise be hidden in corporate files. The tetracycline experience therefore can serve for a model—in its commercial, if not its legal, aspects—for the transformation of the industry as a whole.

Pfizer, the newcomer to integrated production and marketing and the low man on the antibiotic totem pole, employed Robert Woodward of Harvard University to elucidate the chemical structure of Terramycin. Woodward did so, exposing its chemical affinity to Aureomycin and leading a Pfizer scientist to find a new, related drug by removing the chlorine atom from Lederle's Aureomycin. Reflecting this chemical manipulation, Aureomycin acquired the generic name of chlortetracycline, and the new drug was called tetracycline.

Lederle heard about Pfizer's investigations and reactivated its discontinued antibiotic research program. That company produced tetracycline by the same method as Pfizer and filed patent applications in competition with Pfizer. Publication of Pfizer's and Lederle's discoveries led other firms to search their files for evidence that they had previously isolated tetracycline without recognizing its therapeutic properties. Bristol Laboratories and Hayden Chemical, both primarily nonintegrated penicillin manufacturers, found that they had made tetracycline by a different method—one that did not start from chlortetracycline—and filed patent applications also.[28]

All this made for a very intricate situation. Each firm filed both product and process patent applications. That is, they each wanted exclusive use of a new product, tetracycline, and of a new production process, whether the original process starting from chlortetracycline or the alternative one. If—as might easily have been predicted—Pfizer had obtained both product and process patents, and Bristol or Hayden had obtained a patent on its alternative process, then the following condition would have emerged. Pfizer could have produced tetracycline only by getting a license from Lederle to produce chlortetracycline or by getting a license from the patent holder to use the alternative process. Lederle could have produced tetracycline only by getting both product and process patents from Pfizer, and Bristol or Hayden would have needed the use of Pfizer's product patent to exploit its process patent. In any case, cooperation among at least some of these firms would have been necessary for production.

Cooperation there was, but not in this form. Lederle purchased Hayden and its patent application. If Hayden's application for a process patent were to succeed, then Pfizer would be compelled to reach agreement with Lederle to use its product patent, either to get the raw material for its own process patent or to acquire the use of the alternative process. Similarly, if Pfizer got the product patent, then Lederle would need Pfizer's cooperation to exploit its new process patent. Foreseeing this symbiotic relationship, Pfizer and Lederle reached an agreement before the Patent Office ruled on the many patent applications. The agreement eliminated the risk attendant on going through the Patent Office by providing for all the contingencies and by removing some of the disputes that that office was supposed to resolve.[29]

The agreement stipulated that Pfizer and Lederle would determine between themselves who had priority. They resolved on Pfizer, and Lederle withdrew its application for a product patent. However the decision was made, it had the force of logic. If Lederle had the product patent, it had no need for Pfizer and its process patent, and Pfizer had no incentive to reach an agreement that froze it out of the market.

The agreement therefore reduced both firms' risks and guaranteed them both a share of the tetracycline market. The agreement further stipulated that Lederle would provide Pfizer with bulk tetracycline until its own manufacturing facilities were ready. This would enable Pfizer, which had only recently stopped selling solely in bulk, to employ its nascent marketing organization and develop its ability to compete with other integrated firms. Pfizer's sales force had been only ten men in early 1950. It rose to over three hundred by late 1951 as Pfizer promoted Terramycin.[30]

The only remaining competitor was Bristol, which, like Hayden, was almost entirely a bulk supplier of penicillin. While Bristol had a sales force, it was still small, comprising no more than forty detail men.[31] Bristol asked Lederle and Pfizer for licenses, but was told it could have them only under the condition that it renounced bulk sales. Bristol refused, since its sales force was too rudimentary for the company to generate large sales without using other packagers and marketers. It already was apparent to Bristol that it could not compete with firms that had large marketing organizations, but it was not yet clear that the manufacture of drugs in bulk did not generate the magnitude of profits that integrated production, packaging, and sale did.

Having failed to get licenses on terms it liked, Bristol decided to produce tetracycline anyway. In addition, it agreed to supply Squibb and Upjohn with bulk tetracycline. Squibb and Upjohn in return agreed to bear the costs of any litigation arising from patent conflicts with Pfizer. Bristol was a marginally profitable maker of penicillin; by itself it did not have the resources to fight with Pfizer over patents. Squibb and Upjohn had the resources but no means of entry against Pfizer's will. The arrangement gave Bristol the financial strength and the other two firms the legal position to enter the tetracycline market.

Tetracycline had been discovered in 1952. Bristol began production in mid-1954. The Patent Office had not yet decided if tetracycline was patentable, which depended on whether the drug was new or whether it had been obtained previously in the course of producing chlortetracycline. This issue resolved into the question of whether tetracycline could be recovered from the intermediate fermentation products used to produce chlortetracycline under Lederle's patent. The answer to this technical question is unclear, but it does seem clear that Pfizer withheld information damaging to it and structured the experiments carried out during the Patent Office's investigations in ways favorable to it. Pfizer received the product patent in early 1955, but the evidence for it did not appear strong enough to withstand a court challenge by Bristol and its backers. Pfizer reached an agreement with Bristol under which Bristol would accept no more bulk purchasers and with Squibb and Upjohn—even though neither produced bulk tetracycline and neither therefore needed a license to operate—specifying that they too would not sell tetracycline in bulk. With Bristol eliminated as a potential challenger, Pfizer's patent was now secure.

The stakes in this game were high. The price of broad-spectrum antibiotics—the tetracyclines and chloramphenicol—had fallen by two-thirds between the end of 1948 and the end of 1951. They then remained unchanged until the fall of 1961. Even the entry of Bristol and its backers in 1954 did not disturb the market price.[32] The cooperative agreements and licensing arrangements of the early 1950s were able to arrest the price decline.

Prices cannot fall forever; the question is when they stop. If prices had fallen to the level of long-range costs by the end of 1951, there would be no reason to think that the legal stratagems just chronicled had any effect. But if costs were far below the price, then profits were high, and we could conclude that the legal actions were indeed potent. Manufacturing costs for tetracycline were below 10 percent of the wholesale price throughout the 1950s. Did other costs—marketing, advertising, overhead—bring the figure for total costs enough to approach the price, or was there a considerable profit? The data in table 4 give the answer.

These data were compiled in the course of court action questioning the propriety and legality of the actions just chronicled. As such, they are as reliable as any such aggregate profit figures, though subject to all the usual caveats about arbitrary classifications and allocations. Given the magnitudes involved, the caveats are of relatively little import. Lederle obtained a comfortable 20 percent rate of profit on its entire drug business. This is slightly above the 18 percent profit rate shown for the drug industry in 1956 when the FTC and the Security and Exchange Commission (SEC) reports began to list the drug industry separately.[33] However, the firm earned a 35 percent profit rate on antibiotics, and almost nothing—3 percent—on all other drugs. The contrast is even sharper than that. Because Lederle lost money on its sales of penicillin and sulfonamides, the profits from antibiotics came exclusively from the manufacture and sale of chlortetracycline and tetracycline.[34] Lederle's 20 percent profit rate on drugs, therefore, consisted entirely of profits on its patented tetracyclines.[35]

Table 4. Lederle Laboratories' sales, costs, and profits, 1955 (dollars in millions).

Item	All drugs	Antibiotics	All other drugs
Net sales	123.2	81.0	42.2
Costs	104.5	63.7	40.8
Income after taxes	18.7	17.4	1.3
Capital employed	93.5	50.0	43.5
Return on capital (%)	20	35	3

Source: Peter Costello, "The Tetracycline Conspiracy: Structure, Conduct and Performance in the Drug Industry," *Antitrust Law and Economic Review,* 1 (Summer 1968): 40.

Lederle's tetracycline sales did not come as a great surprise to the firm. It spent $2.5 million advertising Achromycin in 1955, of which over $1 million went for personal visits to physicians. A market research study in Wisconsin reported that forty-seven out of the fifty-five doctors studied had been visited ("detailed") on behalf of Achromycin in 1955, and the drug was prescribed by almost all the fifty-five doctors who prescribed any drugs at all.[36] Because the prescription-only restriction delineated the market so precisely, Lederle was able to send a representative to visit personally almost every potential customer, that is, prescriber.

More generally, Lederle and the other producers of broad-spectrum antibiotics belonged to what we may call the broad-spectrum antibiotic cartel.[37] The cartel—by explicit or implicit means—determined the market price for these drugs, holding it constant for a decade. But it did not specify market shares for each producer of tetracycline or for tetracycline as opposed to the other drugs. Sales went to whichever company attracted them, and the companies increased their marketing efforts to maintain or increase their market shares. The companies did their own advertising because their interest in advertising and marketing exceeded the interest of a packaging firm. The drug producers gained from the ability to sell their increased production at a price above its cost, and they consequently wanted more advertising than independent packagers would have supplied. In addition, they wanted to advertise their own brands to enhance their market shares.

The end of patent licensing (other than the restricted licensing within the cartel) therefore increased advertising for two reasons. First, since the returns to advertising were composed of both manufacturing and selling profits and because they were not shared with other producers, the firms realized higher returns from each dollar of advertising expense than independent packagers of generic drugs. Second, since the patent monopolies were in fact only memberships in an oligopoly or price-fixing cartel, advertising was an important determinant of market shares within the cartel. The first reason emphasizes the role of advertising in increasing the demand for the new antibiotics at a given price. The second reason emphasizes its role in allocating a given demand among competing suppliers. There is no way of telling which effect—demand "creating" or demand "diverting"—was more important.

The line of causation went the other way as well; advertising to doctors increased the pressures to end patent licensing. The drug companies sent their personal representatives out to visit doctors, and it was natural for these representatives to take along samples of their firms' products to aid in their promotion. All this would have been much harder if the actual products were produced by other firms under license. The licensing firms' representative could not have simply recommended his firm's product; he would either have had to distinguish between the licensees or commend them all equally to the doctors. It was far simpler not to have the issue arise.[38]

High profits lead to rapid growth, and access to the tetracycline patents promoted the growth of these firms. Lederle was the largest seller of antibiotics in the mid-1950s, while Bristol was one of the smallest, but the effects of tetracycline production on growth can be seen as well in one as the other. Bristol had a detail force of only 40 men when it began to sell tetracycline under its own name in 1954. It had increased this force to 130 men by the end of 1956. By this time too, Bristol had introduced seven new product forms of tetracycline in an effort to differentiate its product from its competitors'. In the words of its president: "None of these [product variations] would qualify as a major scientific advance, but they were practical and useful improvements. They lay in such areas as making liquid suspensions more stable, making liquid forms simpler and more pleasant for the patient to take, combining injectible forms with a superior local anesthetic, and the like."[39]

The importance of tetracycline for Bristol was that it enabled the company to transform itself from a bulk supplier of drugs to an integrated producer that combined the discovery and development of new drugs with the sales of these drugs to doctors and pharmacies. Pfizer, which only began to package its own drugs in 1950, must also have expanded its sales force primarily to market the profitable tetracycline. Not only did this drug earn large profits for its producers in the 1950s, it encouraged their growth and their reorientation from manufacturing firms to the integrated innovating, producing, and marketing firms that we see today.

Transformation of the Drug Industry

The story of tetracycline is dramatic and well-documented. Its legal aspects are the exception in the drug industry, but its economics extend to the industry as a whole. The three elements needed for the creation of a market were present throughout the industry: the new technology extended beyond antibiotics, patent protection was available for many new drugs, and the combination of a patent monopoly and a vertically integrated company meant high profits and rapid growth. While the connection between a single product and profits or growth cannot be documented in general as it can with Lederle and Bristol, several kinds of information confirm indirectly the generality of the story.

First, a similar stepwise development in the treatment of drug patents took place (with less publicity) in steroids about five years later. The first steroids, cortisone and hydrocortisone, were not patented. The first synthetic steroids, prednisone and prednisolone, were introduced in 1955. They were patented, but the patents were licensed widely. Only with the second generation of synthetic steroids and the birth control pills in the late 1950s was the pattern of exclusive production widespread.[40] Exclusive production replaced unrestricted patent licensing throughout the drug industry, and other drug firms grew as rapidly as the producers of broad-spectrum antibiotics.

Second, the five firms involved with tetracycline were among the largest dozen or so drug producers at the end of World War II, and they occupied roughly the same place in the industry a quarter-century later after the size of drug firms had risen dramatically.[41] The drug industry was transformed after the war from an industry of small firms into one of large firms (see table 5).[42] It is worth noting that the growth in firm size started well before the 1962 Drug Amendments and showed no sign of acceleration afterward. If anything, the rate of growth of the largest firms' collective market share slowed after 1962 as it began to approach 100 percent.

The diminution of the smaller firms' market share was not accomplished by driving them out of the industry, as table 5 shows. Nor did the growth of the largest firms' share reflect the dominance of any single firm.

Table 5. Market share and number of drug firms by size of assets, 1948–1973.

	Share of total market receipts by size of assets (%)			Number of firms by size of assets		
Year	$1–10 million	$10–100 million	Over $100 million	$1–10 million	$10–100 million	Over $100 million
1948	22	56	7	82	22	1
1953	19	48	23	92	25	3
1958	17	45	28	101	29	5
1963	11	20	61	138	31	14
1968	6	9	83	147	26	21
1973	3	4	92	119	21	30

Source: *Sourcebook of Statistics of Income* (Washington, D.C.: Internal Revenue Service, 1948–1973).

The rise in the market share of the largest size class was accompanied by a rise in the number of firms in that class. The experience of the five firms marketing tetracycline was not unique.

Third, other firms that had previously manufactured and sold drugs only in bulk followed the example of Pfizer and Bristol and began to package their drugs for wholesale or retail druggists and to advertise them to doctors. For example, Merck, which had not been integrated when it introduced streptomycin in the 1940s, merged with Sharp & Dohme in 1953 and began to market its own packaged products.[43] More generally, drug firms grew by adding functions, not by expanding their producing establishments. Table 6 shows the share of total value added in drug manufacturing by size of establishment for the same time period as table 5. The increase in the size of drug firms finds no echo in the very stable size of productive establishments. The table also indicates that the growth of firms did not result from combining many different productive establishments. No small group of firms was expanding its share of the productive establishments in the industry. Instead, we must conclude that drug firms were performing many functions other than manufacturing drugs by the 1960s. And, while each firm derived the bulk of its revenues from a small number of drugs, the total number of drugs introduced was very large.[44]

Erythromycin is another antibiotic isolated in the early 1950s. It was

Table 6. Percentage of total value added of drug firms by size of employment, and concentration ratios, 1947–1972.

	Percentage of total value added by number of employees[a]					Concentration ratios[b]	
	100–249	250–499	500–999	1,000–2,499	2,500 and over	4-firm	8-firm
1947	15	14	16	16	23	28	44
1954	13	12	15	16	32	25	44
1958	14	13	21	11	33	27	45
1963	11	13	15	27	26	22	38
1967	5	18	18	28	27	24	40
1972	5	18	18	28	27	25	43

Sources: U.S. Bureau of the Census, *Census of Manufactures*, vol. II, *Industry Statistics* (Washington, D.C.: Government Printing Office, 1947–1972); U.S. Bureau of the Census, *Census of Manufactures*, Special Report Series, *Concentration Ratios in Manufacturing* (Government Printing Office, 1967–1972).

a. These data are for SIC 2834; they are virtually unchanged if SIC 283 or the share of receipts is used, when available, in place of share of value added.

b. Share of industry sales of largest four or eight firms. All establishments belonging to a firm are counted as a single observation.

produced and sold in slightly different forms by Eli Lilly and Abbott Laboratories. Even though it competed in use with penicillin and the tetracyclines and was produced by firms that did not make tetracycline, its introduction did not lead to price competition with the makers of that drug. The price of tetracycline remained steady during the 1950s, despite a sustained drop in the prices of penicillin and streptomycin that left their 1960 prices approximately one-tenth of their 1950 prices. The price of erythromycin remained steady also, which must have contributed substantially to the profit and growth rates of Lilly and Abbott.[45]

New sulfa and related drugs were introduced during these years also, but they did not pose the same competitive problems for their discoverers as did the new antibiotics. Unlike the antibiotics, these new drugs had therapeutic properties very different from one another, and a patent on a single drug was worth correspondingly more. Hoffmann-La Roche introduced sulfisoxazole, a sulfa drug particularly well suited to the treatment of urinary infections because of its solubility in urine, under the brand name Gantrisin in 1949. It was promoted by the then novel device of ads written on scratch pads.[46] The success and spread of this kind of device suggests the importance of combining advertising with production of a new drug. Hoffman-La Roche was not giving any therapeutic information of value on its scratch pads; it was reminding doctors of the existence of a new drug. As with the tetracyclines, this was an essential part of creating a relatively price-inelastic market for the new drug.

Sulfisoxazole, like sulfanilamide, was used against infections, but doctors noticed that sulfa drugs also increased the output of urine. Investigators then experimented with sulfa derivatives to find those with diuretic effects but relatively few other effects. As a result of this search, Lederle was able in 1953 to introduce acetazolamide, a diuretic sold under the brand name Diamox. Further research led to the thiazide diuretics, of which chlorothiazide, introduced by Merck Sharp & Dohme as Diuril in 1957, was the first and most important. These drugs are used today to combat fluid retention in disease and high blood pressure.[47]

Another side effect of sulfa drugs was to lower blood-sugar levels by stimulating the pancreas to decompose sugar—precisely what diabetics cannot do. Experimentation led to the oral antidiabetic drugs in the 1950s, beginning with tolbutamide, introduced by Upjohn as Orinase in 1957. It was followed by the longer lasting chlorpropamide, introduced by Pfizer as Diabinese in the following year. As with the diuretics, these sulfa derivatives were produced under patent monopolies by one or two firms who earned high profits and financed rapid growth from their sale.[48]

The research techniques and the points of view that produced new antibiotics and sulfa drugs also produced other new drugs in this period. The steroids have already been mentioned. The market for cortisone and its successors has grown sharply since the early 1950s, as these powerful anti-inflammatory agents have been used to alleviate suffering in conditions ranging from dermatological diseases, allergies, and asthma to rheumatoid arthritis and hepatitis. As related steroids, they have also found use in birth control.

The first of the new tranquilizers, reserpine, was isolated from an Indian plant known as Rauwolfia serpentina or snake root in 1952. The following year Ciba Pharmaceutical introduced it as Serpasil, a nonhypnotic sedative particularly useful with schizophrenics. The firm spent almost $2 million advertising Serpasil in 1954, almost half of which went for detailing. The wisdom of this allocation was shown by a marketing study in 1955 that revealed that "the great majority of Serpasil prescribers [in the observation group] remembered having been detailed on Serpasil, and all but two said that they had received samples of the product. In contrast fewer than half of the non-prescribers were detailed or received samples."[49]

Unhappily for Ciba, chlorpromazine, a synthetic competitor of reserpine, had been developed in France in 1950. It was derived from a dye, methylene blue, much as sulfanilamide had been derived from a dye in the 1930s. Ehrlich had noted that this dye had antimalarial properties, and it was studied during World War II for that purpose. Derivatives lacked the antimalarial action, but turned out to be antihistamines. Looking for better ones, the French group found chlorpromazine with its manifold effects on the central nervous system. The license to produce it in the United States was offered to two firms who refused it and then to Smith Kline & French who accepted. This firm began to market chlorpromazine as Thorazine in 1954 for use in the management of psychotic disorders. Thorazine replaced Serpasil in that market, and reserpine is now used primarily for the treatment of high blood pressure.[50]

As this brief survey has illustrated, the typical large drug company grew during the 1950s by introducing new products for which it held patents or patent rights. The new drugs were sold by aggressive advertising campaigns, and their profits contributed to the expansion of the producing firms. The combination of integrated operations and patent protection meant new drugs, high profits, growing sales, and growing firms in the 1950s.

Lederle's brands of tetracycline, Achromycin and variants, still accounted for 38 percent of its drug receipts in 1960. Pfizer obtained 33 percent of its 1960 receipts from sales of Terramycin (oxytetracycline) and Tetracyn (tetracycline). Parke-Davis was even more dependent on its patented antibiotic in 1960; 45 percent of its sales came from chloramphenicol. Lilly, by contrast, was somewhat more diversified, receiving a more modest, but still important, 16 percent of its 1960 sales from erythromycin.

The derivatives of the sulfa drugs were equally important for their discoverers and producers. Merck Sharp & Dohme had 39 percent of its 1960 sales in Diuril and its variant, Hydrodiuril. Upjohn received 20 percent of its 1960 sales in Orinase, and Smith Kline & French gathered 18 percent in Thorazine and another 15 percent in the related Compazine (prochlorperazine). Each of these drugs was a critical factor in the profitability and growth of these firms.[51]

While the growth of drug firms was unmistakable, it is worth noting that there is no evidence that their average profitability has been increased by the changes just chronicled. Internal Revenue Service data on after-tax profits of different sized drug firms and of the industry as a whole show no discernable trend over the period 1948–1973 (see table 7).

Despite the difficulties of interpreting IRS data, which conform to tax rules rather than to economic concepts, this observation is not contradicted by other evidence. Profit figures from the quarterly FTC-SEC reports are generally higher than the IRS figures for the period when they

Table 7. After-tax profits on equity in the drug industry from two sources, 1948–1973 (percent).

	IRS profit data				
	By size of assets				FTC-SEC profit data
Year	$1–10 million	$10–100 million	Over $100 million	Total	
1948	15	17	31	17	—
1953	10	10	10	10	—
1958	14	15	14	14	18
1963	11	14	15	14	17
1968	11	16	16	16	18
1973	9	12	10	10	19

Sources: *Sourcebook of Statistics of Income* (Washington, D.C.: Internal Revenue Service, 1948–1973); U.S. Federal Trade Commission and U.S. Securities and Exchange Commission, *Rates of Return for Identical Companies in Selected Manufacturing Industries* (Washington, D.C.: Government Printing Office, 1958–1973).

overlap, suggesting that the IRS data miss an increase in drug firm profits after World War II. (The dramatic discrepancy between the two sources in 1973 appears to reflect the different rules by which they processed the data.)[52] But this suggestion is opposed by the work of several authors who have corrected the accounting rates of return for the drug industry by re-defining expenditures on advertising and on research and development as investments. This adjustment allows for the lasting effect of these two ac-tivities on sales in calculating the "economic rate of return."

The profitability literature was surveyed by Clarkson, who offered a set of corrected estimates of the rate of return of a sample of industries for 1959–1973. Starting from the FTC-SEC data, Clarkson found that his correction reduced the return on net worth in the pharmaceutical indus-try by over five percentage points. This reduction did not, however, bring profits in the drug industry down to the average level for manufacturing. Within Clarkson's sample, pharmaceuticals profits as corrected remained more than two standard deviations above the mean. A more recent study by Grabowski and Mueller reached essentially similar conclusions. Start-ing from initial profitability estimates lower than Clarkson's, they esti-mated that profits in the drug industry were actually 3 percent lower than reported in their source materials. But since the other industries in their sample also had lower reported rates than in Clarkson's, a substantial profit differential between the drug industry and most other industries remained. In both studies, the drug industry was the most profitable, both before and after the corrections.[53]

In other words, these studies do not show that the drug industry earned only a competitive rate of return. They do show that the consistently high profit rates shown in the FTC-SEC data (table 7) probably overestimate the corrected or economic return. This finding in turn negates the pre-sumption that since the profits were so high in the 1960s, they must have risen in the 1950s.

One intriguing possibility must be mentioned, even though it cannot be tested by the methods used to date. Drug companies began to invest heavily in intangible capital—advertising and research and develop-ment—in the 1950s. If their accounting rates of return did not vary as they made this change in expenditures, then their economic rate of return had the following pattern. Just after the change, the economic return was higher than the accounting rate because the new expenditures, considered to be expenses in calculating the accounting rate, were in fact investments out of economic returns and because the stock of intangible capital was not yet large enough to offset this increase. After the change was in effect for a while, the growth of the intangible capital lowered the economic rate of return by spreading the profits over a larger base, making the economic return fall below the accounting rate. Consequently, there may have been a temporary surge of economic profits in the drug industry around 1960.

The restricted proposition that profits in the drug industry were high after World War II, but not higher relative to other industries than before, is supported by Stigler's study of manufacturing rates of return on corporate assets for 1938–1956. He found that the amount by which profits in the drug industry exceeded the average fell between 1938–1947 and 1947–1956. It was 3.7 percentage points in the first period and 2.5 in the second.[54] This finding is clouded by a change in the Standard Industrial Classification's definition of the drug industry in 1947, but it suggests that an increase in relative profitability around 1960 may have been only the recapturing of a differential lost in the immediate postwar years.

Taken together, the data just presented show that the size of drug firms increased dramatically at the same time as the firms reallocated their expenditures toward research and marketing, but that this change was not accompanied by overt signs of increasing market power. Neither concentration ratios nor relative profitability rose. The changes in drug firms can be accounted for simply by technological and regulatory conditions, but the apparent lack of change in the industry conflicts both with a priori expectations and with the experience of other industries in response to technological and regulatory changes. It is the generality of the process that produced this apparently paradoxical result. Patents conferred market power on their holders, but competing patents restricted the power of any single one. The increase in profitability that might have come from drug patent monopolies was dissipated in high advertising and research expenditures, with the results just described.

The Role of Doctors

All the new drugs just described were prescription drugs. The 1938 FDA prescription-only regulation and the 1951 Humphrey-Durham Amendment to the Federal Food, Drug, and Cosmetic Act that wrote the regulation into law divided the drug business into two, and almost all new drugs were placed in the prescription-only class. Their great potency made them dangerous in the eyes of the FDA and the drug firms. The layman was not allowed to choose among them; only doctors could do so, and only on a case-by-case basis. As a result of the FDA's regulation, these fruits of modern technology enhanced the doctor's power to heal the patient, as opposed to assisting sick people to heal themselves.

Could it have been any different? Most newer drugs are dispensed by doctors in this country, and the information necessary to their use "appear[s] only in such medical terms as are not likely to be understood by the ordinary individual."[55] But with a different set of regulations, many prescription drugs—antibiotics and analgesics, for example—could have been purchased over the counter or on the recommendation of a nurse or pharmacist. World travelers, in fact, are often amazed by the ease with which they can buy drugs in different countries.[56] The question of whether such a world is preferable to the one we live in—as well as the question of how that decision should be made—will be deferred until later. At this point, it ought only to be acknowledged that our present system is not an inevitable result of technology. It is the joint result of technological and regulatory change.

The transformation in the relationship between the drug companies and the public can be seen in the companies' advertising expenditures. Two estimates of the allocation of advertising expenditures for drugs can be found in table 8, one preceding the changes and one following. The

Table 8. Percentage distribution of drug advertising expenditures among media, c. 1930 and 1972.

	Percentage of drug advertising expenditure	
Medium	c. 1930	1972
Newspapers	64	a
Popular magazines	26	a
Technical journals	2	13
Direct mail	5	5
Detailing	a	51
Samples	a	11
Other	3	20[b]

Sources: C. Rufus Rorem and Robert P. Fischelis, *The Costs of Medicines,* pub. no. 14 of the Committee on the Cost of Medical Care (Chicago: University of Chicago Press, 1932), p. 153; David Schwartzman, *Innovation in the Pharmaceutical Industry* (Baltimore: Johns Hopkins University Press, 1976), p. 202.

a. Included in Other.

b. Schwartzman's estimate increased to include over-the-counter drugs by adding a 1969 estimate of OTC advertising, inflated by 10 percent to make it comparable to 1972. U.S. Congress, Senate, Hearings before the Subcommittee on Monopoly of the Select Committee on Small Business, *Advertising of Proprietary Medicines,* 92nd Cong., 1st sess., to 93rd Cong., 2nd sess., 1971–1973, pt. 1, p. 361.

earlier estimate was prepared in the course of a survey of medical costs published in the early 1930s. The authors do not specify a date for these estimates—they thought in terms of a "steady state" in the midst of the Depression—but they refer clearly to a time before the emergence of a legal division between prescription and over-the-counter drugs and before the appearance of the postwar wonder drugs. The second estimate was prepared recently, well after the industry transformation had taken place. It would be preferable to bracket this technical, legal, and commercial revolution more closely, but reliable estimates of advertising expenses are rare, and the distribution of expenses probably did not change much in the 1930s and 1960s. Total drug advertising expenses rose from 3.0 to 7.4 percent of sales between 1950 and 1960, but only to 8.8 percent by 1970.[57]

An important caveat to these data is that the two estimates do not refer to the same industry. Before 1938 the drug industry included all firms making and selling drugs that were of interest either to doctors or to the public. With the drug market split by the prescription-only regulation, firms had to choose which set of customers they would produce for and sell to. The breakdown of postwar estimates of advertising expenses covers only the pharmaceutical industry, that is, the makers or sellers of medicinal drugs. Most of these drugs are sold by prescription only, and advertising of over-the counter drugs to the general public is shown in the "other" category. This category therefore overlaps to an unknown extent with newspapers and popular magazines. It probably can be thought of as television in the 1970s.

The change in the composition of advertising was dramatic. Newspaper advertising, which had been the dominant mode of drug advertising before the World War, virtually disappeared. Advertising in popular magazines also appears to have vanished, but a better breakdown of the "other" category in 1972 might show this mode of advertising to be still important. Other advertising directed to consumers rose, but the share of advertising to consumers (as opposed to doctors) fell from 90 percent in 1930 or so to 20 percent in 1972. Before World War II, drug companies allocated only about 10 percent of their advertising at doctors. By the 1970s, doctors were subject to a barrage of ads from the drug companies.

Detailing became the dominant mode of advertising drugs to doctors. This mode of communication was not unknown in the drug industry before the rise of the integrated drug firm: wholesale druggists began to send out traveling salesmen to pharmacists in the late nineteenth century, and some drug manufacturers sent their representatives out also to herald the introduction of new products.[58] But these drummers typically were employed by different members of the industry and they visited different customers from modern detail men. Since most manufacturers sold mostly in bulk, the advertising to the public was done primarily by firms further down the production and marketing process. And since doctors did not control the purchases of most drugs, the advertising was not directed at them.

The share of prescriptions in total pharmacy sales rose from 12 percent to 40 percent in the quarter-century following 1940, and the proportion of drugs packaged in final form by their manufacturer rose equally dramatically. The result was to encourage drug advertising directly to doctors— primarily detailing—which saw its major increase well before 1972. Pfizer created its sales force in 1950–51 to sell Terramycin, for example, and Bristol created its force five years later to sell tetracycline. Eight antibiotic producers spent 44 percent of their advertising budgets on detail men and an additional 11 percent on samples in the mid-1950s. Doctors were reporting that they received much of their information about new drugs from detail men by then, and the twenty-two largest drug companies were spending almost 60 percent of their advertising dollars on detailing by 1961.[59] The revolution in advertising expenditures was over by this date.

The growth of detailing was accompanied by a growth in advertising in technical journals. This alternative, less costly approach to the doctors is equally important in understanding the development of the drug industry. Drug advertising in medical journals had not been prevalent before World War II, and it had not provided the main support either for journals or for the AMA (through its journal). The growth of this form of advertising raised important policy problems for the AMA.

In the years following its 1901 reorganization, the association made a variety of abortive efforts to raise the quality of drug advertising. The first effective program did not start until 1929 when the AMA Council on Pharmacy and Chemistry initiated its Seal of Acceptance program. Under this program, the council tested drugs in its laboratories and evaluated proposed advertisements. Only those drugs that met council standards received the seal and with it the ability to advertise in the *Journal of the American Medical Association* (*JAMA*) and related medical journals.[60]

The AMA's quality-control program for drug advertising was in force during the postwar technological revolution. The association apparently thought it was not getting enough of the new "wonder drug" advertising in its journals, because it hired a market research firm, Ben Gaffin and

Associates, to see if revenues could be raised. The study, completed in 1953, led to changes that netted a 3,600 percent rate of return on its cost in increased drug ads, according to its authors. While advertising from other sources remained constant, *JAMA* pages devoted to drug company ads doubled in the mid-1950s. The increase was obtained by three changes in AMA practice: including an index of advertisers in its journals, excluding cigarette ads, and dropping its Seal of Acceptance.[61]

The AMA asserted in a published statement that it had abandoned its Seal of Acceptance because of the excessive workload it imposed. But this story, however, plausible on other grounds, fails to mention the Gaffin study. It seems much more likely that the true reasons were those implied by the association's consultant. Basically, the AMA needed cash. It had just been prosecuted for antitrust violation, and the costs of litigation had been large, even if the fine imposed was small. In addition, the association was continuing its opposition to government financing of medical care, another costly venture.[62]

Further evidence of the increased symbiosis between doctors and drug companies comes from a shift in the AMA's point of view that took place at about this time. The association had previously supported—however half-heartedly—the government's attempts to regulate the drug industry, but it now switched to opposing them. This shift can be explained ideologically: the AMA's opposition to socialized medicine implied a hostility to all government activity in the medical field. It can also be explained technically and legally: because the potent new drugs were obtainable only through a doctor's prescription, the previous risks to the public in taking drugs no longer existed. And it can be explained financially: the AMA was becoming more closely allied with a major source of income. Whichever explanation is adopted—and the truth is surely some mixture—the shift of opinion is a natural result of the therapeutic revolution produced by the new drugs and the legal framework that gave doctors control over them.[63]

The legal connection between the drug industry and the doctors was cemented by the FDA's 1938 regulation, but it did not originate there. It already was apparent to the authors of the 1932 survey of the cost of medicines:

In the regulation with reference to therapeutic value, the opinion of physicians is taken as a criterion for the truthfulness of a manufacturer's statement. The situation is, therefore, one in which the medical profession is both an advocate for the restriction of "patent medicine" manufacture and a judge of the evidence submitted. Society has allowed the medical profession to be the judge of its economic competitor, the "patent medicine" industry.[64]

"Society" also allowed doctors to gain control of the fruits of postwar drug technology and to reap the economic rewards of this control. New competition for doctors was not allowed to surface.

The 1938 regulation creating prescription drugs and the postwar therapeutic revolution had together totally transformed the drug industry by 1960. New technological opportunities led to patent monopolies, while the regulation reduced the elasticity of demand. Maximization of monopoly profits with very inelastic demand led to monopoly production in preference to patent licensing. The existence of shared patents and of competing patents on similar drugs led to vertical integration, larger firms, and increased advertising in the pursuit of larger market shares. The increased advertising and research stimulated by this competition reduced the profits of the newly integrated firms—albeit not to the competitive level—and probably led to some "excessive" advertising, if not "excessive" research and development. It also increased the symbiotic relationship between doctors and the drug firms.

Historically, the advent of a new technology and a new marketing strategy in other industries has led to the emergence of a small number of dominant firms. The introduction of machine-made cigarettes in the 1880s changed American smoking habits and led to the industry dominance of the American Tobacco Company. The introduction of roll photographic film at about the same time changed that product from a producer good used by professional photographers into a consumer good used by amateurs and led to the market dominance of Eastman Kodak.[65] The emergence of general purpose digital computers led to the present contrast between IBM and its competitors. Yet the large drug firms today are the successors to the firms that were large before World War II, and the concentration ratio in the drug industry remained virtually unchanged after the war.

Concentration did not rise in the drug industry because the nature of the technical change in drugs was not the same as in the other industries mentioned. No single drug dominated the industry in a way comparable to Kodak's roll film. While patents conferred temporary market power on the discoverers of new drugs, many different drugs were discovered and promoted. The existence of numerous patent monopolies worked against the emergence of a dominant firm. The new technology was a method of research rather than a method of production, and that method could not be patented.

FIVE

Doctors and Drugs

D OCTORS WERE APPOINTED the consumers' agents in choosing "dangerous" drugs shortly before World War II. The appellation *dangerous* does not mean toxic in this context, but rather potent; doctors were to prevent the misuse of potent drugs by patients. During and after the war, the number of drugs in this category multiplied at a spectacular rate. With the new drugs came a reorganization of the drug industry toward integrated, innovating drug producers who advertised heavily to doctors and who exploited the limitation of their market to establish personal relations with potential customers.

The reaction of individual doctors to these developments can be seen in their prescribing habits. A new relationship between doctors and drug manufacturers began to take shape in the mid-1950s, with the appearance of integrated firms, and lasted until the mid-1970s, when the increasing availability of generic products began to threaten it.[1]

To make an instrumental choice among drugs, doctors need to know, first, their effects on the patient—the benefits and the possible adverse reactions—and, second, their financial costs to the patient. A rational choice results from comparing the benefits and costs of competing drugs. Yet it turns out that doctors know neither comparative benefits nor comparative costs. Comparative benefits, in fact, are often not known at all. It follows that prescribing and taking drugs are risky actions not susceptible to instrumental behavior. Instead, doctors choose drugs by reference to medical "customs."

Evaluating Drug Effectiveness and Risk

Once doctors have graduated from medical school, passed through their internship and residency, and begun to practice, they have accumulated a great deal of information on drugs. Given the need to prescribe drugs for specific circumstances, they are able to narrow their attention to a thera- peutical class of drugs without research. Investigation, if undertaken, is to inform the choice of drugs within a class, rather than between different classes. If undertaken at all, such investigation undoubtedly starts with the *Physicians' Desk Reference.*

The *PDR* is distributed annually to all practicing physicians, free of charge. It contains descriptive articles on approximately twenty-five hun- dred drug products, identified by brand name and listed according to manufacturer. Its organization differs from that used in most other drug compendia, which classify products by their active ingredient and group them by therapeutic class or chemical similarity. A variety of indexes in the *PDR* let doctors go from generic name or therapeutic class to descrip- tions of specific drugs, but the organization of the book does not encour- age a doctor to discover which drugs are chemically or therapeutically equivalent.

The drug descriptions in the *PDR* are strictly regulated by the Food and Drug Administration. The agency's regulations on the adequate la- beling of prescription drugs have been interpreted to include all material distributed with the drug, even if not physically attached to the drug's container. The required labels—too extensive to be written on the side of a reasonable pill container—consequently have come to be written on "package inserts," descriptive circulars included with a drug. And the FDA requires that the drug descriptions in the *PDR* make "verbatim use of the approved labeling."[2] The *PDR*, in other words, is a compilation of package inserts. Written and financed by the contributing companies and given to doctors, it is a kind of group advertisement.

Doctors rely on the *PDR* far more than any other drug data compen- dium. According to a 1973 survey of ten thousand doctors, they consult it more than once a day on average (7.5 times a week), while not consulting any rival volume as often as once a week. Asked which drug compen- dium they considered most useful, an overwhelming majority (89 per- cent) of doctors listed the *PDR*.[3]

The *PDR* by its nature does not contain useful comparative material. The drug descriptions are reproduced from circulars designed for a con- text in which comparison between drugs is not appropriate, since the package insert is meant to be read after the product is purchased. In addition, the inserts are the same for closely related drugs. Not only do they talk of "tetracycline," as opposed to a particular brand, but they talk of "the tetracyclines," that is, all of the chemical compounds based on the tetracycline molecule. Finally, the organization of the volume itself discourages comparisons by scattering rather than grouping the descriptions of analogous or chemically equivalent drugs.

What happens when a doctor decides to inquire more deeply? Let us change the question from what doctors typically do to what they could do. The casual nature of most doctors' approach to comparative drug information cannot be evaluated until we see the potential results of a careful investigation.

The first step in a more serious inquiry would be to consult another compendium or text, like Goodman and Gilman's *Pharmacological Basis of Therapeutics*. It is worth noting that half the doctors in the 1973 survey reported that they never look at Goodman and Gilman and that the remainder refer to it only a few times a month on average. The contents of this volume consequently are not fresh in the minds of many doctors.[4]

Goodman and Gilman is organized by therapeutic classes and therefore provides more information relevant to a choice between similar drugs than does the *PDR*. Within a class, drugs are described by their generic name, which communicates no information about which brand to prescribe. In addition, drugs are grouped in classes and described together. (The *PDR*, by contrast, lists each brand of a drug separately but has the same FDA-approved information for each.) Goodman and Gilman's chapter on antibiotics, for example, notes that the seven available tetracyclines are very much alike, permitting the author to discuss them as a class. The clear implication is that it does not matter in most situations which tetracycline is prescribed. The doctor, however, still has to choose one to write a prescription. The information that the drugs are therapeutically equivalent does not mean that the choice among them need not be made; it means instead that it must be made on other grounds.

To facilitate choices among nonequivalent antibiotics, an extensive table gives first, second, and third choices for use with specific diseases. The diseases are identified by the microorganism involved, so the table is useful only after a culture has been taken and analyzed. And anywhere from two to eight different drugs are recommended for any given disease (since up to three different drugs are listed under each "choice") with only the most limited information about relative effectiveness. What is the consequence of going from the first-choice to the second-choice drug? By how much is the effectiveness of the therapy reduced? The headnote of the table has only this to say:

Presentation of choices of specific agents for the treatment of various infections is always provocative of discussion and disagreement because such choices often represent the distillate of personal experiences that may not duplicate those of others. In addition, the current availability of a number of drugs that are approximately equally effective makes an order of choice very difficult, if not impossible. To complicate matters, sensitivity patterns of a number of microorganisms often vary with the hospital or clinic in which they are isolated.[5]

In other words, no more detailed information is to be expected, and even the information in the table may not be relevant to a particular clinic or hospital. On the other hand, there appears to be little expectation that the effectiveness of the therapy will be much affected by the choice of drug.

One antibiotic is separated out for special treatment. Chloramphenicol, one of the first antibiotics discovered after the war, can cause a fatal anemia reaction in some patients. Only one in forty thousand or more courses of therapy will produce this reaction, according to Goodman and Gilman, but their volume still states that chloramphenicol should be avoided where possible and monitored carefully when used. This cautionary remark is only a pale imitation of the prominent warning notices in the *PDR*. But the *PDR*, although stating clearly that this drug should not be used for trivial infections, does not repeat Goodman and Gilman's estimate of the risk. Doctors who stop with the *PDR* know only that the risk exists: they do not have the information necessary to decide whether it is worth taking or even whether it is larger than the risk with comparable drugs. Doctors who consult Goodman and Gilman get an estimate of the risk, but not of the comparative effectiveness of chloramphenicol in treating various microorganisms. The information is hard to evaluate.[6]

Other compendia are consulted less frequently and tend to give less information than Goodman and Gilman. The *Merck Manual* and *Drugs of Choice* are alternative sources, but they tend to rearrange the information in the *PDR* rather than supplement it. *AMA Drug Evaluations* contains many blunt statements about the ineffectiveness of many drugs, but two-thirds of doctors surveyed never look at it. The political conflicts that have surrounded this volume may have reduced its credibility.[7]

The Medical Letter, a newsletter begun in 1959, regularly summarizes the professional literature on drugs from a well-informed, skeptical viewpoint in four to six typewritten pages. With a circulation of over a hun-

dred thousand—or one out of three doctors—this letter is a wide dissem-
inator of drug information, but it is hard to know whether it is a useful
reference tool. The 1973 survey of doctors did not treat it as such, asking
only if people read the newsletter as it appeared and not if they ever used
it for reference. For lack of better information, I will follow the survey's
lead and treat *The Medical Letter* as a periodical rather than a compendium.

The doctor who wishes more information than found in compendia
must dip into the periodical literature. This literature is vast and varied;
no typical path through it can be charted. Instead, a few examples must
suffice to demonstrate its scope and limitations. The literature on a well-
known adverse reaction, the risk of getting fatal aplastic anemia from
taking chloramphenicol, and the literature comparing different tetracyclines show how medical journals have described an important and an
apparently not-so-important problem.

Chloramphenicol was introduced in 1949. Reports of reversible, non-
fatal anemia associated with its administration began to appear almost
immediately, and reports of fatal aplastic anemia emerged in 1952. The
FDA instituted a nationwide survey of anemia in that year which showed
that anemias related to chloramphenicol were not more fatal than other
anemias. Nevertheless, the FDA issued a warning against the use of
chloramphenicol in 1952 and required it to be included in the drug's labeling. The warning was strengthened in 1961.[8]

The nationwide survey was continued by the American Medical Association, and reports from it appeared at odd intervals. A 1954 report on
1,448 cases of anemia concluded that "no statistical inferences can be
drawn from the data collected." A 1962 report supported "the contention
that chloramphenicol has a definite toxic action on the bone marrow,"
but did not give an estimate of its frequency. A 1967 report said that its
"best guess" for the risk of getting aplastic anemia from chloramphenicol
was one in 100,000.[9]

This "best guess" was taken from a 1961 article in a minor journal
which contained the first serious attempt to evaluate the risk. The probability of the reaction was estimated by dividing the number of people who
had both taken chloramphenicol and contracted aplastic anemia by the
total number of people who had taken chloramphenicol. The numerator
was taken from the AMA survey. The denominator—the number of people at risk—was estimated by dividing the sales of chloramphenicol by
the average dose. The average dose was assumed to range from 3 to 8 g,
depending on the type of administration. The estimate was made for two

years, showing a risk of one in 156,000 for 1958 and one in 227,000 in 1959.[10]

This method was utilized in a study published in 1964, where the average dose of chloramphenicol was assumed to be 4 g. The resulting estimated risk was one in 60,000, noticeably higher than in the 1961 article.[11] The 1964 article prompted resolutions on chloramphenicol in the California legislature and a further study to evaluate the risk incurred when taking this drug. The new study started by considering all California deaths in an eighteen-month period. Of these 225,000 deaths, the authors classified 60 as caused by aplastic anemia. Searching back through the medical records of these 60 people, they discovered that 10 of them had been treated with chloramphenicol—8 within a year of death—while 50 had not. They then estimated the number of people taking chloramphenicol in their sample period by dividing the amount sold by the average dose, assumed to be either 4.5 or 7.5 g.

The authors then had four basic numbers: the total population of California, the number of Californians who had taken chloramphenicol (two estimates), the deaths from aplastic anemia without exposure to chloramphenicol (50), and the deaths from this disease after exposure to this drug (10, or 8 if exposure within a year is considered). Dividing 50 by the total population of California gave the proportion of Californians dying from aplastic anemia without taking chloramphenicol: one in 524,000. Dividing 8 by the two estimates of chloramphenicol users gave two estimates of the proportion of chloramphenicol users who died from aplastic anemia within a year of taking the drug: one in 40,800 and one in 24,500. The first of these is thirteen times as large as the proportion of people not taking chloramphenicol who died from aplastic anemia. It is also the source of the estimated risk reported in Goodman and Gilman.[12]

The transition from the proportion of people dying from aplastic anemia to the estimated risk of dying from this disease under various conditions is easily made, but an argument is needed to justify it. Such an argument might go like this: Assume that there is a fixed probability of contracting and dying from aplastic anemia within a year of taking chloramphenicol and that this probability may differ from the probability of death from aplastic anemia without exposure to this drug. To estimate the former, we need to define a random sample of people, such as everyone living in California in a given eighteen-month period. We then need to divide the sample into chloramphenicol users and avoiders and examine the first group to see how many died in the indicated way. Dividing this number by the number of chloramphenicol users gives an estimated probability of dying from aplastic anemia within a year of taking chloramphenicol. This estimate may not equal the actual probability, of course, since the incidence of aplastic anemia in any given group of people may not equal the average for the population as a whole. But we can estimate a set of "confidence limits" from the sample size within which the true probability would lie in nineteen out of twenty experiments of this kind.[13]

The authors of the study in question did not perform this experiment, but—if their estimates are accurate—they arrived at the same numbers. Even though they did not identify all the chloramphenicol users, they did calculate the ratio of those users who died in the indicated way to the total. Their numbers can be regarded as if they came from such an experiment, and confidence limits for their estimates can be calculated. They calculated the 95 percent confidence interval surrounding 1/40,800 as extending from 1/132,900 to 1/24,100. Similarly, the proportion of nonusers who died from aplastic anemia may be regarded as an estimate of probability of dying from this disease without exposure to chloramphenicol. This estimate lies in a 95 percent confidence interval extending from 1/725,800 to 1/410,800.[14]

This study, published in 1969, is a very fine one. It provides clear and complete descriptions of what was done, and it contains a clear probability model which it uses to calculate confidence intervals for its estimates. Nevertheless, three important limitations need to be emphasized. First, it appeared fully twenty years after chloramphenicol went on the market. The FDA required warnings on chloramphenicol labels in 1952—long before the extent of the risk from taking it was known. This policy, in other words, was based on only the most informal assessment of the danger to patients.

Second, there is no assurance that the estimated probabilities equal the true probabilities. In fact, there is every reason to suspect they do not. We have reasonable assurance that the true probabilities lie within the estimated confidence intervals, but we do not know where. If the true risk of dying from aplastic anemia after taking chloramphenicol lies at the upper end of its confidence interval while the true risk of dying from this disease without exposure lies at the lower end of its confidence interval, then the increased risk from taking the drug is only three times the risk for the population at large. Conversely, if the true probabilities lie at the opposite ends of their respective confidence intervals and the higher estimated average dose is more accurate than the lower one used in the discussion thus far, then the risk to users is fifty times as large as the risk for the unexposed population. It makes a lot of difference whether chloramphenicol increases the risk of dying from aplastic anemia by three or fifty times, but the data in this article cannot say which it is. Given that the population of California—the original "random sample"—was 17 million at the time of the survey, it is hard to see how tighter confidence intervals could be obtained in a study of this type.

Third, there is a paucity of comparable studies with which to compare this one. All kinds of drug reactions, some of them fatal, are reported in the literature, but few studies provide estimates of their relative frequencies or their incidence among users and nonusers of the drugs involved. Comparable data on the relative effectiveness of different drugs in the treatment of given ailments are equally scarce, and the doctor who endeavors to utilize the results of this study to make a therapeutic decision is hampered by the lack of complementary material with which to integrate it.[15]

For example, penicillin is widely thought to be among the least toxic of drugs.[16] But absence of toxicity apparently does not mean absence of risk. According to Goodman and Gilman again: "Penicillin is thought to be the most common cause of drug allergy ... About 0.002% of patients treated with these agents [penicillins] die from anaphylaxis. It has been estimated that there are at least 300 deaths per year due to this complication of therapy."[17] Anyone facile with decimal points will note that 0.002 percent is the same as one in 50,000. This is well within the confidence interval for the risk from chloramphenicol; in fact, it is close to the point estimate of one in 40,000 reported in Goodman and Gilman. Penicillin risk is indistinguishable from chloramphenicol risk![18]

Yet the *PDR* and other sources display prominent warnings about chloramphenicol, while mentioning the risk of penicillin only in passing. The doctor searching for the basis of the chloramphenicol warnings would be forced to conclude that the warnings are misplaced; the epidemiological literature on drug reactions does not justify singling out chloramphenicol. Penicillin is also "dangerous"; perhaps other antibiotics are, too. The technical literature does not bear a clear relationship to the warnings in the *PDR* or even in Goodman and Gilman.[19]

It also does not compare the risks of taking chloramphenicol or other antibiotics with risks from sources unrelated to drugs. For example, one need only drive about seven hundred miles to make the risk of dying in an automobile accident equal the risk of dying from taking chloramphenicol or penicillin.[20]

The doctor who tried to discover the basis for the warning on the chloramphenicol package insert, therefore, ultimately would be frustrated. No attempt to evaluate the prevalence of the risk appeared for a decade after the warning was issued in the early 1950s, and even the careful study published almost two decades after the warning appeared provides only limited information. The estimate of the risk still has a high variance, and it is hard to compare with dissimilar data in the literature.

Because the information, such as it is, took so long to accumulate, a doctor who based a decision on his memory of an old article could be seriously misled. Alternatively, a doctor who followed the path of inquiry just described, only to find such limited information, is unlikely to undertake many other such projects.

Bioavailability and Clinical Equivalence

The example of chloramphenicol illustrates the limitations of available information when important differences between drugs are at stake. The example of tetracycline illustrates the opposite: how little guidance the literature gives the doctor trying to choose between apparently identical products. Drug compendia, it will be recalled, discuss all tetracycline compounds as a class, yet there have been several different kinds of tetracyclines and several different brands of tetracycline itself available right from the start. Doctors searching for information to guide a choice among tetracyclines find many more articles than their colleagues investigating the epidemiology of chloramphenicol, but hardly more guidance.

The different brands of tetracycline were advertised vigorously. Each drug company asserted that it had made some slight modification in the capsule that enhanced the drug's absorption by the patient. One firm added citric acid; another, metaphosphate; another, glucosamine. Others introduced a tetracycline phosphate complex, a slight modification of the tetracycline molecule itself. The firms' claims were based on articles in the professional literature showing that capsules modified in these ways were indeed absorbed more readily into the bloodstream of experimental subjects.

The articles demonstrating differences began to appear in 1953. Four years later, in 1957, two articles appeared showing that the results observed were not due to the causes cited by the experimenters. It turned out that a common filler used for tetracycline capsules, dicalcium phosphate, retarded the absorption of tetracycline into the bloodstream. In some cases the advertised additives offset the effects of dicalcium phosphate; in others a different filler had been used. Plain tetracycline hydrochloride was absorbed as readily as any modified version as long as dicalcium phosphate was not present.

The discovery that the well-publicized "improvements" in tetracycline amounted to no more than undoing the drug companies' own clumsiness prompted a chorus of editorials in the professional literature. *The New England Journal of Medicine* led off in January 1958, followed by Maxwell Finland and Charles May in other medical journals during the same year. *The Medical Letter* devoted two pages of its initial issue to "buffered tetracycline." In addition to repeating that the companies' claims were based on error, *The Medical Letter* noted: "To the physician, the important thing is that elevations even of the order claimed have no real clinical significance. Because of the great differences in absorption among patients, the recommended dosages of antibiotics make allowance for low absorption by some patients."[21]

These conclusions were echoed by experiments done after the identification of dicalcium phosphate as a depressing agent. The concluding sentences of one experimental article cogently summarize the state of knowledge in 1959: "The magnitude of observed differences between tetracycline preparations are largely of academic interest and have little, if any, significance in terms of tetracycline therapy. The best tetracycline preparation appears to be unembellished tetracycline hyrochloride."[22]

The tetracycline literature of the 1950s represented one step foward and one step back. First there were differences among different brands of tetracycline and related compounds, and then there were not. Increasingly clearly, the technical literature assured doctors that any existing differences lacked clinical significance. Doctors apparently could not go far wrong in prescribing any tetracycline, but they were, by the same token, deprived of therapeutic guidance in making the choice.

The speed of tetracycline absorption into the blood stream rose to prominence again a decade later as the patents on tetracycline began to expire. New firms entered the market, and generic tetracycline sold by small firms became available. A new set of experiments searched for differential rates of absorption, and a new set of articles appeared. The test was old, but the terminology was new. The experiments were now about "bioavailability," and they were testing for "bioequivalence." The only difference between the bioavailability experiments of the 1970s and the blood-level experiments of the 1950s was the subject matter. The early investigators were testing different formulations by the major manufacturers; the later ones were testing the same formulations by large and small drug firms.

A 1971 article that tested oxytetracycline from all eleven domestic manufacturers is typical of the bioavailability literature.[23] The authors gave one 250 mg pill to each of a hundred healthy, fasting subjects. But taking one pill differs from the normal dosage of four pills a day for ten days; a pill that was not absorbed well in a few hours might nevertheless be indistinguishable from others after repeated doses. In addition, the clinical use of tetracycline is for sick patients; it is not clear how the absorption by healthy patients relates to this use.[24] And most patients continue to eat while taking tetracycline. This, too, changes the speed of its absorption. For all these reasons, the results of this test do not translate directly into useful clinical guidance.

The article reported that the products of three manufacturers were not significantly different from Terramycin, the standard of reference, but that seven did result in lower concentrations of oxytetracycline in the subjects' blood streams. The doctor who tried to use these results for guidance in prescribing oxytetracycline, however, would find some obstacles. The experimenter obtained his samples from manufacturers, but the doctor identifies drugs by their distributor. Not only are the manufacturers and distributors of generic drugs often distinct, but a given manufacturer may supply more than one distributor and a given distributor may buy from more than one manufacturer.[25] Doctors could conclude from this article that Terramycin is preferable to some other oxtetracyclines, but they could not identify the "bioequivalent" oxytetracyclines that the article shows to exist.

A 1972 article tested three brands of tetracycline against one another. Because only one lot of each brand was used and because the variation within brands was not known, the manufacturers were identified as A, B, and C. A footnote supplied the names for the curious, but only one of them (Lederle) appears in the PDR. Single doses of tetracycline were given to most of the healthy, fasting subjects, but a few had multiple doses. The author reported that the results of certain tests correlated well with the results of others, but he neglected to include the correlation coefficients that say just how close these relationships were. Any reader who substituted one test for another on the basis of this article would be injecting an unknown variation into his experiments. The article's conclusions admirably capture the ambivalence in the bioavailability literature: "The single-dose studies presented here conclusively show differences between the biologic availability of A, B, and C in ambulatory healthy subjects participating in these studies. Unfortunately, there is no information on whether these differences would be greater or less in bed patients with infectious disease."[26]

Both these articles present evidence of some differences in the absorption rates among different brands of the same drug, but the evidence does not relate to the conditions under which the drugs are used: the patients were healthy, they were fasting, and they typically took only one pill. And the different drugs tested were identified only imperfectly: the major manufacturer in the market was identified as the source of one sample, but the others—equivalent or not—were not described in a way that doctors could make use of. The only possible conclusion a practicing doctor could draw is to stay with the dominant manufacturer, not as a result of the experimental findings but because of the way the experiments were conducted and the evidence presented.[27]

Just over one hundred fifty experimental articles on bioavailability were published in the professional medical literature in the last decade.[28] They can be divided into three groups by subject matter: antibiotics, digoxin (or digitoxin), and all other drugs. Arraying the characteristics of the articles in tabular form, table 9, verifies the representativeness of the two just discussed.

The two articles limited their attention to blood levels and urine output. They did not ask whether there were therapeutic differences among the tested drugs, even though the earlier bioequivalence debate over tetracycline concluded that the observed differences were therapeutically insignificant. Less than one-quarter of the experimental articles on bioequivalence in the past decade made the transition from blood or urine levels to therapeutic effects. All the others measured absorption or excretion of the drugs by healthy patients, which is only tenuously connected to therapeutic usefulness.

In addition, the samples employed in the tests were small. The median

Table 9. Characteristics of experimental articles on bioavailability by type of drug studied, 1968–1978 (number of articles or subjects).

Characteristic	Antibiotics	Digoxin[a]	Other	Total
Total articles	38	31	93	162
Articles reporting a therapeutic test	6	2	32	40
Median number of subjects per article	12	7	11	10
Articles reporting one pill per subject	23	15	58	96
Articles reporting differences among drugs tested	27	22	50	99
Articles identifying the drugs used	26	24	69	119

Source: See text.
a. Or digitoxin.

number of subjects was small, ten overall, and three-fifths of the articles reported the effects of giving only a single pill to each subject. Since most articles did not report their sample variances, it is impossible to know whether the differences observed would stand up with larger samples. Given the lack of attention to statistical details that pervades this literature, it often is hard even to know if the articles include information relevant to this question.

So even though three-fifths of the articles reported differences in the rate of absorption into the blood stream of the drugs studied, this evidence is hard to utilize. And although half the articles identify the brands or manufacturers of the drugs used, the articles that do so are not always the ones that found differences, and not all the identifications are easily related to the demands of writing prescriptions.

The time pattern of the experimental bioavailability articles is interesting. There was only one article on digoxin before 1972, and the other articles were split evenly between antibiotics and other drugs. Then, in response to the early digoxin article and the controversy it aroused, there were over twenty experimental articles on this drug in the next three years. During these years Burroughs Wellcome changed the way in which Lanoxin, the leading brand of digoxin, was made, and the FDA changed its standards for marketable digoxin to include both more stringent dissolution and bioavailability tests. Despite the flurry of experimental articles, the change in the most popular brand, and the change in the FDA standards, Goodman and Gilman still recommend using a brand of digoxin rather than prescribing generically.[29] The attempts by the FDA to assure the comparability of digoxin from different sources do not seem to have changed recommended prescribing patterns.

The number of experimental articles on drugs other than antibiotics and digoxin rose steadily throughout the decade, from just about two a year to over ten. This was accompanied by a shift of articles out of well-known American journals into less widely circulated and foreign journals, probably in response to the lack of novelty of the newer studies. While the change in journals is understandable, it is not clear how it affects the dissemination of the information in the more recent articles.

There seems to be enough information to worry doctors, but not enough for them to evaluate their unease. Outside of a small number of drugs like digoxin, it may not matter which brand is used or whether generic drugs are used. Dosage levels for most antibiotics and many other drugs are not critical, and no evidence is presented in these articles about quality or purity. Nevertheless, the literature does not allow a doctor to be absolutely convinced of this condition. It is one thing to say that there is no convincing evidence of therapeutic differences; it is another to say that they do not exist.[30]

The ambiguity of this literature reflects an underlying theoretical confusion. Clinical tests have been avoided because the standards to be used in evaluating them are not clear. Disagreement over which drug to use in any specific case has been fostered by the pursuit of imprecise and unformulated goals. As a medical statistician has expressed it: "There is no satisfactory procedure for assessing the safety and efficacy of drugs ... The main difficulty is due to a classic type of scientific error: the development of precise techniques for attaining a goal that is itself unspecified."[31]

Even if we could define what we mean by an "effective" drug, difficulties would remain. Louis Goodman, editor of the authoritative drug compendium, has emphasized that "there are very few drugs, if any, for which we know the basic mechanism of action." In the absence of this information, tests of drug effectiveness—however defined—must be designed to capture all possibilities. Goodman listed twenty drug characteristics—like absorption, distribution, duration of effect, tolerance, toxicity, and interaction with other drugs—that could affect drug "efficacy." He also listed seventeen patient characteristics and nine physician characteristics that could alter the effectiveness of any given drug. Standardization for all these factors, clearly, is a superhuman job.[32]

Research physicians consequently have eschewed epidemiological tests of the comparative effects of different drugs or of different brands of the same drug. A survey of the medical literature on digestive diseases and neoplasms in the decade before 1974 revealed that only 3 percent of the reports on gastrointestinal drug therapy were randomized clinical trials, that is, experiments that could yield statistical evidence on the therapeutic results of using different drugs, brands, or formulations. In four-fifths of these cases, a new therapy was established; only one-fifth reevaluated established treatments in the light of new knowledge and evidence.[33]

A government Task Force on Prescription Drugs reported in 1968, at the beginning of the period surveyed in table 9, that the lack of clinical equivalence among chemical equivalents was "grossly exaggerated." It admitted, however, that clinical equivalence was hard to verify and that bioavailability was used instead. The substitution of this test for a therapeutic one assumes that the clinical effect of the drug is related to the level in the bloodstream over the relevant range. The task force recognized the need for this assumption, but it offered no evidence that it was justified. The earlier literature on tetracycline, it will be recalled, denied the validity of this assumption as applied to that drug.[34]

The professional literature of the next few years did little to support the task force's contention that fears of therapeutic inequivalence among chemically equivalent drugs was grossly exaggerated. Bioavailability and clinical or therapeutic equivalence were still assumed to be related in a simple way. A report on drug bioequivalence by the Congressional Office of Technology Assessment in 1974, near the end of the period surveyed, therefore reiterated the task force's conclusions with more clarity, but without more evidence on therapeutic questions.

The Office of Technology Assessment was asked an economic question: "whether drug products are or can be made sufficiently interchangeable so that price can be a major factor in their selection." Their answer was mixed. For most oral drug products, they said that therapeutic interchangeability was attainable. In particular, "many groups of drugs . . . are customarily given in doses that insure concentration in the blood well in excess of the minimum effective concentration." For these drugs, the issue of bioequivalence is not major. Even if different pills result in varying levels of absorption by the blood, the therapeutic effect of all the pills will be the same. On the other hand, there exist some drugs where the range between the minimum dosage that is therapeutically effective and the maximum dosage that does not produce significant toxicity is very narrow. Cardioactive drugs—like digoxin—anticonvulsants, and chloramphenicol were given as examples. (Chloramphenicol causes a dose-related anemia in addition to the fatal aplastic anemia discussed above.) The report recommended that an "official list of interchangeable drug products" be drawn up and that drugs be classified into two groups according to whether bioavailability was therapeutically important.[35]

The Office of Technology Assessment succeeded in stating the question clearly, but not in providing answers. The professional literature in the years between the two reports just described appears to have clarified the issues at hand without providing any more clues toward their resolution. The reader of either report is left with the impression that bioavailability is not an important issue in general, but that it may be important in some specific—and largely unspecified—cases. Until the time when bioavailability's importance can be sharply delineated, therefore, no doctor can confidently ignore it.

Doctors' Knowledge of Drug Prices

One alternative basis for choosing among drugs is cost. In an ideal world, the benefits from different drugs would be evaluated in light of the costs.

For different brands of the same drug having no therapeutic differences, the costs alone would affect the choice. But it turns out that doctors do not know much more about the comparative costs of drugs than about their comparative benefits. The parallel between benefits and costs is not exact, however: Comparative costs are known. Pharmacists, who buy and sell drugs, know their own prices and have access to industry publications that inform them of others'.[36] But doctors do not avail themselves of these publications.

None of the medical publications that discuss benefits lists prices. *The Medical Letter* occasionally discusses costs, but not in any great detail. Whatever information doctors have on drug prices must have come from somewhere other than the voluminous medical literature.

The FDA sponsored a large-scale survey in 1973 to find out how much doctors used its publications and whether they would like and use additional information. Fortunately, the survey was not limited to this topic. For each of fifteen different types of source material, the questionnaire asked doctors which of six different kinds of information they looked for and how often they consulted each of the sources listed. There were just over ten thousand replies.[37]

Of these ten thousand doctors, 30 percent indicated that they never looked for cost information at all, whether from peers, ads, articles, or whatever. These respondents were not administrators or researchers: 88 percent of them listed patient care as their primary activity, and 37 percent listed this as their sole activity.[38] The proportion of doctors who said they looked for drug cost information in each of the listed sources is shown in table 10. Even though only 70 percent of the doctors are represented there, each respondent could check as many cost information boxes as he chose, and the percentages add up to over twice 70 percent.

Only detail men and pharmacists are used as sources of drug costs by more than a quarter of the doctors who ever seek cost information. This is understandable, since any doctor who looked for drug cost information in the other sources listed would fail to find any. Newsletters (like *The Medical Letter*) and other doctors are not used nearly as intensively as detail men and pharmacists, but they are consulted on costs more often than other sources.

The extent to which sources other than detail men and pharmacists are consulted can be gauged by other evidence in the questionnaire. Almost no doctors—less than 5 percent in most cases—who said they looked for cost information in any of these sources said that they used the source in question for that purpose alone. Most, in fact, said that they used the

Table 10. Percentage of doctors seeking drug cost information from various sources, 1973.

Source	Weighted by specialty	Unweighted[a]
Medical journal articles	9	8
Periodical newsletters	17	12
FDA *Drug Bulletin*	7	6
Package inserts	5	4
Journal advertisements	6	4
Direct mail advertisements	6	4
Textbooks	5	4
Compendia or formularies	10	6
Peer colleagues	22	16
Consultants	14	9
Detail men	54	44
Drug information centers	4	3
Pharmacists	53	41
Hospital staff meetings	10	8
Other professional meetings	11	8

Source: U.S. Food and Drug Administration, unpublished survey responses, 1973.

a. The firm conducting the survey weighted each response by the ratio of the estimated total number of doctors in each of six medical specialty categories to the number of responding doctors in that category. The implicit assumption is that doctors differ by medical specialty in how and where they obtain drug information. See U.S. Congress, Senate, Hearings before the Subcommittee on Health of the Committee on Labor and Public Welfare, *Examination of the Pharmaceutical Industry,* 93rd Cong., 1st and 2nd sess., 1973–1974, pt. 5, pp. 1573, 1582, 1621.

source in question for all the possible different types of information. This pattern contrasts sharply with the replies for detail men and pharmacists. One-fifth of the doctors who asked detail men about costs asked for no other information, and only one-third of those who did so asked for all possible kinds of data. Fully half the doctors who queried pharmacists about drug prices asked for no other information, and only 13 percent— far, far less than for any other source—asked for the whole range of information listed in the questionnaire. The small percentages in most rows of table 10, therefore, are probably overestimates of the true values. Many doctors singled out detail men and pharmacists as sources of drug cost information; no more than a handful among the 10,000 did the same with any other source.[39]

An estimate of how intensively the primary sources of drug cost information were used appears in table 11, which shows the frequency of con-

Table 11. Frequency of contact with sources of drug cost information by doctors using each source for cost information, 1973 (percentage of doctors).

Source	Contacts per week					
	0	1	2	3	4 or more	Total
Detail men	18	31	23	10	19	100
Pharmacists	29	39	16	6	10	100
Peer colleagues	7	28	24	12	30	100

Source: U.S. Food and Drug Administration, unpublished survey responses, 1973.

tact by doctors who reported seeking cost information in these sources.[40] Half the doctors who recorded seeking cost information from detail men consulted them once a week or less, and two-thirds of doctors seeking cost information from pharmacists consulted them once a week or less. While detail men are contacted more frequently than pharmacists, their information is less precise and less objective. Doctors who seek drug cost information seldom avail themselves of informed, disinterested sources.

As a result, doctors seldom have an accurate sense of drug costs. A 1970 survey of Palo Alto physicians asked them to choose a favored drug for urinary tract infections and then estimate its retail price. A correct answer was defined as one falling in the range of prices in "representative retail pharmacies." Only one-third of the doctors polled gave a correct price by this standard. When asked to identify the more expensive drug in fifteen pairs of commonly prescribed anti-infective drugs, half the doctors chose correctly in eleven or more cases. Since random guessing would yield a correct score of seven, this finding suggests that the doctors polled knew between one-third and one-half of the relative price comparisons. The first test suggests that one-third of doctors knew the price in question, while the second suggests that each doctor knew approximately one-third of the prices asked about. The two tests are consistent: if doctors knew approximately one-third of common drug prices and the identity of this one-third is determined more or less randomly, then asking doctors about any specific price should yield approximately one-third correct answers. Doctors are not totally ignorant of drug prices, nor would we expect them to be. But their knowledge is sharply limited. Asked about common drug prices, they reveal ignorance more often than knowledge.[41]

Other tests of physicians' price knowledge are scarce, both because of the multitude of prices that could be asked about and because everyone writing in this area appears to assume that doctors do not know drug prices.[42] For example, the conclusion of the 1968 Task Force on Drugs said that the doctor is *not* the patients' "expert purchasing agent." "In the view of the task force, this concept is not valid: in most situations, a purchasing agent who purchased without consideration of both quality and price would be unworthy of trust."[43] The task force, like so many other public and private groups, was intent only on stigmatizing doctors. Their conclusion, therefore, was purely negative: doctors are not capable of providing a reasoned choice among the alternative drugs available. But the task force, again typifying the literature, did not tease out the implications of this negative assertion.

The FDA appointed doctors to be the consumers' purchasing agent for "dangerous," that is, potent, drugs in 1938. This appointment was written into statute in 1951, and it does not ever seem to have been controversial. But doctors are not expert purchasing agents for consumers because they lack the knowledge to fulfill that role. To some extent, this is because the needed information does not exist, but even the information that exists is often not utilized. The question for public policy, consequently, is whether society is well served by the 1938 arrangement.

How Doctors Choose Drugs

Doctors do not and cannot exhibit instrumental behavior when prescribing drugs. They act instead in the customary mode. Persistent references in the literature to "prescribing habits" show that this attribution is not new, but its implications have not been adequately explored.[44]

Recall the characteristics of customary behavior. People acting in this mode tend to conserve what they think of as historical behavior. They evaluate actions in terms of the actions themselves, not their consequences. Social interaction is very important, both for the transmission of custom within the community and for the opportunity for reciprocal actions that it provides. Reciprocity, not exchange, is the dominant form of interpersonal communication.

Applied to drug use, habitual or customary behavior varies among physicians. Since different doctors do not perform the same optimizing calculations and since they were trained in different places, there is no reason to expect them to prescribe the same drugs for the same diseases. When doctors evaluate the prescribing patterns of others, the presence of customary behavior leads them to examine the prescriptions themselves, not their effects. The prevalence of this mode makes the medical community important in several ways. Place ("status") within this community is important in determining adherence to its customs, and membership in the community is important for influencing behavior. In fact, the marketing of drugs is conducted by "penetrating" this community and exploiting the reciprocity among its members.

It is easy to document the diversity of actions by doctors. The variety of antibiotics used in the treatment of various conditions is recorded in table 12. (The main use, of course, is in prescriptions, but the table also reports hospital orders of privately practicing physicians, office administrations, dispensing by doctors, and doctors' recommendations.) For example, 16 percent of the times when drugs were used for respiratory disorders, tetracycline was the choice. In no case were as many as half the drugs used for a given disease contained in a single specific category of drugs!

The diversity revealed by table 12 does not result from aggregation—from simply lumping together diseases for which drugs are prescribed. Each classification of this table contains several diseases, but no matter how finely the diseases are divided, doctors still use a wide variety of drugs for each one. A breakdown of diseases within the class accounting for the largest use of antibiotics appears in table 13. Half of antibiotic uses are for respiratory diseases, but no single drug is used predominantly for any single respiratory ailment. The categories of skin or cellular diseases, which account for 9 percent of antibiotic uses, are shown in table 14. This table shows an exception to the general rule of diversity: tetracyclines are clearly the drugs of choice for acne. Yet acne is unique among the conditions listed in that it is not an infectious disease, and even here one-third of the uses are for other antibiotics. With few exceptions, therefore, doctors differ widely in the drugs they choose for any given disease.

Although free from problems created by aggregating diseases, these data cannot distinguish between two types of diversity. There is no way to know whether the same doctor is using different drugs for the same disease—so that the tables reproduce the behavior of each doctor sampled—or whether each doctor consistently uses the same drug for the same disease, but a different one from many other doctors. In the first case, doctors may be responding to differences among patients or diagnoses not shown in the underlying data. For example, since antibiotics are organism-specific, the dispersion of tables 12 through 14 may reflect a range of disease-causing microorganisms. The data do not exist to test this hypothesis or even to show whether cultures were made in each case to identify the organism. In the second case, if doctors vary among them-

Table 12. Percentage of times given drugs were used for various conditions, 1979.

	Condition[a]								
Drug	Respiratory disorders	Central nervous system, sensory organ disorders	Special conditions without sickness	Diseases of skin or cellular tissue	Genitourinary disorders	Infective parasitic disorders	Digestive disorders	Circulatory disorders	Accidents and injuries
Tetracyclines	16	4	11	38	23	10	21	10	11
Chloramphenicol	b	1	2	b	b	1	2	b	1
Cephalosporins	7	6	42	9	21	7	25	14	30
Erythromycins	21	12	5	15	3	10	7	14	12
Ampicillins	14	22	13	5	27	10	15	10	11
Amoxicillins	9	30	1	1	4	3	2	4	4
Other broad-spectrum penicillins	b	b	2	1	6	1	1	b	1
Streptomycin	b	0	b	0	b	1	b	1	0
Aminoglycosides	1	b	9	b	7	5	10	3	4
Other broad- and medium-spectrum antibiotics	2	b	4	12	1	1	3	2	2
Penicillin V and VK	12	9	2	5	1	25	5	18	6
Penicillin G	16	12	5	5	6	25	8	19	9
Antistaphylococcal penicillins	1	1	3	7	7	1	5	5	6
Other penicillins	b	0	0	0	0	0	b	0	0
Total	100	100	100	100	100	100	100	100	100

Source: *National Disease and Therapeutic Index* (Ambler, Pa.: IMS America, 1979).
a. Conditions listed are all those for which more than 1.5 percent of all antibiotics were used. No more than 5 percent of any single antibiotic was used for a condition not listed.
b. Less than 1 percent.

Table 13. Percentage of times given drugs were used for respiratory diseases, 1979.

Drug	Respiratory diseases[a]				
	Acute pharyngitis	Acute upper respiratory infection, multiple sites	Bronchitis, unqualified	Acute tonsillitis	Acute bronchitis
Tetracyclines	9	19	25	3	27
Chloramphenicol	b	b	b	0	b
Cephalosporins	3	4	7	5	9
Erythromycins	21	25	24	14	23
Ampicillins	11	16	14	12	14
Amoxicillins	9	9	12	8	8
Other broad-spectrum penicillins	b	b	b	0	b
Streptomycin	b	b	b	b	b
Aminoglycosides	b	b	b	b	b
Other broad- and medium-spectrum antibiotics	2	2	2	1	2
Penicillin V and VK	23	10	5	26	5
Penicillin G	22	15	10	29	11
Antistaphylococcal penicillins	b	b	b	1	1
Other penicillins	0	0	0	0	0
Total	100	100	100	100	100

Source: *National Disease and Therapeutic Index* (Ambler, Pa.: IMS America, 1979).
a. Five largest subclasses of respiratory disease.
b. Less than 1 percent.

selves, then the tables show the extent to which doctors disagree on the treatment of specific diseases. More research is needed to analyze the diversity of physician behavior.[45]

In addition to exhibiting considerable diversity in their own prescribing patterns, doctors evaluate the prescribing habits of other doctors by examining the prescriptions themselves, not by asking whether the patients got well or whether they were treated at the lowest cost. In some studies, panels of experts reviewed the medical records and ranked the prescriptions according to whether they would have acted similarly. These studies did not measure the health of the patients; they convened a

Table 14. Percentage of times given drugs were used for diseases of skin or cellular tissue, 1979.

Drug	Acne	Other cellulitis abcess	Other local skin infection	Impetigo	Boil and carbuncle
		Skin or cellular tissue disease[a]			
Tetracyclines	67	8	8	4	8
Chloramphenicol	[b]	1	2	0	0
Cephalosporins	0	24	23	5	14
Erythromycins	11	9	17	33	30
Ampicillins	[b]	13	9	6	9
Amoxicillins	0	3	2	1	0
Other broad-spectrum penicillins	0	1	3	0	0
Streptomycin	0	0	0	0	0
Aminoglycosides	0	3	6	0	0
Other broad- and medium-spectrum antibiotics	21	4	3	0	3
Penicillin V and VK	[b]	8	6	27	10
Penicillin G	0	11	15	17	11
Antistaphylococcal penicillins	[b]	15	16	6	15
Other penicillins	0	0	0	0	0
Total	100	100	100	100	100

Source: *National Disease and Therapeutic Index* (Ambler, Pa.: IMS America, 1979).
a. Five largest subclasses of skin or cellular tissue disease.
b. Less than 1 percent.

"council of elders" to evaluate adherence to the group's norms. In other studies, doctors were ranked by the extent to which they prescribed chloramphenicol. Again, no evaluation of risks and benefits was made; doctors were ranked by their adherence to the custom of not using chloramphenicol.[46]

Other studies vary in the metrics they apply to the observed prescribing patterns, but they share the characteristic of examining the prescriptions instead of their effects. As in the rankings by experts and by chloramphenicol usage, there is a hypothesized effect of "bad" prescriptions, but this is not tested in the evaluation. For example, one study used computers to screen prescriptions for "irrational" patterns. A computer program surveyed prescription records and noted prescriptions in which the dosage prescribed or the frequency with which a drug was used exceeded a predetermined norm or in which the concurrent usage of different drugs violated another preset norm. (The norms were set sufficiently wide so that relatively few prescriptions were found to be "irrational" by this measure.) Another study surveyed hospital administrations of three drugs to see if usage accorded with the indications in the *PDR*. The study found that the majority of uses for each drug were in conflict with the *PDR*'s indications, but argued that the actual use of one drug was superior to the *PDR*'s recommendation. This conclusion, while emphasizing the limitations of the medical literature, tends to obscure the implications of the test. In a theoretical essay, one author elevated the examination of prescriptions rather than therapeutic effects from a practical procedure to a preferred mode of action. Since regulation covers medical care, not health, doctors should be judged by what they do, not by what happens to the patient.[47]

The classic study of new-drug adoption by Coleman, Katz, and Menzel examined the diffusion of an unnamed drug without relating diffusion to effectiveness. No comparison with other drugs was attempted. No data were collected, therefore, that could show the impact of differential effectiveness on the rate of adoption. The authors never asked about the results of using the new drug; they were concerned solely with the relation of the choice itself to the doctors' place within the medical community. They noted that the drug they studied was the third in a sequence of related drugs—and indicated this by the nom de plume they gave to the drug, Gammamyn—but did not address the question of whether this drug offered substantial improvement over the older two.[48]

This study is typical of the literature. More accurately, it set the pattern for subsequent inquiries. A recent survey of the literature of prescribing habits cites only one article on the question of whether therapeutic effect had an effect on the adoption of new drugs. This study found that therapeutic advantage was important, but that it accounted for only slightly over half the reasons given by physicians for adopting new drugs. And since this reason is a highly approved one in the medical community, this estimate undoubtedly is a major overestimate of the true influences of therapeutic advantage.[49]

The diversity of prescribing patterns and the emphasis on process rather than results in evaluating these patterns reveal the customary nature of prescribing behavior. The importance of the medical community in determining prescribing habits provides further evidence of customary behavior because membership in a community serves a vital function for a person acting customarily. It is in reference to the community that customs are validated, and it is through reciprocal relations within the community that customs change.

In the presence of risks, adherence to community norms also functions as a kind of insurance policy, protecting the community member in time of trouble. If a doctor's patients suffer because of adverse reactions from chloramphenicol or penicillin, because of an inadequate dosage of some other drug, or because of the doctor's decision which drug to use, his first line of defense is to rally the medical community around him. A doctor adhering closely to the customs of this community is in a far better position to do this than a deviant, experimental physician.

Adherence to medical custom is also a legal defense. To the extent that prescribing patterns get to be codified in FDA-approved literature, they acquire some of the status of law. A doctor may legally prescribe a drug for unauthorized uses, but anyone in the chain of distribution who suggests it be so used is guilty of violating the law. If misadventure follows, the doctor's failure to follow the approved label's instructions may render him liable to malpractice judgments.[50]

Coleman, Katz, and Menzel, examining the role of the medical community in the adoption of a new drug, found that usage diffused according to two quite distinct patterns among physicians who were and were not members of a professional community. The rate at which use of the new drug spread among isolated doctors decreased steadily during the first six months it was available, but remained level or even increased during the same period among doctors integrated into a medical community. The authors explained this by reference to two processes. One involved a constant rate of adoption for each person, leading to a decreased rate for the population as a whole as fewer and fewer doctors were left to make the change. The other was analogous to an epidemic, where the risk of "infection" spread both according to who was at risk and how many "carriers" were around. The authors did not attempt to delineate the precise nature of the "infection" in this model.[51]

Assume for the moment that the "infection" consists solely of information. This approach minimizes the influence of social forces and maximizes the appearance of instrumental behavior. Even so, the pattern of diffusion confirms the dominance of customary behavior in two ways. First, published information of all sorts was equally available to integrated and unintegrated doctors. The contagion model assumes, however, that only information from colleagues increased the probability of adopting the new drug. Second, the time period involved was too short for any comparison of the new and old drugs. The information being transmitted must have been about the custom itself—"I use this new drug ..."—rather than about its relative effectiveness. Even if practicing doctors were engaged in the business of testing the relative therapeutic benefits of new drugs, which they are not, there was not enough time for them to have learned anything of value.

This seminal study confirms the customary nature of prescribing habits. It does so both by the way it formulated the question and avoided interdrug comparisons and in the conclusions it reached. The role of the medical community is all important in altering prescribing habits.[52]

Prescribing habits, then, are customs of the medical community. They are transmitted through the institutions of the community—education, clinical training, professional conversations. And they are conserved by these same activities, along with the risk of professional disapproval for dissidents. These customs are also functional; doctors can alleviate distress in ways undreamed of before Ehrlich. There must be connections between the customs of the medical community and the effects of these customs on patients. A brief survey of several such connections serves to put the last characteristic of customary behavior in drug prescribing—the importance of detail men—in perspective.

The first and loosest connection is personal experience. Doctors prescribe drugs and observe patients. They then evaluate the clinical effect of giving a certain drug to a given patient and obtain guidance for future prescriptions. The prevalence of this activity is shown by the multitude of journal articles reporting exactly this process.[53]

Despite its popularity, this mode of gathering information is singularly inefficient, if not actually misleading. Practicing doctors cannot run controlled experiments on their patients. They do not have large enough samples or the necessary statistical training to test even moderately complex hypotheses. And all the conceptual problems of evaluating drug reactions in formal medical research appear as well in the "experiments" of practicing physicians.

If doctors were to limit themselves to a small number of drugs, then they might be able to accumulate useful information on their effects. But doctors avail themselves freely of the wide variety of available drugs. With approximately a thousand chemical entities on the market, sold often under multiple names or by multiple vendors or in combination, doctors find it hard to restrict themselves to a small number of drugs. No matter how many prescriptions they write, doctors average under a dozen a year for each drug (or brand of drug) used (see table 15).

Table 15. Average number of drug products specified by doctors with different volumes of new prescriptions, year ending June 1976.[a]

Number of drug products specified	Percentage of doctors using this number of drug products	New prescriptions per doctor (average)	New prescriptions per drug product per doctor[b] (average)
1–50	0.8	305	8
51–100	5.7	832	10
101–150	20.4	1500	12
151–200	23.0	1664	10
201–250	16.1	2240	10
251–300	14.1	3226	12
301–350	8.4	3692	11
351–400	6.3	5299	14
401–500	3.9	5924	13
501 and over	1.4	11095	20

Source: *Audatrex* (Ambler, Pa.: IMS America, 1976). Reproduced with permission from *Drugs and Health: Economic Issues and Policy Objectives* (Washington, D.C.: American Enterprise Institute, 1980).

a. Based on a panel of 491 doctors. A drug product is a drug or brand of drug.

b. Data were obtained by approximating the entries in column 2 by a continuous gamma distribution (by minimizing the sum of squared deviations between the observed and estimated distributions), estimating conditional means of that distribution for the intervals in column 1, and dividing the entries in column 3 by these conditional means. If the entries in column 3 were divided by the midpoints of the intervals shown in column 1—that is, if the distribution of column 2 is assumed to be linear in the intervals—the estimates in column 4 would be the same except for the first two rows and the final one where the midpoint is undefined. In the first two rows, the alternate estimates are closer to 12 than those in the table. The overall range possible under any assumptions (for all entries except the last) is only from 8 to 16.

For example, doctors who used between 50 and 100 different drug products in the year ending in June 1976 wrote an average of 830 new prescriptions during the year. This in an average of only 3 new prescriptions (as opposed to refills) for each of 250 working days; these doctors prescribed far below the average of their colleagues. It is also an average of only 10 prescriptions per drug. At the other end of the spectrum, doctors who used between 400 and 500 different drug products wrote an average of almost 6,000 new prescriptions during the year, or an average of just under 24 new prescriptions on each of 250 working days. But they used each drug on average only 13 times during the year. Despite the difference between the two groups in the volume of prescriptions, the frequency with which they used any single drug product was remarkably constant, as it was throughout almost the full range of doctors.

Doctors who use a drug a dozen times in the course of a year cannot evaluate its benefits and costs relative to those of other drugs even if they try. And while the rate of a dozen prescriptions a year is only an average, deviations to one side are matched by deviations to the other. For example, consider a doctor who uses 200 different drug products and writes 2,000 new prescriptions a year—a median doctor in table 15. If he uses 30 drugs most of the time, say, once a week, he uses these 30 drugs in 1,500 of his new prescriptions. This leaves 500 other new prescriptions spread among 170 other drugs. Each of these other drugs therefore is used an average of only three times a year, hardly enough to gather any information on patient reactions at all. Acknowledging that physicians use some drugs more than others only emphasizes the point that doctors have very limited experience with most of the drugs they use.[54]

The second connection between doctors' prescribing habits and their clinical effects comes through the advice of community "elders"—teachers, respected practitioners, conference and seminar participants. To the extent that these leaders of the medical community are in touch with drug research, they communicate the best knowledge available. But the research results—as noted above—are imprecise and hard to evaluate. There is no guarantee that any given "elder" is in touch with this research or has the training to understand it. And the information comes to the practicing doctor with a lag of unknown duration. This link between prescribing customs and clinical effects contains much more information than the first, but it is still a loose connection.

The third channel for clinical information is quite different. The drug companies, recognizing the customary nature of prescriptions, have introduced their agents, who are not themselves doctors, into the medical community. Only three-fifths of the doctors surveyed by the FDA admitted having contact with detail men, so the influence of these company representatives cannot be universal. Nevertheless, detail men visit many doctors, establish personal contacts with them, and provide information to them. If the stories are to be believed, they also do favors for doctors, possibly including performing surgery on their patients.[55]

Detail men shower doctors with gifts and "reminder items." They gave away almost two hundred gifts per doctor in 1973, though each item was of curiously little value. The gifts in 1973 averaged less than fifty cents apiece in value, while the reminder items cost less than a quarter.[56] Their function is not to impart something of value; it is to establish a relationship and a basis for reciprocal action.

Reciprocity is the key to the relationship between detail men and physicians. The detail man gives freely to the doctor, and the doctor feels obligated to reciprocate. But he cannot give information or gifts to the detail man; he can only prescribe the company's drugs. When he cannot or will not do this, he feels guilty and may even *apologize* to the detail man.[57]

One empirical study attempted to evaluate the influence of detail men through interviews with over four hundred doctors at two medical conventions. The author distinguished two effects on drug choice. The first, called "compliance," shows the effects of reciprocity with the detail man. The second was risk reduction, which would lead a doctor to choose a company he trusted independently of the detail man. He found that preference for a detail man was more highly correlated with the choice of a drug than preference for a company when "safe" drugs were at issue, but not when "risky" drugs were considered. He concluded that doctors were influenced by their relationship with detail men in choosing among "safe" drugs and by their concern for drug risks in the choice of other, more dangerous drugs.[58]

Although the studies that have been done have tended to focus on what doctors know as opposed to what they do, the few investigations just reported suggest a certain behavior pattern. Doctors seeing detail men tend to prescribe drugs from the detail men's firms after the visits, but this tendency is tempered by two influences. The doctor is more likely to follow this pattern for drugs he sees as therapeutically equivalent than for those in which he sees some difference. Also, the preference induced by any one detail man is replaced by another preference when the doctor sees another detail man. The more frequently doctors are visited, the more often they change their prescribing patterns. Each drug is prescribed roughly to the degree that a doctor is visited by detail men from the originating firm—roughly in order of the drug company's advertising expenses.[59]

It follows that doctors are not loyal to specific drug companies. For example, doctors who write more prescriptions for antibiotics use antibiotics from more different drug manufacturers (see Table 16). Larger prescribers write more prescriptions for the products of each manufacturer, but they do not confine themselves to a small group of manufacturers even within a single therapeutic classification. Almost three-quarters of the doctors surveyed prescribed antibiotics from more than five different drug firms.

As with the diversity with which different drugs are used, this pattern is evident at any level of detail. The number of different brands of plain tetracycline used by doctors is shown in table 17. A doctor who writes as few as five new tetracycline prescriptions a month (sixty-seven per year) typically uses two different kinds of plain tetracycline, and those few doctors

Table 16. Number of manufacturers whose antibiotics were specified by doctors with different volumes of new prescriptions, 1976.[a]

Number of manufacturers whose antibiotics were specified	Percentage of doctors using antibiotics from this number of manufacturers	New antibiotic prescriptions per doctor (average)	New antibiotic prescriptions per manufacturer per doctor[b] (average)
1	2	22	22
2–3	10	57	23
4–5	16	130	29
6–7	17	215	33
8–9	17	432	51
10–11	16	657	63
12–13	11	904	72
14–15	7	810	56
16 and over	5	1092	—

Source: *Audatrex* (Ambler, Pa.: IMS America, 1976).

a. Based on a panel of 505 doctors.

b. Averages were calculated by assuming that doctors in each cell were divided equally between the two numbers of manufacturers in each cell.

Table 17. Number of kinds of plain tetracycline specified by doctors with different volumes of new prescriptions, 1976.[a]

Number of kinds of tetracycline specified	Percentage of doctors using this number of kinds of tetracycline	New tetracycline prescriptions per doctor (average)	New prescriptions per product per doctor (average)
1	45	32	32
2	29	67	34
3	16	109	36
4	6	175	44
5	2	298	56
6 and over	1	295	—

Source: *Audatrex* (Ambler, Pa.: IMS America, 1976).

a. Based on a panel of 482 doctors. The discrepancy between the first rows of this table and of table 16 reflects the different groups reported. Doctors who used only one antibiotic product may not have used tetracycline, and doctors who used only one tetracycline may also have used other antibiotics.

who write close to one new tetracycline prescription a day use five or more different kinds. Doctors do not choose a "best" tetracycline and stay with it. Given the assurances of rough equality between them, doctors who use this drug heavily use several different brands or alternate between brand-name and generic tetracycline.

The prescribing habits of doctors are characterized by diversity. Doctors use many different drugs in the course of the year, including similar drugs from many different manufacturers and different drugs for the same diseases. They use far too many drugs to have accurate information on their comparative costs and benefits even if this information existed. Doctors consequently follow the customs of the medical community in choosing drugs to prescribe. Like all customs, these are sustained by the institutions of the community. And like most customs, they are also functional. Nevertheless, the prevalence of customary behavior indicates that the link between prescribing habits and the therapeutic effects of drugs is weak. In the words of a prominent student of drug marketing: "We hypothesize that examination will show that while the medical reward (optimum patient care) does exist for rational drug therapy, at present time there are no real social rewards. Yet it would appear that at least two kinds of social rewards do exist for non-rational therapy (at least overprescribing)—client approval and dissonance reduction via rereading advertisements for drugs already prescribed."[60] To the list of dissonance-reducing influences, we can add conversations with detail men.

The large drug companies are aware of this process; they worked out its implications in the years just after World War II. Provided by law with a limited and identifiable group of potential customers and selling products about which full information was impossible to acquire, the major drug companies appreciated the role of custom and of reciprocal personal relationships in drug choice. They saturated the market with their representatives who established personal relations with many potential customers and gained thereby the ability to influence their customary behavior.

The drug companies' awareness of the important role served by the relationships established between their detail men and physicians can be seen in many ways, of which the amount of money they spend on detailing is only the most obvious. In open-ended interviews about research plans, management personnel from major drug firms repeatedly referred to their company's "franchise." At the level of discovery and production, the drug firms' personnel have experience in areas represented by their current products. At the equally important level of marketing, their detail men have personal relationships with doctors who use the kind of drugs they already produce. Selling a new drug to these doctors would be easier than selling it to doctors with no previous personal connection with the drug firm, according to the respondents, because new personal relationships would not have to be created. The existence of drug firms' "franchises," consequently, is partly the result of using reciprocal personal relationships in the marketing of drugs.[61]

Consumers, legislators, and regulators do not seem to be as well-informed as the drug firms. They preserve the assumption underlying the FDA's 1938 regulation and the 1951 amendment to the Federal Food, Drug, and Cosmetic Act. In this view, doctors make the educated choices that consumers are unable to make, but the evidence that doctors cannot and do not make informed choices among competing drugs casts doubt upon the viability of this position. At the same time, however, the limitations of available knowledge also cast doubt on the alternative concept of the sovereign consumer. At this point, we can say only that while the traditional argument for the present regulatory structure for prescription drugs is suspect, a reasonable alternative is not immediately apparent.

SIX

The Postwar Expansion
of Drug Regulation

THE PRESENT REGULATORY STRUCTURE for pre-
scription drugs is not simply the result of administering the 1938 Food,
Drug, and Cosmetic Act. In response to the therapeutic revolution and
the doctors' reaction to it, drug regulation changed substantially after
World War II. The most visible and dramatic changes were embodied in
the 1962 Drug Amendments, but this legislation cannot be understood in
isolation. Its role in the distribution of medicinal drugs becomes clear
only in the context of the concomitant changes within the Food and Drug
Administration and of the litigation and administrative rule making that
followed it. It is to this story that I now turn.

It is worth emphasizing that it is a story. Regulation, like most other
aspects of the human condition, is not static. The 1938 changes came in
response to events of the 1930s. They were followed by great technological advances and an industrial transformation. The effects of the prewar
regulatory changes in the postwar environment became apparent only
over time. As they did become apparent, or at least as some people observed them, the question of drug regulation was reopened. Not only is it
a story, therefore; it is a story without an end.

Passage of the 1962 Drug Amendments

Expansion of the FDA began in the mid-1950s. As a 1955 Citizens' Advisory Committee noted, the agency employed a smaller enforcement

staff in 1955 than it had in 1941.[1] The FDA had maintained a roughly constant size through the early years of the Great Depression. Its size increased rapidly in the late 1930s, presumably as a result of the 1938 legislation. But the growth of the FDA, measured by the change in personnel, was sharply arrested by the war and did not resume afterward. As advisory committees will, this one argued that the FDA needed more money. The committee's voice was heeded, and the agency expanded rapidly in the next decade. It was almost five times as large in 1966 as it had been a decade earlier (see Table 18).

Observers of the drug market commonly view the 1962 amendments to the Federal Food, Drug, and Cosmetic Act as a turning point in the FDA's activities, but it is clear that the change had begun well before they were enacted. While consistent data on the FDA's drug activities are not available, it is hard to believe that the agency's growth in the late 1950s had bypassed those departments working on drugs.

The FDA's functions were still overwhelmingly regulatory throughout this rapid expansion. At its start, in 1954, fully one-third of the agency's appropriation for drugs and devices was used to enforce compliance with one regulation: the 1938 drug prosecutions were to ensure control over restricted drugs, and the number of prosecutions typified by the suit against

Table 18. FDA appropriations and personnel, 1926–1976.

Fiscal year	Appropriations (thousands of dollars)	Personnel
1926	1,288	460[a]
1931	1,616	541
1936	1,922	518
1941	2,550	875[a]
1946	2,838	948
1951	6,025	1,185
1956	6,144	1,065
1961	20,454	2,112
1966	58,660	4,994
1971	87,503	4,615
1976	207,805	6,362

Source: U.S. Office of Management and Budget, The Budget of the U.S. Government, and Appendix (Washington, D.C.: Government Printing Office, various years). For earlier appropriations, see Lauffer R. Hayes and Frank J. Rugg, "The Administration of the Federal Food and Drugs Act," Law and Contemporary Problems, 1 (December 1933): 24n.

a. Interpolated by regressing deflated appropriations on personnel estimated for the twenty-four years between 1929 and 1966 for which both sets of data were available.

Sullivan's Pharmacy had risen from an annual average of about eleven in the late 1940s to over a hundred a year in 1953 and 1954. Even though the size of the FDA stagnated after World War II, it was enforcing a major change in the way medicinal drugs were distributed. At the conclusion of its expansion in 1966, the FDA still spent ten times as much on regulatory compliance as it did on scientific evaluation.[2]

The changes from a conventional industry to one in which most purchases had to be professionally directed was complete by the time Senator Estes Kefauver opened his famous hearings on the drug industry at the end of 1959. Kefauver's initial interest in drugs was unrelated to the expansion of the FDA. His concern was the market power and high prices in the drug industry, and the drug hearings were part of a larger series on administered prices. He succinctly summarized what he considered the distinguishing feature of the drug market: "He who orders does not buy, and he who buys does not order."[3]

Kefauver's hearings exposed the nature—or rather, the lack—of competition in the market for new, patented drugs and made headlines out of the enormous spread in the prices and manufacturing cost of those drugs. The senator introduced legislation in 1961 designed both to foster competition among drug companies and to increase FDA surveillance over drug manufacturing and new drug introductions. The bill amended the Sherman Antitrust Act to make private patent settlements like the one for tetracycline into per se violations of the law. In addition, an important provision of this proposed legislation—perhaps the most significant for Kefauver—introduced compulsory patent licensing into the drug industry. Companies discovering and patenting new drugs would be required to license other firms to produce and sell their patented drug after three years at a royalty no greater than 8 percent of sales.[4]

Another section of the proposed law amended the Federal Food, Drug, and Cosmetic Act to change the criterion for a new drug to be marketed from "safe" to "safe and efficacious in use." The efficacy requirement was added after the safety requirement wherever it appeared in the description of the new drug application (NDA) and its approval.

A succession of notable physicians testified on this part of the bill in July 1961. They agreed that the ordinary doctor in clinical practice could not evaluate the efficacy of drugs. Charles D. May, editor of *Pediatrics* and author of an important article on the role of advertising in the marketing of antibiotics, argued that "a collection of impressions," such as those gathered in the course of clinical practice, "will not furnish the truth." Louis Goodman, coeditor of Goodman and Gilman's *Pharmaco-*

logical Basis of Therapeutics, characterized the American Medical Association's argument that doctors are the best judges of a drug's efficacy as "most specious." And Louis Lasagna, who has become a staunch critic of the FDA in the 1970s, said: "Modern therapeutics is too difficult and too dangerous for today's doctor to go it alone. He needs help." Other prominent doctors agreed.[5]

Despite the support of these physicians, Kefauver's bill had an unpromising legislative history. President John F. Kennedy supported new drug legislation in his Consumer Message of March 1962, but did not mention either Kefauver's bill or compulsory licensing. The bill's licensing provision was removed in subcommittee, and the whole bill was rewritten before it was reported out of the Judiciary Committee in July 1962. Protesting the absence of compulsory licensing and the extensive rewriting, Kefauver refused to floor manage "his" bill. It did not seem to have any other support.

The administration, which had participated in the rewriting of the Senate bill, introduced its own drug bill into the House under the sponsorship of Congressman Oren Harris of Arkansas. The House bill lacked both compulsory licensing and extensive support.

But these moribund bills were not yet dead. As in 1906 and 1938, drug legislation was given a new lease on life by public perception of a threat to health. Three days after the Senate Judiciary Committee reported out its bill, the *Washington Post* broke the thalidomide story.[6]

A drug company had applied to the FDA for approval of thalidomide as a new drug in September 1960. In the absence of an objection from the FDA, on the grounds either that the drug was not safe or that the application did not contain enough evidence of safety, the NDA would have been approved automatically after sixty days. But Dr. Frances Kelsey, the FDA examiner, kept returning the application to the company each sixty days on the grounds of insufficient information. Even without firm evidence of danger, Dr. Kelsey refused to let the application take effect.

Meanwhile, phocomelia—a condition where children are born without hands or feet—began to appear with alarming frequency in Germany and other European countries. Thalidomide was identified as the source of the outbreak late in 1961, and the drug was withdrawn in several countries. The NDA to the FDA was withdrawn in March 1962 without having been approved.

The FDA did not have authority to supervise the clinical testing of drugs under the 1938 law, and thalidomide had been distributed in America for this purpose (over 2.5 million tablets to more than twelve hundred doctors). Despite the absence of marketing in America, therefore, consumption of the test drug and of thalidomide purchased in Europe resulted in a small, but highly visible, outbreak of phocomelia in this country.

News of this "near miss" in the United States would have surfaced in time, but Kefauver's staff discovered the problem as it was happening and turned their findings over to the *Washington Post*. The news created public support for the drug legislation pending in the Senate, although the bill would have done little to prevent the kind of problem posed by the thalidomide tragedy. It was reconsidered and reworded in committee and reported out again in August.

Among other revisions, the committee reworked the efficacy requirement for approval of a new drug. The word *efficacious* was replaced by *effective,* and the revised bill stated that the claims of effectiveness in the NDA or thereafter had to be supported by "substantial evidence," a term defined in the bill. The committee had taken to heart the admonitions of the doctors testifying for the bill a year before and had distinguished between the practicing doctor's "collection of impressions" and the evidence of effectiveness required in the bill. The committee considered two standards, "preponderant evidence" and "substantial evidence." The latter was the weaker, according to the committee, as it did not require agreement among experts for approval of a new drug. This agreement was not considered necessary as long as there was "substantial evidence" of effectiveness.[7]

Although the effectiveness requirement was somewhat stronger than before, the patent provisions were still missing from the revised bill. Kefauver tried to introduce a new compulsory licensing proposal on the floor of the Senate, but it was tabled on the Kennedy administration's orders and the bill passed without any patent provision at all.

The House bill was sped along by a second drug problem originating with William S. Merrell, the same company that manufactured thalidomide in America. Merrell had obtained FDA approval in 1959 to market a new drug called MER/29. After some months, reports of adverse drug reactions began to come back to the firm and to the FDA. The agency did not think it had the power to order the drug off the market, but the company withdrew it voluntarily. Subsequently, the FDA discovered that Merrell had not included all its data in the NDA and sued it for fraud. This story surfaced in late 1962 and spurred the House to approve a drug bill, although the new bill did not change the law's provisions respecting the submission of safety data to the FDA.[8]

The Kefauver-Harris bill was signed into law on October 10, 1962. Although it differed significantly from Kefauver's original bill—most notably in its lack of strong provisions to lower the price of brand-name drugs—it strengthened the government's regulation of both the introduction of new drugs and the production and sale of existing drugs.

The 1962 Drug Amendments made three important changes in the way new drugs were approved for sale. Besides changing the standards for approving a new drug, it made the FDA into an active participant in the approval process. Instead of letting a firm's NDA take effect automatically if the FDA did not object, the new law required affirmative FDA approval before marketing could begin. In addition, the amendments gave the FDA jurisdiction over the testing of all new drugs before they were approved for marketing. A drug firm had to apply to the FDA for approval of its procedures for testing an investigational new drug before it could undertake the tests needed to file an NDA. Silence by the FDA was deemed to be approval at this stage, even though it was not for the NDA. The testing of drugs like thalidomide could no longer be undertaken without prior notification of the FDA.

The new law also made three important changes in the regulation of existing drugs. First, it required drug firms to adhere to standards of good manufacturing practice which would be specified by the FDA. Periodic inspections were to be undertaken to ensure compliance. Second, the amendments required firms to use generic names in addition to brand names on drug labels and advertisements, and gave the FDA the authority to designate generic ("official") names if intervention was needed to make the names convenient for general use. Third, the FDA was empowered administratively to withdraw approval already granted to an NDA for a variety of listed causes, including that the drug was unsafe, that new evidence or methods showed it to be unsafe, a "lack of substantial evidence" of effectiveness, and material misstatements in the application. The penultimate provision meant that all approved drugs would have to meet the new standards, particularly the effectiveness standard, even if they had been approved for sale before 1962. The application of the new effectiveness standard was delayed for two years after the law's enactment to allow the drug firms to adjust to the new conditions.[9]

These provisions represent a continuation of an FDA policy that is visible since the turn of the century. The earliest attempts to guarantee that all drugs were effective had been declared unconstitutional by the Supreme Court in *U.S.* v. *Johnson* (1910) on the basis that therapeutic effectiveness was a matter of opinion. The term *effective* had appeared in an early draft of the Humphrey-Durham Amendment to the Federal Food, Drug, and Cosmetic Act, but it had been removed before passage. The FDA's concern with efficacy in 1962 was a straightforward extension of the Pure Food Act of 1906.

It can be argued that safety and effectiveness are related and that the legislative thrust of the 1962 amendments can be linked to the thalidomide tragedy. The connection is tenuous, however. First, the problem with thalidomide was safety; adding an effectiveness requirement is an exceedingly costly way to strengthen the safety provision. Second, no one disputes that thalidomide is an effective tranquilizer. Efficacy tests would not have kept it off the market, except for the time needed to perform them.

Manufacturing standards, naming practice, and other provisions, similarly, were unrelated to the thalidomide problem. Only the requirement for FDA approval—or at least the absence of FDA objection—for drug testing can be seen as a response to that episode.[10] As in 1906 and in 1938, the public response to a dramatic health hazard produced new drug legislation. And, as in these earlier episodes, the legislation reflected the concerns of the FDA more than the concerns of the public.

Effectiveness and "Innocuous" Drugs

The FDA had tried in its early years to extend its authority over therapeutic claims for drugs. This attempt had been turned back by the Supreme Court on the grounds that therapeutic claims were opinions, not facts, and therefore not susceptible of administrative control. Under the 1938 act, the FDA extended its control over drug labeling by insisting that safety was inextricably combined with efficacy in the case of toxic drugs for life-threatening diseases. Its control over claims of effectiveness was still limited, however. It could not stop a toxic drug just because its effectiveness claim was exaggerated. More significantly, it could not refuse to clear an "innocuous" drug. It could seize such a drug after it was marketed for misbranding if its label claimed some benefit would emerge from using it, but it could not prevent it from reaching the market.[11]

An innocuous drug—one that has no effects at all—clearly is not dangerous. The FDA's concern for these drugs reveals that something beyond physical safety was at issue. As in 1906, the government wanted to assure consumers of value for their money, to protect consumers from unwise purchases.

The asymmetry between safety and efficacy introduced by Holmes's opinion in *U.S.* v. *Johnson* and emphasized by the 1938 law could no longer be justified by 1962. Therapeutic claims had acquired the status of fact, capable of being demonstrated by scientifically trained experts. The law therefore could be extended to give the FDA authority to approve or disallow all therapeutic claims by manufacturers before a drug was put on the market, as well as the consequent ability to prevent "innocuous" drugs from ever being sold.

The 1962 Drug Amendments also continued the trend toward reliance on experts begun with the FDA's 1938 regulation creating a class of non-narcotic drugs available only by prescription. The new law did not say drugs had to be effective. It said there had to be "substantial evidence" of efficacy, defined thus:

The term "substantial evidence" means evidence consisting of adequate and well-controlled investigations, including clinical investigations, by experts qualified by scientific training and experience to evaluate the effectiveness of the drug involved, on the basis of which it could fairly and responsibly be concluded by such experts that the drug will have the effect it purports or is represented to have under the conditions of use prescribed, recommended, or suggested in the labeling or proposed labeling thereof.[12]

This is not a definition at all. The passage describes a procedure for deciding if there exists "substantial evidence," to consist of "investigations . . . by experts . . . on the basis of which it could . . . be concluded by such experts that the drug will have the effect it purports . . . to have." In other words, the experts are to decide what kind of evidence they would like to see and then go get it. The procedure is no more explicit than that.

This delegation of responsibility to experts acquires added significance when we consider that the law contains no further definition of effectiveness. The closest thing to a definition is in the passage just quoted: a drug is supposed to have "the effects it purports or is represented to have . . . in the labeling . . . thereof." A drug is effective or not depending on what its label says! A pharmaceutical rose, by any other name, is *not* a rose. The experts, by insisting on changes in the drug's label, can change the effectiveness of that drug. The implications are clear. If a drug has any desirable effects at all, the process of getting FDA approval will be centered on the label.[13] The experts, through their manipulation of drug labels, will affect not only which drugs are marketed, but also what they are used for.

The relations between this provision and the FDA's 1938 regulation mandating prescription sales for some drugs are complex. On the one hand, the new provision extends consumers' reliance on the medical community by restricting their freedom to choose drugs even more than the 1938 regulation did. On the other hand, it undercuts the older regulation by implying that the doctors who write prescriptions need to have their choices restricted by experts. The FDA delegated authority to doctors in 1938, but it turned to experts in 1962.

There are now two sets of decision makers dictating to consumers what drugs they should take. Consumers are dependent on what their doctors say, and the doctors' choices are dependent on what the government's medical experts say. The 1962 law tacitly admits that ordinary doctors practicing medicine are not qualified to choose among drugs for their patients. They need the direction provided by a restricted choice of drugs and explicitly approved labels.

This extension of FDA authority reflects an additional erosion in the legislative belief that markets protect consumers. Not only can consumers not rely on the general market to weed out inferior products, they cannot even rely on the highly educated medical market—that is, practicing physicians—to weed out worthless drugs. The government, not the market, will weed out worthless products and misleading labels.

This administrative safeguard was not designed to end with a drug's approval for marketing. In particular, useless drugs introduced before 1962 were not to be allowed a natural economic death as doctors discovered their lack of efficacy and stopped prescribing them; they were to be forced off the market by FDA action. This provision emphasizes the legislative conviction that doctors cannot evaluate drugs in the course of their clinical practice and that the normal process of economic learning cannot take place.

Over four thousand drugs had been introduced between 1938 and 1962. Even the rapidly growing FDA could not hope to evaluate all of them for effectiveness while still performing other activities. The agency therefore contracted with the National Research Council of the National Academy of Sciences to undertake this evaluation. Known as the Drug Efficacy Study, the investigation started in 1966 and ran for three years.[14]

The actual work was done by thirty panels of experts, each consisting of six members. The National Research Council's report to the FDA said of these panels that they "were composed of physicians with academic affiliations, for the obvious reason that these best met the legal qualification of 'experts qualified by scientific training and experience to evaluate the effectiveness of the drug involved.' "[15] Panel chairmen were selected from nominations by professional and medical societies, and panel members were then selected by the panel chairmen. The chairman of the Panel on

Psychiatric Drugs commented after the study that he was not unhappy with the panel, but neither was he happy about having six people in a position to adjudicate for the country, with all its varied opinions and patterns for practice. Yet he said, "There was no strain in our group, which proves that I probably didn't select a wide enough range of people."[16] If this panel's experience was typical, the disagreement anticipated in the Senate's choice of "substantial evidence" over "preponderant evidence" failed to appear among the experts.

The law classified drugs as either possessing or lacking "substantial evidence" of effectiveness, but the FDA asked the National Research Council to use a fourfold classification scheme with intermediate categories of "probably effective" and "possibly effective." These additions softened the distinction between effective and ineffective in much the same way that the 1938 prescription regulation softened the dichotomy between safe and unsafe drugs. The expert panels in turn added two more categories. In one they recognized that a drug was effective but less so than some other. The law made no provision for such comparative judgment, but the panels regarded this omission as "an irrational limitation on medical judgment." In the other new category, the panels rated some drugs as "ineffective as a fixed combination," an ideological opposition to fixed-combination drugs that was a clear expression of a particular academic view of medicine.[17]

The panels started with the literature on the drugs being reviewed, as submitted to them by the drug companies, but they also relied on "the informal judgment of the panel," meaning the clinical experience of the panel members and their peers, when the literature seemed inadequate.[18] Because the law was based on the assumption that such clinical experience was not a valid indication of effectiveness, this decision process undermined the conceptual basis for the Drug Efficacy Study itself. It was further undermined by a circular reliance on the market as shown in the following passage from the study's report:

The final arbiter of the value of a drug is the consensus of the experience of clinical physicians in its use in the practice of medicine over a period of years. Approval of a new drug for release to the market is only a license to seek this experience. When the panels were faced with this situation, they have sought to grant liberty but to restrain license by assigning a rating of "probably effective" or "possibly effective" on the basis of their own clinical experience with the drug and their evaluation of the opinions of their peers.[19]

The Drug Efficacy Study, therefore, while performed by scientifically trained experts, was admittedly unscientific. To an unknown extent, the experts relied on the very market they were supposed to contain and on their own subjective experience.

This procedure clearly was within the scope of the law. The law defined "substantial evidence" to be whatever the experts would accept. If they were willing to rely on their own experience, that experience constituted "substantial evidence." Nevertheless, it seems curious to replace reliance on the clinical experience of some doctors with reliance on the clinical experience of other doctors.

This apparent circularity derived from the law's call for "adequate and well-controlled investigations." It was not clear what this new element in the evaluation of drugs consisted of, though it was clear that ordinary clinical experience did not qualify. As the call for its use did not immediately bring forth an instantaneous stream of appropriate investigations, the expert panels were called upon to make judgments on drugs on such evidence as they could find. And for part of the task, they were forced to fall back on the clinical experience the law was designed to supplant.[20]

Congress had attempted to extend the scope of the government's evaluation of drug descriptions to include therapeutic effects. Even though ultimately allowed by the courts, this attempt initially ran afoul of the same problem that plagued the similar attempt after 1906. The Drug Efficacy Study could not rely on undisputed facts about these effects, because there were not enough of them. The FDA procedure therefore allowed a rather homogeneous group of medical "elders"—if the psychiatric panel was at all typical—to codify their customs into federal regulations. These customs included taboos on some classes of drugs—like fixed combinations—as well as traditions specifying the uses of various drugs.

The proscription of combination drugs by the Drug Efficacy Study illustrates the process. The expert panels declined to approve combinations unless the joint administration of the component drugs produced a greater effect than the sum of their separate administrations. This position can be justified on the grounds that individual determination of the desired ratio of the two drugs is preferable to a fixed ratio, but it also can be opposed on several grounds. Given the scarcity of careful studies, it is unlikely that the quantitative criterion for acceptance was usable. Further, the concept of effect was not well defined. Not every prescription is filled, and not every pill purchased is taken. Reducing the complexity of a prescription by reducing the number of pills prescribed may well increase the probability that it will be followed. If so, a single fixed-ratio pill may have more effect than two separate pills providing a specially designed ratio. But the expert panels apparently did not consider probability of use to be part of the effectiveness standard required by law. A panel of clinical practitioners might have chosen differently. (The policy was modified under protest to say only that each drug in a combination had to contribute to the total effect and that the joint dosage had to be safe and effective for a significant population of potential users.)[21]

The extent of customary medical behavior was diminished; the extent of command behavior, increased. This kind of change, which omits the intermediate stage of instrumental, searching behavior, is normally the result of a cataclysmic shock to the society involved. No such event occurred in the late 1960s, the period of the Drug Efficacy Study, but this is the wrong period to examine. The study was initiated by the Drug Amendments of 1962, which were passed in response to the thalidomide disaster. That unhappy episode was the shock that extended the reach of command behavior in drug prescribing. Even though the problem with thalidomide had nothing to do with efficacy, the replacement of customary by command behavior was the direct response.

Once started, the movement toward command behavior was not limited to the Drug Efficacy Study. Even before that study was completed, the FDA moved to close what it regarded as loopholes in the 1962 law. The law exempted drugs not subject to the Federal Food, Drug, and Cosmetic Act from its requirements. This clearly exempted drugs introduced before 1938, but it left the so-called "me-too" drugs in an ambiguous position. The FDA had adopted the position between 1938 and 1962 that a new drug closely related to an existing drug did not need to have an approved NDA of its own, but could piggy-back on that of the existing drug by means of an "old drug determination letter" from the FDA (hence the term, *me-too*). Since a "me-too" drug lacked an approved NDA, the FDA's approval of its NDA could not be revoked. But it seemed inconsistent to revoke approval of one drug's NDA and leave its "me-too" followers on the market.

The FDA consequently announced early in 1968 that:

The Food and Drug Administration's conclusions on the effectiveness of drugs are currently being published in the *Federal Register* as Drug Efficacy Study Implementation (DESI) Notices ... Many drug products which are identical to, related to, and similar to the drug products covered by these notices have been marketed under different names or by different firms during this same period or since 1962 without going through the new-drug procedures of the Academy review ... Even though these products are not listed in the notices, they are subject to these notices.[22]

While the "me-too" drugs arguably were covered by the 1962 law, drugs introduced before 1938 clearly were exempted from the standards of that law by grandfather clauses in the 1938 and 1962 laws. Nevertheless, the FDA did not stop by including the "me-too" drugs under the new standards. At about the same time as the "me-too" announcement, it unveiled a review process similar to that of the Drug Efficacy Study for over-the-counter drugs, grandfathered and nongrandfathered alike.

The FDA's argument for reviewing grandfathered drugs had three steps. First, grandfathered drugs were exempted only from the new-drug provisions of the 1938 and 1962 laws. They were subject to the rest of the laws, and specifically to the rules on misbranding. Second, any grandfathered drug determined to be misbranded automatically became an unapproved new drug: it could not be sold with the erroneous label, and it would need an approved NDA for any new label or formulation. Consequently, third, a review of grandfathered drugs' effectiveness was needed to determine whether they—like ineffective drugs whose NDA had been revoked—were unapproved new drugs. In other words, the FDA extended its jurisdiction over misbranding, which had been restricted to statements about ingredients in 1910, to statements about therapeutic effectiveness as well in 1968. The complexity of the FDA's reasoning shows how difficult it was to circumvent the Supreme Court ruling of fifty years' standing.

In addition, the FDA said it would review therapeutic classes, not individual drugs as in the Drug Efficacy Study. The limits of the FDA's resources, the large and growing number of over-the-counter drugs, the small number—about two hundred, according to the FDA—of active ingredients in these drugs, the expenses and slowness of litigation on individual drugs, and the consequent unevenness of timing in drug removals, all were cited by the FDA in support of its decision. As if in summary of its position on both grandfathered drugs and therapeutic classes, the FDA declared, "The same scientific and medical determinations involved in reviewing the safety and effectiveness of non-grandfathered OTC drugs are also involved in determining whether grandfathered drugs are misbranded and thus are properly made in a single proceeding that will apply across the board to all products in a single therapeutic class."[23]

Citing efficiency, fairness, and scientific reasonableness, the FDA brought all the drugs that had been exempted, whether accidentally or purposely, from the effectiveness provisions of the 1962 law under the jurisdiction of those provisions in 1968. It was still implementing those provisions by the slightly circular Drug Efficacy Study at the time, and the legal basis of both activities was unclear. As might be expected, they were challenged by the drug industry in the courts.

The Drug Industry's Response

The drug industry had been an interested, if limited, participant in the Drug Efficacy Study. After being invited to submit written materials on drug effectiveness, drug manufacturers were invited to a conference in 1966 with the chairmen of the review panels to discuss the proposed guidelines for the panels. But requests that manufacturers be allowed to make presentations to the panels and to question their summary of the evidence were refused. The panels did have the option to request additional information from the manufacturers, but they rarely did so. The industry was denied the right to intervene in the review process, and the panels did not invite the industry (or anyone else) to participate with any regularity. The Drug Efficacy Study relied on the published literature and the accumulated wisdom of the panelists.[24]

The study's procedures and conclusions were contested as soon as the FDA attempted to implement them. The challenge centered around Upjohn's suit against the FDA to prevent the agency from withdrawing approval of Panalba and several related products, which led to both an important court decision and a new regulation redefining "substantial evidence."

Upjohn had combined two antibiotics—tetracycline and novobiacin—in a single drug formulation in the mid-1950s. This product, Panalba, became a commercial success, but it fell into the Drug Efficacy Study's classification "ineffective as a fixed combination." Since this category was one of the two added by the study's staff to those provided by the FDA, its legal status was unclear. When the FDA moved to ban Panalba from the market on the basis of the efficacy study's findings, Upjohn brought suit.

The FDA gave first notice of its intent in December 1968 and withdrew approval of Upjohn's NDA for Panalba and several related products the following June. Upjohn sued in a federal district court and obtained a stay of the FDA's actions within a month. An oral hearing before the FDA commissioner followed, and the agency reaffirmed its original ruling in September. On the same day, the FDA also issued new regulations defining the statutory term, "substantial evidence."[25]

Upjohn pursued its case in a federal court of appeals where it presented a complex of issues. The company protested the FDA's refusal to hold an evidentiary hearing, that is, a hearing with cross-examination of the expert panel that had provided the "factual" basis for the FDA's action and of any other relevant witnesses as well. The FDA replied that Upjohn was not entitled to an evidentiary hearing unless it *first* came forward with "substantial evidence" of the drug's effectiveness. This reply raises questions of both substance and procedure. Was the FDA arguing that Upjohn needed to prove its point before the hearing rather than in the hearing? And what is "substantial evidence"?

Upjohn argued that a drug's acceptance and use by practicing physicians could qualify as evidence of its effectiveness. In the context of the case, the company needed only to argue that such commercial success was enough evidence of effectiveness to justify an evidentiary hearing. But it was clear to all concerned that the definition of "substantial evidence" was important for substance (which drugs could be marketed) as well as for procedure (whether a hearing was needed). Issues of substance and procedure were inextricably intertwined.

The court ruled that Upjohn was not entitled to an evidentiary hearing unless it first established "reasonable grounds" for it. Citing congressional testimony and opinion, the court followed the FDA's argument that commercial success did not constitute legally acceptable evidence of effectiveness: "We hold that the record of commercial success of the drugs in question, and their widespread acceptance by the medical profession, do not, standing alone, meet the standards of substantial evidence prescribed [in the law]." Upjohn had "to demonstrate that it had available and was prepared to submit proof of adequate and well-controlled studies meeting the statutory definition of substantial evidence, in support of its claim for the effectiveness of its drugs." The phrase "adequate and well-controlled study" had not been defined in the law, and neither the FDA's actions nor the Drug Efficacy Study had clarified its meaning. Nevertheless, again following the FDA's lead, the court ruled that none of the fifty-four documents submitted to the FDA by Upjohn in support of its drugs qualified as an "adequate and well-controlled study."[26]

Just as light can be seen either as waves or as particles, this conclusion can be seen as either procedure or substance. From the former point of view, the FDA was seeking ways to implement the recommendations of the Drug Efficacy Study. If the agency's every action was to be subject to a lengthy evidentiary hearing, withdrawing approval of NDAs would be difficult if not impossible in many cases, both because of the inherent complexity and cost of such a hearing and because appeals from evidentiary hearings could be frequent. One lesson of the Panalba case was that the drug companies would use the avenues open to them to protest, retard, and, if possible, reverse FDA decisions harmful to them. The FDA therefore wanted a court decision restricting the grounds on which the companies could object to its actions.

To help the court impose this restriction, the FDA had issued regulations defining "adequate and well-controlled investigations" on the same day it had finally banned Panalba. The agency was doing its best to make sure the next court case would be fought in an environment more favorable to its rulings than that existing during the Panalba case. The attempts to use regulations for this purpose were contested by the drug industry in a variety of court challenges that were not resolved until 1973, and the issue of how closely the FDA could shape the NDA process by regulation was not settled until then.

Upjohn, and the drug companies in general, were opposed to this extension of FDA authority. They did not claim the right to market any drug they wished, although the logic of their position moved in that direction. But they did want to preserve considerable freedom in what they could market and to prevent the government from arbitrarily, as the drug firms saw it, depriving them of the right to sell specific products.

The FDA won a complete victory on procedural grounds. The court ruled that the agency could decide without a hearing which evidence it would allow in the hearing. It could, for example, decide without a hearing that Upjohn's evidence for Panalba and the other drugs was not even worth contesting in a formal proceeding. The burden of proof had shifted. The FDA did not have to prove that its administrative ruling was justified; Upjohn had to prove it was not.[27]

At this point the issue of procedure merges into the issue of substance. If the FDA was to decide what evidence satisfied the law's requirements, it needed criteria by which so do so. The decision to withdraw approval of Panalba was made on the grounds of the Drug Efficacy Study panel's recommendation, which was based on the literature submitted to it by Upjohn and the panel members' "own clinical experience with the drug and their evaluation of the opinions of their peers."[28] To the extent that the decision rested on the clinical experience of the panel members, Upjohn surely was entitled to examine them on that experience. In fact, since the written report of the panel did not say how they had arrived at their decision, Upjohn was entitled to know how important clinical evidence was to the decision to withdraw Panalba's NDA.

The use—or the possible use—of clinical evidence by the panel posed additional problems for the FDA's position because the court explicitly ruled that clinical evidence compiled in the course of ordinary medical practice did not fit within the statutory definition of "substantial evidence." It did so both in its statement that commercial success was not evidence of efficacy and in its rejection of Upjohn's written submissions to the FDA. The FDA was consequently in the uncomfortable position of trying to implement a decision arrived at through a kind of evidence that it would not allow to be used to oppose its decision.

In other words, in order for the FDA to enforce its Panalba decision and others like it, it had to disqualify part of the evidence used by the Drug Efficacy Study when it reappeared in the industry's challenge, and do so in a way that did not invalidate the Drug Efficacy Study itself. The mechanism for doing this was a new regulation that spelled out the meaning of "adequate and well-controlled investigations." This regulation initially was promulgated simultaneously with the final banning of Panalba, but a court challenge from the Pharmaceutical Manufacturers' Association kept the final regulation from being issued till May 1970.[29]

The regulation said that the "adequate and well-controlled investigations" cited by the statute as "substantial evidence" had to include a formal test with explicit objectives, selection procedures for both subjects and control groups, observation and recording methods, and statistical analysis. Every study needed a carefully defined control group fitting into one of four possible categories. The drug being tested could be compared with a placebo or with another drug known to be active from past studies. Or, the effects of the drug being tested could be compared with the known results of no treatment or with historical data on the course of the ailment without this drug. The FDA clearly tried to spread its net wide to allow a variety of tests—so wide in fact that it would be hard to disallow any clinical investigation on the basis of inadequate controls, since the study could be allowed in as an example of historical or no-treatment controls. Clinical experience was ruled out for its informality and lack of explicit objectives and methods, rather than for its lack of controls.[30] As an author at Smith Kline & French saw it: "FDA officials, eight years after the law empowered them to do so, finally promulgated and retroactively applied specific standards for the conduct of controlled clinical trials. In this process, 'substantial evidence' of effectiveness took on a new and expanded meaning. The once good standing of adequate, documented clinical experience was swept away."[31]

Independently of the FDA's victory in the Panalba case, this regulation was destined to have a long-run impact. By clearly disqualifying ordinary clinical experience from the "substantial evidence" of the statute, the FDA decreased the range of evidence the drug companies could use to argue for permission to market their products. The legal challenges to the new regulation reached the Supreme Court in 1973, but the court sustained the regulation on procedural grounds and on its consistency with the 1962 act. The court stated that if the FDA had to hold hearings for all disallowed drugs and uses, "It could not fulfill its statutory mandate to remove from the market all those drugs which do not meet the effectiveness requirements of the Act." Carrying the case further, the court declared, "Only paralysis would result if case-by-case battles in the courts were the only way to protect the public against unsafe or ineffective drugs." The issue was not simply unsafe drugs; it was "unsafe or ineffective" drugs. The FDA had the clear right to prevent innocuous drugs from ever reaching the market.[32]

These cases also confirmed the legality of the FDA's acts eliminating the impact of the grandfather clause. The drug firms involved had claimed variously that their drugs wre not "new drugs" because they had been on the market before 1962 or that they were not covered by the act because they had not had approved NDAs, that is, they were "me-too" drugs. On the first issue, the court noted that the law defined a "new drug" as one that was not "generally recognized" to be safe and effective in use. It admitted that the term "generally recognized" was not defined in the statute, but it accepted the FDA's claim that it was at least as strong a requirement as the "substantial evidence" requirement for approval of an NDA. In the court's words: "We accordingly have concluded that a drug can be "generally recognized" by experts as effective for intended use within the meaning of the Act only when that expert consensus is founded upon "substantial evidence" as defined in 505 (d) [of the Act]."[33]

In short, if a drug did not have the qualifications to pass the post-1962 tests for an approved NDA, it was a new drug without an approved NDA and could not legally be sold. The only exception recognized by the FDA and the courts appeared to have been drugs that had *never* been regulated by the FDA either under the 1938 or the 1962 laws. In practice, that meant that only unchanged forms of drugs introduced before the therapeutic revolution were not subject to the effectiveness standards of the 1962 amendments and the 1970 regulation.[34] This is not a large class of drugs.

With the conclusion of these cases, the 1970 regulation was secure. The FDA had finally translated the "substantial evidence" requirement of the 1962 law into a description of testing procedures rather than a delegation of authority to a group of "experts." As the drug industry correctly saw, it represented a change in procedure not only from before 1962, but also from the Drug Efficacy Study itself. The 1962 law increased the difficulty and therefore the cost of introducing new drugs to the market and of defending old ones. But it did so over the course of eight years: only in 1970 was informal clinical evidence definitively excluded from "substantial evidence."[35]

Unnoticed in all this legal controversy was the relationship of the 1970 regulation to the 1938 regulation. The earlier one had appointed physicians as the judges of which drugs were appropriate for individuals to take. The later one said that physicians were not able to discriminate efficacious drugs from useless ones. The 1970 regulation undercut the 1938 regulation equally with the government's case on Panalba.

This apparent reversal of policy exposes the government's ambiguous stand on the central issue of drug regulatory policy: who gets to choose which drug a person can take. Starting in 1906, the FDA and its precursors gradually increased their ability to affect this determination. Unable to make borderline decisions, or unwilling to face the implications of doing so, they incorporated doctors into the decision process in 1938. As a result of technological change unforeseen at that time, the doctors rather quickly assumed a major role in the choice of medicines for people. The FDA apparently was dissatisfied with this arrangement, whether because of the evidence that doctors could not act instrumentally in their choice of drugs or because it reduced the agency's ability to direct the purchase of drugs. Whatever the reason, the FDA moved in the 1960s to take back some of the control over drug purchases that had been delegated to doctors.

The FDA's announced concern with "innocuous" drugs sheds important light on this process. The problem with "innocuous" drugs is not that they are dangerous. They are only innocuous. The FDA did not want them off the market to maintain the safety of the population, but rather to protect consumers from wasting their money, that is, from making bad purchases. This goal, it will be recalled from the earlier history, was precisely the same as Harvey W. Wiley's in 1906. If doctors were behaving instrumentally and had adequate information, they could have protected the consumers for wasting their money. But because doctors had not provided the level of protection that the FDA wanted, the agency used the opportunity afforded by a drug disaster to exert more control over the process of drug selection, much as it had done in 1938. (The parallelism is in the laws, rather than in the regulations; both the 1938 and the 1962 laws extended the criteria by which the FDA could exclude a drug from the market.) It is important to stress the continuity of drug policy because much of the recent discussion of drug regulation has assumed that FDA policy originated in 1938 and was at that time motivated entirely by concern for drug safety. It is more accurate to view the emphasis on safety in the 1938 law and the delegation of responsibility to doctors as aberrations in the trend of drug policy.The 1962 amendments and the 1970 regulation emerge as mainstream elements of this trend.

The FDA's attempt to extend its control further over the distribution of drugs proved unsuccessful. It attempted to restrict the distribution of methadone, an analgesic and antitussive agent useful in the detoxification of heroin addicts, to approved channels, primarily approved maintenance treatment programs and approved hospital pharmacies. A circuit court ruled that this limit on the distribution of a drug exceeded the FDA's legislative authority and disallowed it.

The court summarized the FDA's argument as follows:

The FDA contends that where there exists a documented pattern of drug misuse contrary to the intended uses specified in the labelling, the drug is unsafe for approval unless controls over distribution are imposed. As a corollary, it asserts that for a drug such as methadone, for which there is substantial evidence of misuse, the FDA must have the power to restrict distribution to avoid the dilemma of either disapproving a drug with important thereapeutic benefits or of placing on the market a drug likely to be misused. The FDA claims that section 355 (d) authorized restricting distribution to a prescription-only basis before the FDA was explicitly granted that authority in 1951, and that the regulations at issue differ only in degree from a prescription-only restriction.[36]

The FDA's capsule history was accurate. It did restrict distribution of some drugs to a prescription-only basis well before it had explicit legislative authorization to do so. It acted to avoid banning altogether drugs that could be beneficial if not misused. And it did so to limit misuse of drugs: overuse of barbiturates and underuse of sulfa drugs.

The court, however, did not accept the FDA's history, and it denied the parallel between the prescription-only regulation and the restricted distribution of methadone. It maintained that the methadone restrictions differed from the prescription-only restriction in not involving complex medical knowledge and diagnostic skills. This argument, supportable for 1976, is not accurate when applied to 1938, when the prescription-only regulation was introduced. The drugs available at that time did not require complex knowledge to administer—in fact, the regulation itself was an important factor in drawing the distinction between medical and lay knowledge. To the extent that the court was relying on history to refute the FDA's argument, it was skating on thin ice.

The court also argued that "there would be almost no limit to the FDA's authority were its view accepted."[37] This position has more support. The FDA expanded its authority in 1938 by making regulations that went beyond the law's intent. The extension was permitted by the courts and written into law in 1951, creating the precedent for FDA leadership in the extension of its authority. The growth of regulation defining "substantial evidence" of effectiveness may be interpreted as following this precedent, although the regulation appears closer to the legislative intent than did the 1938 regulation. The methadone restrictions clearly followed this precedent, and the circuit court objected, at least partly on the grounds that the FDA had to be more tightly bound by its legislative mandate.

The methadone litigation marks the limit of FDA authority in the 1970s. The agency could make it as difficult as it wanted to place a drug on the market, but it could not interfere with doctors' rights to choose among the drugs approved for marketing. Having granted doctors a large role in the distribution of medicinal drugs, the FDA did not seem to be in a position to monitor that role very closely. In the tradition of the Harrison Anti-Narcotics Act of 1914, that control—for a specified list of drugs—was vested in the Justice Department by the Controlled Substances Act of 1970.[38]

SEVEN

Recent Changes in the Drug Industry

T HE REGULATORY CHANGES of the 1960s took place as the drug industry was continuing its evolution. The new regulations have been given credit—or more usually, blame—for the changes, but many of the changes were independent of the efficacy requirements. In particular, the patent laws and other government programs appear to have had as much effect on the shape of the drug industry as the Federal Drug Administration's regulation.

The Decline in New-Drug Introductions

The increase in the FDA's size, its legislative mandate, and its regulatory specificity raised the cost of introducing new drugs to the market. The number of drugs introduced in the 1960s and 1970s was far smaller than in the 1950s (table 2). But while it is clear that increasing the cost of introduction will act to reduce the number of new drugs on the market, it is not at all clear how much of the actual decrease in the rate of drug introduction can be laid at the door of the FDA. A summary of a debate on this question by one of the participants concluded "that regulation has had a significant negative effect on the rate of innovation," but "that nonregulatory factors have had some negative impact on drug innovation, and further analysis, particularly of the research depletion hypothesis, would seem to be warranted."[1]

According to the research depletion hypothesis, the new opportunities opened up by the discovery of the sulfa drugs and antibiotics in the 1930s and 1940s were all exhausted by the time the 1962 Drug Amendments were passed—in effect, the therapeutic revolution was over by 1960. After that time, the industry began to return to its prewar pattern of marketing existing drugs rather than discovering new ones. The effects of the regulatory changes just chronicled are, therefore, inextricably mixed with the effects of the depleted store of drugs to be discovered.

There does not seem to be any strong evidence to support this hypothesis. International comparisons offer only partial evidence because increasing the cost of entering the American drug market—far and away the largest national market—must affect the profitability of drug research everywhere in the world. A decline in drug innovation in other countries, therefore, may reflect the regulatory tightening inside the United States rather than research depletion. Moreover, American drug companies do not seem to have decreased their research expenditures in response to a presumed lack of opportunities. Yet there is an inherent plausibility about the hypothesis that keeps it alive without much evidence in its favor.[2]

The most careful study of this question to date was done by Steven Wiggins. He assumed that increased regulatory stringency could affect the rate of new drug introduction either by raising the cost of introducing them, thereby decreasing the number of new drugs that would come from a constant research expenditure, or by discouraging research expenditures themselves. Wiggins followed the lead of earlier investigators in using the length of time it took the FDA to process an NDA as the index of regulatory stringency. This index rose rapidly during the 1960s to a peak in the early 1970s, closely following the pattern of the continually rising approval standards (see table 19). Wiggins did not, however, derive his estimates from the data shown in table 19. He derived the analogous measure for each of several therapeutic classes and made his estimates primarily from comparisons among classes.[3]

Wiggins found that the increase in regulatory stringency during the 1960s roughly doubled the amount of resources needed to get a drug onto the market. This estimate is virtually identical to those found by earlier investigators. While similar answers do not necessarily indicate accuracy—all the authors may have made a common mistake—they do give us some confidence in the results.[4] In addition, Wiggins found that increased regulatory stringency has a powerful effect on the volume of research expenditures, with the result that his estimate of the total effect of regulation on new drug introductions is considerably larger than that of other investigators.

Table 19. FDA processing time from NDA submission to approval, 1962–1978 (months).

Year of approval	Processing time
1962	17
1963	18
1964	22
1965	25
1966	31
1967	36
1968	31
1969	44
1970	29
1971	19
1972	17
1973	29
1974	21
1975	26
1976	23
1977	27
1978	20

Source: Data supplied by the Center for the Study of Drug Development, University of Rochester Medical Center, Rochester, N.Y.

It is not correct, however, to attribute the reduction in the rate of new drug introductions during the 1960s to the increased regulatory stringency. The problem is that the drop in new drug introductions preceded the increase in regulatory stringency, whether measured by the legal history or by the index in table 19. Instead, it appears that the fall in new drug introductions in the early 1960s was concentrated almost entirely in central nervous system drugs, and within that class, in tranquilizers. Two possible reasons for this specific movement come to mind. First, the thalidomide disaster that led to the passage of the 1962 Drug Amendments must also have discouraged the introduction of similar drugs that might have had similar adverse effects. Second, Hoffman–La Roche's phenomenal success with Librium and Valium reportedly was achieved in part by successfully patenting the chemicals that might have become the competition for these drugs, an action (if actually undertaken) that would have reduced the rate of introduction of minor tranquilizers. The evidence does not exist to discriminate between these or other hypotheses, but the role of tranquilizers in the overall fall in new drug introductions is clear.[5]

The sharp decline in new drug introductions during the early 1960s therefore can be explained along the following lines. The tragedy that produced new legislation also discouraged (possibly in combination with other, nongovernmental stimuli) the introduction of new tranquilizers. Since many such drugs had been introduced in the late 1950s, the reduction in this class translated into a large decline in the overall rate of new drug introductions. If the regulatory climate had not changed, the rate of new drug introduction might well have picked up as people recovered from the thalidomide scare or as advances in technology opened up new areas for drug research. But the increased regulatory stringency of the late 1960s prevented such a resurgence of new drug introductions. In short, the thalidomide tragedy was the proximate cause of the decline in new drug introduction, acting quickly through its effects on the direction of drug industry research and more slowly through the governmental regulatory process.[6]

The reduced rate of new drug introductions in the United States has thrown the international character of the modern drug industry into high relief. Several of the leading drug firms in the world are not American. Although lists of large drug firms differ in their rankings, Hoffman–La Roche (Swiss), Hoechst (German), and Ciba-Geigy (Swiss) are always among the top half-dozen. In two lists of international drug firms, American firms accounted for just over half of the top twenty firms (eleven and thirteen), but only a quarter of the next twenty.[7]

Roughly half of world drug production took place in the United States at the time the 1962 Drug Amendments went into effect (see table 20). This share fell during the 1960s, although the relationship of this change to the new law is as difficult to specify as that of the decline in

Table 20. National shares of world pharmaceutical production, 1963 and 1970 (percent).[a]

Country	1963	1970
United States	49	43
Japan	12	17
France	10	8
Germany	8	10
Italy	6	7
United Kingdom	6	4
Canada	3	3
Other	6	8

Source: Sanjaya Lall, *Major Issues in the Transfer of Technology to Developing Countries: A Case Study of the Pharmaceutical Industry* (New York: United Nations Conference on Trade and Development, 1975).

a. Data reflect location of production, not of producing firms' home offices.

Table 21. Domestic and foreign sales of drug firms headquartered in the United States, 1956–1976 (percent).

Year	Domestic[a]	Foreign[b]
1956	88	12
1961	73	27
1966	71	29
1971	66	34
1976[c]	60	40

Source: *Annual Survey Reports* (Washington, D.C.: Pharmaceutical Manufacturers' Association, 1977), p. iii.

a. Drugs in finished human dosage forms only.

b. Drugs in finished human and veterinary dosage forms.

c. Eliminating veterinary forms from international data raises domestic share to 62 percent.

American new drug introductions. In addition, an increasing proportion of the sales of firms headquartered in the United States has been abroad (table 21). This proportion includes both exports and the production of foreign subsidiaries, so the data in the two tables are not quite compatible. To the extent that they do show the same process, however, the foreign sales data of U.S. firms suggest that the trend toward international activity antedates the 1962 amendments. Like the increase in firm size (shown in table 5), the shift to foreign markets is a long-term process only partly caused by the 1962 legislation.

The current debate over the loss of American leadership does not focus on the location of production; it deals with the location of research and the first introduction of new drugs. Data relevant to the question can be found in table 22, which, unlike those in table 20, reflect the nationality of the firm rather than the location of the research or the introduction. The prominent place of Switzerland in this table is courtesy of Hoffman–La Roche and Ciba-Geigy, not domestic Swiss activity.

American firms discovered about half the drugs counted by the Organization for Economic Cooperation and Development in the years from 1950 to 1967. These include only drugs sold in three or more major national markets. The other data source, which ranks all new drugs equally, shows the share of the United States in the discovery of these drugs to be markedly lower and to have decreased only slightly over time. In addition to urging caution in the use of data on multinational companies, the divergence between the two sources points up the problems of data pertaining to the whole drug market.

Not all the drugs initially discovered by American firms were intro-

Table 22. National shares of new drug discoveries and initial introductions, selected years (percent).

Country	Discoveries[a]			Initial introductions	
	1950–1967[b]	1961–1963	1971–1973	1961–1963	1971–1973
United States	49	26	23	16	7
Japan	1	8	10	8	10
France	8	19	22	19	24
Germany	11	15	11	19	7
Italy	1	4	10	6	9
United Kingdom	7	7	4	11	10
Switzerland	15	10	8	7	6
Other	8	11	12	14	27

Sources: *Gaps in Technology: Pharmaceuticals* (Paris: Organization for Economic Cooperation and Development, 1969); E. von Ries-Arndt, *"Neue Pharmazeutische Wirkstoffe,"* *Pharmazeutisch Industrie,* 37 (1975), reproduced in Barrie G. James, *The Future of the Multinational Pharmaceutical Industry to 1990* (New York, Wiley, 1977), pp. 73–75.

a. Data reflect location of discovering firms' home offices.
b. Includes only drugs sold in at least three of eight national markets.

duced first in America. The share of such drugs also has fallen sharply between the two periods shown, a phenomenon termed the "drug lag." The United Kingdom and "other" are the only areas that consistently introduced more drugs than they discovered in the periods shown in table 22.

Data on research expenditures reveal that more and more research by American drug firms is being done abroad. Less than 10 percent of company-funded research and development by members of the Pharmaceutical Manufacturers' Association was done abroad a decade ago; the current share is close to 20 percent.[8] The decline in the number of drugs initially introduced in America antedates this shift, suggesting that the movement toward internationalization is one response to the pressures of increased regulation, increasingly complex drug technology, and public pressure on prices. In the words of an international survey of the drug industry: "The 'Belle Epoque' of the post-1945 period has ended for the pharmaceutical industry."[9]

The effects of tighter regulation on health and welfare are even harder to measure than its effects on drug innovation. The generally favorable view of drug regulation from within the government has been opposed by two prominent commentators. Sam Peltzman criticized the 1962 Drug

Amendments from an economic point of view; William Wardell, from a medical.

Peltzman's study had two parts. He argued first that the 1962 amendments restricted the number of new drugs—new chemical entities (NCEs), to be precise—presented to the American public. He made the argument by contrasting the actual number of NCEs in each year after 1962 with a predicted number based on the extrapolation of pre-1962 trends. Then he argued by an entirely separate analysis that this change was extremely costly to the public, amounting to about $300 or $400 million a year. The estimate was derived by comparing the costs and benefits of the 1962 amendments. The benefits were assumed to come from faster learning about ineffective drugs which reduced the money wasted in the learning process. The costs were the losses in benefits attributable to the amendments' effect in reducing the demand for drugs. Since the demand for new drugs did not fall over time relative to the demand for old drugs, either before or after 1962, the benefits were pronounced negligible. And, since Peltzman's estimated statistical procedures interpreted the fall in the number of NCEs introduced after 1962 as a fall in the overall demand for drugs, the costs were seen as large.[10]

Both parts of this argument are wrong. The comparison of the number of NCEs introduced in the 1960s with the extrapolations from the 1950s assumes that the 1962 Amendments had an immediate impact on introductions. However, the amendments took effect gradually over many years and did not cause the drop in new drug introductions in the early 1960s; the law itself did not represent a radical change in the way the FDA processed new drug applications.[11] It is clear, therefore, that the discrepancy between the actual number of NCEs introduced in the decade after 1962 and Peltzman's prediction overestimates the results of the 1962 law. His estimate failed to capture the history of those years.

Peltzman's estimate of the putative benefits of the law was based on the assumption that people could learn from experience which drugs were effective and which were not. But this is not how knowledge about drugs is accumulated. It is no wonder that Peltzman found that the demand for new drugs did not fall relative to the demand for old drugs as people learned which ones were ineffective.

His estimate of the benefits is based on two assumptions, neither of which is justified. He assumed that the effect of the 1962 law was to reduce the demand for drugs, when it clearly was to reduce the supply of drugs. The increased testing required to get drugs approved increased the cost of producing marketable drugs; the impact of the law on demand is exceedingly hard to know. And he assumed that the demand for drugs has the same welfare properties as the demand for bread or other simple products. But, since consumers do not select their own drugs, there is no warrant for this assumption. We may presume that people derive benefits from drugs, but the association between this benefit and the price they pay for the drugs is hardly close. For example, the cost of visiting a doctor to get a prescription must be added to the price of the drug in order to calculate the full cost to the consumer. Isn't this total cost more relevant to consumer welfare than the price of the drug alone?[12]

Wardell approached the problem of drug regulation from an entirely different perspective. In a series of articles collected into a monograph, he examined individual drugs that were available in either Britain or America and discovered a phenomenon he called the "drug lag." Comparing the date at which drugs were introduced in the two countries. Wardell asserted that a given drug typically was introduced into the American market later, with a lag depending on the type of drug it was. In a late study in the sequence, Wardell argued that the drug lag may have peaked in the early 1970s and begun to decline after about 1972.[13]

The demonstration of a drug lag corresponds with the first part of Peltzman's argument. Both authors asserted that the 1962 Drug Amendments and its accompanying regulations reduced the supply of new drugs in America. One article of Wardell's then went on to echo the second part of Peltzman's argument—that this change was costly to Americans. Wardell approached the problem indirectly. He started by acknowledging the impossibility of getting a direct measure of comparative benefit from new drugs as Peltzman had tried to. In his words: "A situation has arisen in which we now have methodology available which, while defective, is being used to estimate the total harm of drugs to the community; but we have no comparable methodology available for measuring the total benefit of drugs to the community." Making strength out of a weakness, Wardell found the solution to the last half of this sentence in the first part. He argued that there must have been some benefit to the new drugs, since "it can be assumed that recent judgments in the United Kingdom about drug approvals are based on reasonable evidence of therapeutic activity." He then argued that there was not an "excessive hazard" from the new drugs: "since most serious drug toxicity can be shown to stem from older, well-established drugs, there appears to be no foundation for the customary belief that new drugs represent the greatest hazard." Given the existence of an assumed benefit and the inferred absence of a significant cost, Wardell concluded that the drug lag was costly to the United States.[14]

Wardell's argument is not quantitative, and it does not result in a dollar cost of drug regulation to the United States. (No such measurement is really possible.) As a result of this unavoidable uncertainty, there is room for legitimate disagreement with Wardell's conclusions. He talked of "excessive" hazard and "serious" drug toxicity. Other people may choose other words with which to evaluate the same literature.

On the assumption that Wardell's terms are justified, it is instructive to look at the structure of his argument. He appears to be saying that the United States is foregoing some benefit at little or no cost. Two interpretations of this statement immediately come to mind. The United States may be acting irrationally, in which case the information contained in Wardell's studies might be expected to reduce the irrationality. To the extent that the drug lag has been reduced and to the extent that this was the result of Wardell's work, this expectation has been realized. Alternatively, there may be a cost that Wardell has not recognized. Wardell discussed drug toxicity, so the added cost must refer to something else.

A possible extra cost is contained in the passages already quoted from the Supreme Court's opinion in *Weinberger* v. *Hynson, Westcott and Dunning.* The court was analyzing ways "to protect the public against unsafe *or ineffective* drugs" (emphasis added).[15] Wardell discussed protection from unsafe drugs; he did not consider protection from ineffective drugs. But a principal aim of United States government policy in the 1960s—whose roots can be traced back through FDA statements and actions to the Progressive period—was to protect people from the risk of buying innocuous, ineffective drugs. The cost of obtaining the benefits from newer drugs may have been a looser regulatory framework that would have decreased the protection against ineffective drugs.

Wardell wrote in the tradition of the Drug Efficacy Study—considering the effects of drugs when used in laboratory settings. The FDA, though, is concerned with the use of drugs in the course of ordinary clinical practice. From their viewpoint, it is so hard to understand the changes brought about by the discovery of new drugs, whether good or bad, that command behavior is indicated. With the approval of both Congress and the federal courts, the FDA has moved to take more and more control over drug marketing. Wardell appears to assume that doctors will act instrumentally in their choice of drugs and pick the most appropriate ones in each case. His argument therefore supports the position that doctors—not the FDA—should make the decision whether to use a given drug. His assumption about doctors' behavior, however, is subject to the criticisms raised earlier, which suggest that doctors can make some, but by no means all, drug decisions in the instrumental mode. Instead, their dominant mode of behavior in this context is customary. The question therefore is how serious is the risk that doctors—acting customarily—will use innocuous drugs if more drugs, both effective and ineffective, are available to them.[16] If most people consider this risk onerous relative to the anticipated gain, then Wardell's assertion of a higher return from the looser regulation would not hold true.

It seems clear that the FDA and the federal courts consider the risk of buying ineffective products to be serious. There also has been a continuing concern since the therapeutic revolution of the 1940s and 1950s that consumers are paying too much for drugs, both because the price of drugs is high and because their effectiveness is lower than their labels claim. This concern has not been quantified, and it has not been compared with the risk of not recovering from an illness owing to the unavailability of a drug. Wardell's writings do not make this comparison; they articulate a medical point of view somewhat at variance with the government's. The two risks are not commensurable in any easy way. One is concerned with monetary payments and a hint of fraud or hucksterism; the other involves the value of human life and well-being.

Despite the difficulty of comparison, a policy choice must be made. The policy stance adopted in the United States has favored protection of those who appear unable to protect themselves over the competing goal of allowing wide and possibly beneficial choices. The discovery of the "drug lag" appears to show that British drug policy has chosen another alternative, that of choice rather than restriction. But this implication, whether intended by Wardell or not, is not true.

Most of the evidence for the existence of the "drug lag" was taken from the 1960s. As the previous discussion shows, this was the time when American drug policy was undergoing important changes. British policy, not in the midst of this process at the same time, can be used as a control, but the inference that British policy toward drugs is fundamentally different from American drug policy is erroneous. British policy has followed the direction of American policy with a lag of about a decade. The evidence compiled by Wardell compared the United States in the midst of policy change with Britain just before a similar change.

The British Medicines Act was adopted in 1968. The Committee on Safety of Medicines, with powers granted by the Medicines Act, was created in 1970 to replace the earlier, voluntary Committee on Safety of Drugs. Compulsory licenses for drugs were introduced in September 1971. British drug policy moved in the direction of substantially increasing governmental control over drugs just at the end of the period surveyed by Wardell.[17]

Although Wardell did not mention this change explicitly in his studies; it appears just below the surface. In a late article in the sequence, he noted that the drug lag was smaller in 1972–1974 (the time period surveyed in the late article) than in the previous decade (the time surveyed in the original article). Wardell commented, "It is conceivable that the narrowing of the differences between the two countries could be due to a more conservative trend in Britain." But he rejected this explanation in favor of one relying on "an enlightening of the regulatory approach in the U.S."[18] The index of regulatory tightness (table 19) provides some evidence of such a change in the United States, but the rejected explanation, increased regulatory tightness in England, cannot be ignored.

Wardell compared American drug policy in the 1960s with a policy in Britain that was not considered satisfactory by those subject to it. The comparison therefore demonstrates that stricter regulation implies fewer new drugs. By its design, it cannot approach the broader question of whether a tighter or looser policy is desirable.

Patent Expirations and Competition

The apparent inability of investigators to reach a clear conclusion on the welfare effects of the regulatory changes initiated by the 1962 Drug Amendments contrasts with the relatively clear picture that emerges of its effect on competition in the drug industry. The 1962 law reduced the supply of new drugs, although it is hard to know by how much, and it therefore favored the producers of existing drugs over new entrants. The latter effect was offset in part by patent expirations, which aided new entrants. And all parts of the drug industry were affected by increased third-party financing of health care.

Because the producers of drugs discovered since World War II tend to be large firms, the restriction in the supply of new drugs aided large firms over small, at least for the duration of their patents. In addition, the increased cost of introducing a new drug made it easier for larger firms to finance this activity and gain thereby a competitive edge. These effects, however, appear to have been less important in the development of the drug industry than the technological and regulatory changes occuring at the time. The therapeutic revolution of the 1950s decisively altered the size of major drug firms before the 1962 amendments were passed. The trend toward larger firms did not accelerate in the 1960s or 1970s; if anything, it slowed down as large firms came to dominate the drug industry (see table 5).

The pace of new drug introductions picked up dramatically in the 1950s. It slowed down after that decade, either in response to the legal changes or to the exhaustion of a limited research opportunity. The result was that the share of marketed drugs manufactured under one or more patents rose during the 1950s and began to fall in the late 1960s as the patents on the original wonder drugs began to expire. Patents have a legal duration of seventeen years, of course, but their commercial life is often considerably shorter. At one end, the patent may be granted before the FDA has given its approval for the drug to be marketed. At the other end, competing firms sometimes begin to manufacture a drug toward the end of its patented life in the expectation that the patent will expire before successful prosecution can be completed. New competition in tetracycline, for example, began several years before its patents expired, since the tangled legal history of those patents made them unusually vulnerable.[19] Increased competition in other drug markets followed.

The proportion of prescription drug sales accounted for by patented drugs has been estimated at about two-thirds of the total throughout the 1930s and 1940s. This estimate seems high, although only a small proportion of drugs were sold by prescription at that time and the allocation of nonprescription sales between patented and nonpatented drugs is not known. The proportion of prescriptions that were for patented drugs rose to over 90 percent during the 1950s in response to the therapeutic revolution. It began to fall thereafter, returning to somewhere near its pre-1950 level by 1972. A 1976 projection estimated that the share of patented drugs in the total will have fallen to 55 percent by 1985.[20]

The absence of effective patents means that any firm maintaining FDA-set quality standards can produce and market a drug, but it does not mean that it can capture a large market share. Many of the drugs now lacking patent protection are sold by brand name, and brand loyalty for drugs can be very strong. In addition, pharmacists choose among manufacturers in filling prescriptions written for a generic drug, and their response to the availability of lower-price generic drugs has been slow.

Less than 10 percent of the sales of unpatented drugs were for drugs identified only by generic name in the early 1970s. As a result, less than 5 percent of the total drug market was accounted for by these drugs.[21] It follows that most sales of unpatented drugs are by relatively large firms, since brand names need to be promoted. For example, the two unpatented drugs with the largest sales in the early 1970s were tetracycline and ampicillin. The top five sellers of tetracycline in 1974 were Squibb, Lederle, Upjohn, Pfizer, and Parke-Davis. The top five sellers of ampicillin were Squibb (again), Wyeth Laboratories, Parke-Davis, Ayerst Laboratories, and Pfizer. And these two drugs were among those with the most competition among suppliers. Their sales were large, and worries about bioavailability were low. The leading suppliers consequently furnished less than 30 percent of the total for each drug, which can be compared with the roughly 90 percent market share for the leading suppliers of digoxin (Burroughs Wellcome) and nitroglycerin (Lilly), where dosage levels and bioavailability are major issues. Nevertheless, the leading suppliers of these antibiotics were still major drug firms. Although smaller, newer firms have entered the market for unpatented drugs, their market shares are still very small.[22]

More detail on the markets for the two top generically prescribed drugs is available (table 23). Of the total new prescriptions written for these two drugs in 1976, over half—but far short of all—were written using only the generic name. Since these prescriptions did not specify a preferred brand or manufacturer, the doctor was allowing the pharmacist to choose which manufacturer to use. And pharmacists acted very differently with respect to these drugs.

Brand-name drug manufacturers supplied the drugs for over 90 per-

Table 23. New prescriptions for ampicillin and tetracycline filled by trade-name manufacturers, 1979 (percentage of total prescriptions).

Prescription category	Ampicillin	Tetracycline
New prescriptions written generically[a]	78.2	63.7
New prescriptions filled by trade-name manufacturers[b]	92.3	57.7
New generic prescriptions filled by trade-name manufacturers	90.7	36.7

Source: IMS America, National Prescription Audit, *Generic Market Reports, 1979: Ampicillin, Tetracycline* (Ambler, Pa.: IMS America, 1980).

a. Excludes 0.7 percent (ampicillin) and 1.4 percent (tetracycline) on which the manufacturer was specified.

b. Trade-name manufacturers of ampicillin were Ayerst, Beecham, Bristol, Lederle, Mallinckrodt, Parke-Davis, Pfipharmecs, Smith Kline, Squibb, Upjohn, and Wyeth. Trade-name manufacturers of tetracycline were the same plus Robins and minus Ayerst, Beecham, Parke-Davis, and Wyeth. Parke-Davis accounted for 20 percent of generic prescriptions for tetracycline without specified brand or manufacturer; Wyeth accounted for 7 percent.

cent of all new ampicillin prescriptions in 1979, but for only about three-fifths of the new prescriptions for tetracycline. This difference is not due to a difference in prescribing patterns by doctors: a greater percentage of the ampicillin prescriptions did not mention a brand or manufacturer. Pharmacists had more rather than less choice in selling ampicillin, and the market share reflects their choice. An overwhelming proportion of the unspecified generic ampicillin prescriptions were filled from brand-name firms, while less than half of the unspecified generic prescriptions of tetracycline were filled with the products of this type of firm. The firms who make the drugs and sell them under the generic name have made a much greater market penetration in tetracycline than in ampicillin.

The reasons for this difference in pharmacist preferences are unclear. As specified in the 1962 Drug Amendments, every batch of both these antibiotic drugs is certified by the FDA, and there is little therapeutic sensitivity to the exact dosage in either benefit or toxicity. Bioavailability worries, therefore, should be limited. Nevertheless, the large manufacturers have succeeded in holding on to the ampicillin market to a far greater degree than the tetracycline market.

The differences between these drugs should not blind us to their similarities. In both cases, over half of the new prescriptions were filled by drugs supplied by trade-name manufacturers. In other words, the large drug firms have succeeded in holding on to a major share of the drug market, even for drugs available on a generic basis for which bioavailability and quality control are not important issues. An increasing concentration of drug sales in the large drug firms is the result.

A study of two drug markets, thiazide diuretics and antianginals, has shown that the first company to market a drug maintains a larger share of the market than would be expected from its price and advertising expenses long after there are many competing sellers of the drug.[23] One explanation of this result follows from the customary behavior of doctors. Having established the custom of prescribing the brand name of the premier firm, doctors maintain this custom long after the patent for that drug has expired. The new brands and generic supplies of the drugs may be as good as the original, but their lower price offers no advantage startling enough to shake the customs of doctors and pharmacists.

Nevertheless, price competition for antibiotics and some other drugs has increased sharply in the past decade. The growth of price competition in antibiotics has been characterized by Schwartzman as "a jungle." The list prices of the leading brands of tetracycline fell from a uniform $30.60 per hundred 250 mg. capsules in 1960 to a range of from $22 to $4 a dozen years later. Ampicillin brands fell from around $26 in 1964 to between $14 and $9 nine years later.[24]

As Schwartzman notes, "The causes of the decline in prices are difficult to assess." The expiration of patents and the growth of generic prescribing must be factors, but the price cuts do not correspond in time with the dates of patent expirations, and the growth of generics has been less important than competition among brand-name drugs. The various informal agreements on price seem to have come apart in the course of the 1960s.[25]

In an alternative interpretation of the price decline, each drug firm acts independently, setting the profit-maximizing price for its product in light of the demand curve for it. A firm with a new, patented product faces a steep demand curve and consequently charges a high price. A firm with an older product produced by several firms faces an elastic demand curve and charges a low price. Over a period of time, therefore, the price of any single drug declines as the number of sellers increases and causes the elasticity of demand facing any single seller to increase also. Evidence of declining prices and increasing demand elasticity for individual drugs is consistent both with this story and with a story that sees the increase in price competition as a diminution of interfirm cooperation. The difference is not in the price behavior; it is whether the tetracycline story shows aberrant or typical drug industry behavior.[26]

In either case, the demand for any single drug product is rendered more elastic by the presence of other competing products, whether other brands or generic forms of the same drug or closely related but chemically distinct drugs. In other words, while doctors and pharmacists generally do not seek drugs with the lowest price, either there are enough doctors or pharmacists in any drug market who act this way to make a difference to sales or drug firms believe that there are enough such doctors or pharmacists. Price is therefore assumed by drug companies to be one determinant of drug demand.[27]

Consider now the price at which a new drug is introduced. If it competes with existing drugs, the preceding assumption implies that sales revenue can be maximized at a price near that of the existing competitors. If the price is too high relative to the competition, only a few doctors will make the switch and revenue will be small. If the price is too low, then there is a higher price at which almost everyone who switched at the lower price would still have switched at the higher price. If drug companies set prices to maximize revenue, they would price the new drug near its existing competition.

This argument exposes a pricing strategy for newly discovered patented drugs. The pricing of generic drugs follows a completely different pattern. These drugs, which have no patent protection and are sold without the benefit of extensive advertising, exist in a roughly competitive market, where the possibility of entry by new producers keeps the price near the cost of manufacturing and distributing the drug. Lack of information limits the rigor of this price competition, and many different prices for apparently identical products can coexist (as in table 3). Current government policy is to encourage this competitive pressure on price.

The combination of these two processes produces a paradoxical result. When the rate of drug discovery is high, most of the existing drugs with which a new drug competes still enjoy patent protection when it is introduced. The prices of the existing drugs are still high, and the new drug has a high price, too. When the pace of drug discovery slows, new drugs are likely to be in competition with older drugs whose patents have expired and whose prices have fallen toward the cost of production. The prices of new drugs in this setting will be lower than the prices of new drugs introduced when the rate of introduction is high. Restrictions on the rate of introduction of new drugs thus have the effect of lowering drug prices on average, even if regulation increases the cost of producing old drugs.

The paradoxical quality of this result may render it unstable. Increased regulation, the story goes, reduces the supply of new drugs by raising the costs of introducing them. But increasing regulation also decreases the price at which these new drugs are sold because the reduced rate of new drug introduction increases the probability that any new drug will compete with existing unpatented, as opposed to patented, drugs. Measures that increase costs and decrease prices must have a depressing effect on profits. It is hard to know whether this is happening—though the drug companies assure us that it is—but such a process could have an increasingly adverse effect on the rate of new drug introductions. If the reduced rate of profit is still high enough to encourage this activity, the change will simply be a reallocation of income. If, however, the anticipation of lower profits leads drug firms to transfer their resources into other lines, then the cumulative impact of increased regulation may be severe indeed.[28]

This argument captures only a general tendency of drug prices and should not be taken as a complete description. Drug prices exhibit wide dispersion, caused in part by uncertainty over possible differences in quality. And competition among patented drugs further complicates the two-tier pricing system outlined here.

Doctors and consumers have switched to newer drugs as they became available, loosening the link between the price of an average drug and the profits of the major drug companies. Price competition is centered on antibiotics, which became less expensive in the 1960s while the price of sedatives and prescription drugs for coughs and colds rose. The net effect was to leave drug prices remarkably stable. Drug prices fell to a trough around 1965 and rose thereafter, accelerating upward after 1970.[29] The aggregate price level rose then, too, and the relative or "real" price of drugs has fallen continuously since 1960. The average cost of prescriptions, however, has risen in real terms, that is, relative to other prices, owing both to an increase in the average size of prescriptions and the use of newer, more expensive drugs (see table 24). The pervasiveness of the new competition is not yet clear.

While the expiration of drug patents led to a decline in the relative price of drugs, growing price competition was accompanied by increased demand which may have moderated the price decline. The rise in the demand for drugs came from many sources, but the increased governmental role in the financing of health care deserves special attention since it led to new programs to reduce drug prices.

Medicare and Medicaid were passed as successive titles of the Social Security Amendments of 1965. They signaled a dramatic change in the federal government's involvement in the distribution of health care, a

Table 24. Nominal and real drug price indexes, 1960–1975 (1967 = 100).

Index	1960	1965	1970	1975
Wholesale prices[a]				
Nominal	106.6	100.4	101.1	126.6
Real	112.3	103.9	91.6	72.4
Retail prices[b]				
Nominal	104.5	100.2	103.5	118.8
Real	117.8	106.0	89.0	73.7
Prescription prices[c]				
Nominal	88.7	95.9	110.7	129.5[d]
Real	100.0	101.5	95.2	111.4[d]

Source: Thomas K. Fulda, *Prescription Drug Data Summary, 1974,* Department of Health, Educaion, and Welfare pub. no. SSS–76–11928 (Washington, D.C.: Government Printing Office, 1976), pp. 36–37.

a. Deflated by wholesale price index.

b. Deflated by consumer price index.

c. National Prescription Audit (IMS America) index deflated by consumer price index; other indexes of prescription drug costs show different values but similar trends.

d. 1974.

change that has been reflected in an enormous increase in the government's health expenditures. The share of personal health expenditures paid for by the federal government rose from 10.2 percent in 1965 to 27.1 percent in 1975 and 27.7 percent in 1978, offsetting a fall in the share of direct payments by consumers. Neither private insurance's nor state and local governments' shares changed significantly during this decade. (The former rose less than four percentage points and the latter not at all.)[30]

The expansion of government health insurance increased the demand for medical care by the poor and the aged,[31] but not by the rest of the population. In fact, to the extent that Medicare and Medicaid raised the cost of medical care by increasing the demand faster than the supply, they may have decreased the quantity demanded by the population not covered.

To evaluate the effect of the increased government financing on the demand for drugs, it is necessary to consider both direct and indirect effects, since most outpatient insurance does not include payments for drugs. Nevertheless, if people see a doctor whom they would not have visited without insurance and then purchase a drug this doctor prescribes, the purchase may be seen as an effect of the insurance even though it is not covered. Formally, assume that the composition of health care is not affected by how it is financed and further that the care given to Medicare and Medicaid recipients would not have been delivered without these programs. Then, almost 20 percent of health care expenditures in 1975 can be attributed to these programs (as a result of the second assumption), as can almost 20 percent of drug expenditures, however financed (as a result of the first assumption). United States sales of American drug firms in 1975 were two and a half times as large as they had been a decade earlier. If sales in 1975 had been 20 percent lower than they actually were, then they would have been only twice as large as a decade earlier.[32] Most of the rapid growth in the dollar value of drugs consumed, therefore, was independent of Medicare and Medicaid, although the growth of government involvement in health care probably moderated the price decline attendant on the expiration of drug patents in the preceding decade.

Even though Medicare and Medicaid have had a relatively minor effect on the demand for drugs and government expenditures for drugs are a small part of total costs of the two programs, these expenditures have been a cause of public concern. Frustrated by the inability to stem the growth of health-related expenditures in any comprehensive way, people have attempted to control those aspects of cost that can be disentangled from the complex web of health care delivery. Drugs fall into this category.

One approach that has been followed in a number of states is to repeal the nonsubstitution laws which prevented pharmacists from choosing which manufacturer's drug they would use in filling a prescription. The hope is that pharmacists will opt for low-cost suppliers, although their incentive to do so is not strong. The federal government's approach is to specify the maximum amount it will pay for a given drug, generally the lowest price available on the market. If a higher priced drug is furnished to a Medicare or Medicaid patient, someone other than the government must pick up the extra cost.

During the therapeutic revolution, almost every state passed an antisubstitution law requiring pharmacists to use the brand of drug specified by the doctor on prescriptions. Drug manufacturers wanted these laws to allow their advertising to the doctors to be effective in determing sales; they were a logical extension of the integration of drug production and marketing. Pharmacists wanted them to limit their liability by defining their role in the new distribution system more precisely. These state laws attacked problems similar to those dealt with by the Humphrey-Durham Amendment on the federal level.

Opposition to these laws began to mount in the 1960s as generic drugs became available and many people, convinced that generic drugs were equivalent to brand-named drugs, wanted to get the cheapest product they could. Not being able to choose prescription drugs for themselves, they wanted to restrict the doctors' power to order expensive drugs for them when cheaper equivalents were available. To be sure, this would simply shift the decision to the pharmacist, not the consumer, but the opponents of the antisubstitution laws assumed that pharmacists were not as much the object of advertisements for brand-named drugs and were more subject to legislative control. Over thirty states had repealed their antisubstitution laws by 1977. Two-thirds of these, however, did not give pharmacists license to substitute whenever they wished; they furnished either a list of substitutable drugs or a list of nonsubstitutable drugs to restrict their actions.[33]

The repeal of the antisubstitution laws appears to be an ideal way to reduce drug costs with little administrative or other expense. The expense of administering the law has not exceeded expectations, but the apparent savings have fallen short—at least in the short run. The savings have proven exceedingly difficult to measure owing to the complexity of retail drug prices, which differ across pharmacies, across customers at the same pharmacy, and across time at the same pharmacy as well. The result has been a continuing conviction that drug costs are lower, with little substantive evidence to support it.[34]

Given this mixed empirical picture, several reasons why the repeal of the antisubstitution laws might have only limited success come to mind. There are many single-source drugs, drugs still under patent protection, for which the new laws are not relevant. Doctors may take advantage of the opportunity provided them in most states of refusing to allow substitution on the prescriptions they write. Pharmacists may prove to be as conservative in their reliance on the major drug producers as doctors. And the variation in retail drug prices from other sources may be large enough to obscure whatever effects the new laws have. All these factors look more important in the short run than in the long, and the effects of the renewed ability to choose among drug manufacturers should become more apparent over time. The limited market penetration of unbranded products shown in table 23 may be only a temporary phenomenon.

At the same time that the antisubstitution laws were being repealed, the federal government announced its plan to limit the amount it would pay for drugs under Medicare and Medicaid. The maximum allowable cost (MAC) program specified the highest amount that the government would reimburse a pharmacy for supplying each drug. This program has the same aims as the repeal of the antisubstitution laws, but approaches it in a different way: instead of allowing more choice and hoping the market will drive down prices, the MAC program tries to lower prices by administrative means. The contrast derives from the difference in the two programs' coverage. The repeal of the antisubstitution laws affects the market for drugs purchased without third-party reimbursement; the MAC program affects the market for drugs paid for by the government. The only discipline possible in the latter type of market is adminsitrative.

The MAC program has had a slow start. Announced informally in 1973 and officially in 1975, the first MAC did not become effective until June 1977. MACs were issued for ampicillin and penicillin in 1977 and for tetracycline, propoxyphene, and chlordiazepoxide in early 1978. Hoffmann-La Roche, whose well-known brand of chlordiazepoxide, Librium, accounted for most of that market of that drug, thereupon challenged the government's authority to set MACs. It is clear that the determination of MACs for individual drugs is a time-consuming, and presumably costly, process. If there is to be extensive litigation over them, this will consume even more resources. The question is whether the government will save more in its drug purchases than it spends administering and defending the MAC program.[35]

Whatever the social merit of the MAC program, the combination of this program with the others already in place has put the drug industry in a peculiar position. With a decrease in the supply of drugs—owing both to the increased cost of introducing new drugs and to the increased monitoring of drug production and use—and an increase in the demand for drugs from various sources, the price of drugs might be expected to rise. But, as table 24 makes clear, the price has continued to fall, and government policy is designed to make it fall even faster. It is still too early to know if any policy, other than the patent laws, will have an important effect.

EIGHT

Uncertainty and Economic Behavior

THE NEXT PART of the narrative has yet to be written. Congress has before it a bill to reform current drug regulation, but history provides only a limited guide to its fate. Passage may have to wait for the next drug disaster, awful though that is to contemplate. And even if the bill passes, the progress of legislation is only a partial determinant of the Food and Drug Administration's behavior. The FDA has maintained a constancy of purpose over time, changing slowly in response to a variety of factors emanating partly from Congress and partly from elsewhere.[1]

The 1938 prescription-only regulation provides the best example of FDA independence from legislative direction. This independence has been underscored recently by a federal judge who declared the regulation invalid on the grounds that it lacked legislative justification. Arguing along lines similar to those I have used, the judge maintained that the regulation was designed to fill a hiatus in the statute, that is, "the area where certain drugs are necessary for the public health but will always be technically misbranded because 'adequate directions for use' are impossible to devise." But, the judge continued, "such administrative action, albeit logical, does not justify judicial addition to the language of the statute." He therefore disallowed an FDA action based on the regulation.[2]

This regulation has been imbedded in subsequent statutes, and the FDA will not let the regulatory structure built on the distinction between prescription and over-the-counter drugs fall in response to this threat to its foundations. Nevertheless, it is as hard to predict how the agency will shore up the foundations of this structure as how Congress will revise the architecture. It is time, therefore, to step back from the narrative and ask where drug policy might go—to ask both about probable directions and about desirable ones.

In order to formulate views about current policy choices, two elements are needed. One must know the history, and one must have a theory or model of behavior to suggest both how people will act in different contexts and how the regulatory context itself can change. The model that follows both illuminates the history and provides guidance for prediction.

A Model of Behavior under Uncertainty

The model begins with the three modes of behavior outlined earlier. The three modes are instrumental (rational or goal-oriented), customary (habitual or traditional), and command (hierarchical). Instrumental behavior is the type that economists assume prevails in market settings, the actions of *homo economicus*. A person or business firm acting in this mode behaves consistently in a fashion that can be described as the pursuit of a definable objective goal. People and firms acting in the customary mode, by contrast, repeat more or less fixed patterns of action in a habitual or traditional way. These customs can and do change over time in response to individual variations that get adopted by the group, to imperfect memories of the past, and to other stimuli. But their predominantly conservative and static nature sets them off from the ceaselessly changing and adapting instrumental activity. Finally, command behavior is either the issuing or the obeying of explicit orders. There must be some sort of inducement to encourage compliance with these orders in order for them to be given and followed. Many types are possible, ranging from the threat of violence to the expectation of social disapproval. In each case, however, the orders emanate from an identifiable source, distinguishing them from amorphous, anonymous customs.

Each mode of behavior entails a characteristic form of personal interaction. When exhibiting instrumental behavior, people barter or buy goods and services with and from one another; the primary interaction is explicit, voluntary exchange. Reciprocity is the characteristic form of personal communication in customary behavior. Like custom, reciprocity is incapable of precise delineation, but the presence of this "social exchange" can be seen and its importance recognized in many situations. In command behavior, people issue and receive orders, such as prescriptions.

Two of these characteristic forms of communication have entered into the legal discussion of contracts. It has been argued that there are two kinds of contracts which need to be recognized—and are recognized—in two different kinds of contract law. The first kind of contract is "transactional." It is the means of implementing an isolated economic transaction of the sort considered in economic theory, that is, of instrumental behavior. The second kind of contract is "relational." It is used in the context of ongoing relations that characterize interactions among known parties. These are the contexts of customary behavior, which can be identified by the type of interaction used.[3]

Because these different modes of behavior are suited to different conditions, it is reasonable to ask whether the conditions favorable to each mode can be described more completely. In addition, different people are likely to use different modes, and it is not unreasonable to ask also whether the kind of people who are likely to use one or the other mode can be described as well. These reasonable requests hide a variety of problems, of course. Neither conditions nor personalities are easy to characterize. And with two factors present, the relationship between each factor and the corresponding mode of behavior will of necessity be complex.

Because change is a fact of life, any context in which people act is subject to change all the time. In addition, the characteristics of change vary from one situation to the next. Its speed, the extent to which it can be predicted, the costs of faulty predictions, even the extent to which the change is apparent, all vary from place to place and from time to time.

A pertinent example may clarify the dimensions along which different types of change can be ranked. Most people are healthy most of the time. They move around, they eat and sleep, they go about their business. Their normal health routines represent familiar paths through activities and variations in how they feel. These repetitive changes are so completely predicted that they are like no change at all. There are few decisions on this subject to be made in the course of daily living, and planning, if it is done at all, is automatic and straightforward.

If a person feels a little unwell, this will destabilize his normal pattern. There will be choices to make about whether to get up or what to eat, whether to take a pill or call a doctor. If the person is not too sick, he will think about what to do. An upset stomach or a cold is not so unusual that he will not have had prior experience to suggest what may work. There are many ways to get information on minor ailments, from calling the doctor to reading a home medical manual. Since the illness is not major, there is the possibility of speeding recovery without much danger of serious damage. There is a modest amount of change from the familiar pattern and an opportunity for reasoned decisions.

A person who is more seriously ill, who is in acute pain or who thinks that something major is amiss, typically will act differently. In this case, major changes are taking place in the body and there is at least potential danger. As the person gets sicker, he will find it less appropriate to decide for himself what to do and more comfortable to seek out an expert to help. Parsons defines the state of "illness" as beginning at the point where the person opts out of his own decision making and places himself in the care of another.[4]

Finally, there may come a point, either because of drastic changes in the person's health or because of changes in the context in which the person moves, that it may not seem worth the effort to look for an expert or an authority figure. It may, paradoxically, be like the state of normal health in which there is little perception of things to do. Extreme change may be so bewildering that it seems like acts of God. For planning purposes, such change may seem like no change at all; it may simply be white noise.

It is very hard to characterize states of health explicitly, as many policymakers have discovered, and this discussion is not intended to do so. It illustrates simply that situations can be ordered according to the amount of change taking place, indexed by its predictability, speed, and magnitude.

Perfectly predictable changes and completely unpredictable changes are like no change. Moderate change is change that is reasonably predictable and which either does not progress quickly or does not threaten disaster. Extensive change is rapid, relatively unpredictable change of important variables. Large losses are possible, but planning can reduce them, at least in principle. If the possible predictions are so limited that only the most general kind of actions are indicated, then the anticipated changes are close to straight noise, and the change becomes a feature of the background rather than a stimulus to predicting, planning, and taking specific actions. The measure of change increases as it becomes more rapid, more costly, and less predictable, up to a point where it is so rapid, costly, and unpredictable that it cannot be dealt with as change. The measure then returns discontinuously to its origin.

This is not strictly true, of course. People generally act differently in a noisy environment than in a perfectly predictable one, even if they cannot make information predictions for the future. For example, they may try to preserve their ability to take advantage of changes in the environment. But this qualification does not pose a problem for the model. The presence of noise indicates that flexibility is desirable, but does not by itself indicate the optimum level. People typically choose this response based on custom, as the traditional reaction or the one prevalent in their peer group at the time. Unpredictable change therefore leads to customary behavior, albeit not to the same customs as the absence of change.

This discontinuity implies that there is a maximum amount of change in this measure. The measure can therefore be confined to the unit interval, with zero as no change or pure noise and one as the maximum amount of change that is still seen as change. Within the interval, change is evaluated as larger if it is more rapid, more costly, or less predictable.

In addition to differences among situations, the model also recognizes differences among people. In this it departs from the substantial body of thought that denies the possibility of distinguishing people in any systematic way. Adherents of this intellectual position do not deny that people differ; they deny that they differ in sufficiently constant ways for their variations to be calibrated. In other words, they argue that the behavior of any individual varies enough over situations that it can be predicted more reliably by the characteristics of the situation at hand than by individual "traits." An article supporting this view succinctly summarized its limited conclusions in its title. It was called: "On Predicting Some of the People Some of the Time."[5]

It is true that personal variations are not amenable to scaling along one or a few dimensions, but the insistence that people cannot usefully be characterized at all seems to go beyond the available evidence. The title just noted suggests the problem. Even people who act consistently will act differently in different situations. A theory that describes behavior needs to be multidimensional, that is, to show the interaction of individual and situation. Within bounds, it should be able to predict everyone's behavior some of the time and even some people's behavior all the time by accurately identifying this interaction. Only if such a theory fails can we conclude that people do not vary systematically.

The personality measure to be described here, therefore, does not need to carry the burden usually thrust upon such measures in personality theory. Alone, it will not predict behavior: each mode of behavior can be practiced by any person—in the appropriate situation. The choice of mode is the result of both personality and situation.

Phrased differently, personality cannot be defined in terms of behavior exhibited. Only in a very extreme case will someone behave consistently in the customary or instrumental mode. The great majority of people will act sometimes in one mode, sometimes in another. The present theory thus differs in structure from the kind of analysis typified by David Riesman's *The Lonely Crowd.* The inner-directed and other-directed personality types described in that book were defined in terms of their actions, with the former acting instrumentally while the latter acted customarily.[6] Reisman confused personality and action, the inputs and outputs of the model being presented here. His discussion increases our understanding of these two modes of behavior, but it cannot enlighten us about how people with different personalities and attitudes select (not necessarily consciously) among the possible modes of behavior.

The dimension of personality that is of interest here can be called *autonomy*. The opposite of autonomous in the present context is *social,* and people are considered to be located in a scale that ranges from complete autonomy to complete social involvement (or zero autonomy).

Autonomous people are concerned with their individual position, with their possessions, and with other symbols of achievement. They are relatively unconnected emotionally with other people or with a group. They seek to get ahead, to change, to advance. They do not look with any longing at a stable place within an established group. At the extreme, they are ambitious, critical, and selfish. If they are not "self-made men," they aspire to that position.

Social people, by contrast, exhibit the opposite attitudes. They are concerned with their interpersonal relationships and desire above all to be located within a stable social framework. They are responsive to the needs of the group and even willing to sacrifice their own advancement for the progress of the group. They are the "good soldiers" of society.

The concept of autonomy is not new, and these brief comments are not meant to add to existing descriptions. Instead, they are the initial steps in finding or devising a measure of autonomy. For if the present model is to have any empirical content, there must be an explicit measure of autonomy to join with the explicit measure of change introduced above. No existing personality scale lies precisely along this dimension, but the Machiavelli scale developed by Christie and Geis and the field articulation scale defined by Witkin measure personality and attitudes along a similar dimension.

Christie and Geis hypothesized that people who agreed with Machiavelli's political directives would act differently from those who disagreed. They evaluated individual acceptance of Machiavellian prescriptions by means of a tabulated questionnaire, characterizing people who agreed with Machiavelli (as transcribed by these modern psychologists) as "high Machs." Individual Mach scores were not correlated with intelligence, but they did correlate well with identifiable behavior patterns. People were characterized as high and low Mach in these terms:

High Machs: The Cool Syndrome
   resistance to social influence, orientation to cognitions, initiating and controlling structure.
Low Machs: The Soft Touch
   susceptibility to social influence, orientation to persons, accepting and following structure.[7]

Witkin and his co-workers identified a similar index of personality, which they termed field independence or articulation. One set of authors using their theory has defined this index as follows:

A person at the global end of the continuum is likely to be characterized as intellectually intuitive, perceptually holistic, emotionally expressive, socially dependent and other-directed, and motivationally diffuse. A person at the articulated end, on the other hand, is likely to be characterized as intellectually analytical and systematic, perceptually discriminating, emotionally self-controlled, socially independent and self-reliant, and motivationally focused.[8]

High Machs and field-articulate individuals are what I have called autonomous; low Machs and field-global individuals are what I have called social. Both indexes are associated with quantitative tests that locate people on the scales defined. At this stage of research, we can assume that the personality measure used here can be indexed by either type of test. And since the tests all have maximum scores, we can assume that the relevant continuum is confined to the unit interval.

   These two dimensions can be put together as shown in figure 1. Indi-

Figure 1

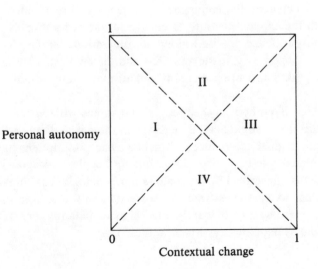

vidual differences are ranked along the vertical axis, with high Machs or field articulation at the top. Differences among situations are ranked along the horizontal axis, with the speed of unpredictable change increasing to the right. Any point in the box represents the combination of a group and a situation with the appropriate characteristics.

Each side of this square can be identifed with a particular mode of behavior. Since there are four sides and only three modes, two sides will be identified with the same mode. If these two sides are adjacent, we can define three areas of unimodal behavior, starting with the edges of the box and going toward the middle. They will be separated by lines that start from the corners of the box and meet at some point, T, in the interior where the three areas touch. Without more specification, it is impossible to say where in the interior of the square this point is. For symmetry and simplicity, I have represented it in the center of the square. Drawing lines from this point to the corners of the square divides figure 1 into equal quadrants. Each quadrant will be characterized by one mode of behavior, and two of them by the same mode.

This procedure is based on a continuity assumption. It assumes that there is only one connected area for each mode of behavior, so that an identification of the edges of the box with a mode of behavior implies a similar identification with the area near the edge. It also implies that the boundaries between areas have roughly the shape shown in figure 1, although there is no reason for them to be straight or to have equal slopes.[9] The continuity assumption can be tested in a preliminary way by examining a few boundary points for their plausibility after the modes of behavior have been filled in.

The left-hand edge shows conditions of no change or white noise. These are the conditions under which customary behavior is used; there is no scope for either instrumental or command behavior. Quadrant I can thus be identified as a region of customary behavior.

The location of customary behavior at the left-hand side of the box raises the question of the relation between custom and habit. I have so far used these two terms interchangeably, but they convey slightly different meanings. Custom refers to activities performed in a group context, while habits refer to individual activities. The difference is not in the stability of the actions. Customs can be very rigid and durable, as they are in certain "traditional" communities. Nor is it in the action's origins. Some habits are the customs of a previous peer group. It seems rather to be in the degree to which the rules that govern custom or habit are internalized. Habitual activity responds to a set of internal guidelines; customary activity, to a set of external—group—guidelines.

Despite the difference between these two terms, it does not seem advisable to distinguish them as separate modes of behavior. They overlap in common usage, so that doctors' prescribing patterns, which respond to group influence and pressure, are spoken of in the literature as "prescribing habits." And this overlap reflects the inherent difficulty of demarcating where habit ends and custom begins. Rather than distinguishing them, it is preferable to include habit in the customary mode of behavior, recognizing that people near the top of the box (along the left-hand edge) will be acting more out of habit, while people near the bottom act more out of custom.[10]

The top of the square shows the behavior of completely autonomous people. Unencumbered by social ties, they act instrumentally in all conditions. Of course, such people exist only in economic theory. The more accurate statement is that more autonomous people will use instrumental behavior in a wider array of contexts than less autonomous people. Quadrant II therefore is the region of instrumental behavior.

The right-hand edge describes behavior at the maximum amount of change that can be understood as change, just before the movement dissolves into chaos and noise. It is not unreasonable to assume that everyone in this position would see some form of hierarchical decision making as desirable. There may well be disagreements about who should be in control and how much authority the controller should have, but the disagreements will be about the nature of hierarchy, not its existence. Quadrant III is the domain of command behavior.

Finally, the bottom of the box shows the activities of completely socialized beings. They are imbedded in a group, and they follow the customs of that group. There is no assurance from the combination of personality and situation that such a group will exist. The argument is rather that if a suitable group does not exist, social people will invent one. Quadrant IV, like quadrant I, is a region of customary behavior.

Identifying the quadrants with the mode of behavior indicated in each and eliminating the redundant boundary between quadrants I and IV yields figure 2. Point T, the sole boundary to all three modes of behavior, is shown at the middle of the square, but this is purely for convenience since we know only that T is somewhere in the interior of the square and connected to three of the four corners. We can speak of points above or below, to the right or left, of point T, but we cannot describe the distance between point T and other points in the box. Consequently, the apparent inference from figure 2 that customary behavior occurs in more situations than either instrumental or command behavior is illegitimate. This may be true, but it cannot be inferred from the diagram.

Figure 2

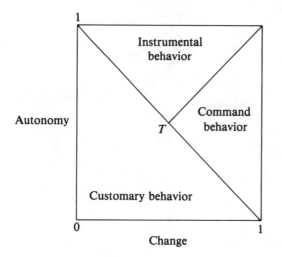

The way in which a mode of behavior is selected varies. It may be the result of explicit choice—of instrumental behavior applied to the choice of mode. This is one extreme. At the other extreme, people may use one or another mode of behavior in a given context because they are unable to conceptualize any other. As far as they are concerned, there is no choice to be made. Between these two extremes lie various combinations of explicit choice and cognitive determinism. The balance between these poles may differ among people and even among situations for the same person.

A rough test of the assumptions underlying figure 2 would be to assess the plausibility of its implications. Let us examine the behavior predicted along a horizontal line above T and a vertical line to the right of T, each of which passes through all three zones (as shown in figure 3). The figure describes equilibrium behavior, that is, behavior that can be sustained under different conditions, so it is more appropriate to compare different people placed along each line than to trace the movement of a single person who moves along the lines. Three points are distinguished on each of them, one in each region.

The horizontal line, ABC, shows the behavior of relatively autonomous people under different circumstances. For the range of conditions typified by point B, the autonomous person behaves instrumentally. But even a quite autonomous person cannot maintain this mode under all circumstances. Finding himself at point A, where there is little variance in the

Figure 3

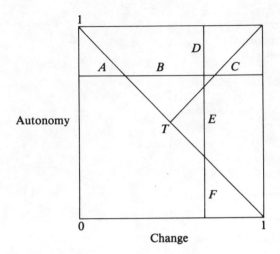

relevant environment, such a person would tend to slip into the customary mode. Ordinary decisions, often repeated, are the stuff of habit or custom, not of repeated calculation. At the opposite extreme, even relatively autonomous people at point *C*, in conditions of rapid change, will acknowledge the inability of single individuals to cope with the changes. They will opt for some kind of delegation of power to experts or professionals who, presumably, are better placed to deal with the difficulties of rapid change.

Doctors, to take a well-educated, reasonably autonomous group, follow medical custom for their "ordinary" cases. With more difficult cases, they do research to seek out an efficacious therapy. And with cases involving changes outside their experience, they relinquish authority to someone higher in the medical hierarchy: they refer the case to a specialist. As the model suggests, the extent of the middle, instrumental, category varies among doctors.

The vertical line, *DEF,* shows the behavior of different people in the same situation, in this case one of extensive change. The most social people, at *F,* follow their customs in the face of change, either ignoring the change or choosing to preserve the group instead of adapting quickly. More autonomous people, at *E,* prerefer a hierarchical system for dealing with the change, opting for the increased flexibility rather than the maintenance of a peer group. The most autonomous individuals, at *D,* choose to "go it alone." The extent of change is not great enough to cause them to abandon their individual efforts to benefit from the changes they see.

In other words, different people might show diverse responses to the same symptoms of illness. Those people most tightly integrated into a social group would deal with their symptoms within the group. More independent people would go to a doctor. But some independent types would try to discover a reasonable course of action on their own. As the model suggests, there is a threshold of symptoms below which doctors are not consulted, and the proportion of people seeing doctors increases with the severity of the symptoms.

This small exercise shows that a plausible interpretation can be given to movements from one region of the box to another, even when there is more than one transition to explain along a single line. The exercise therefore supports the use of continuity assumption to fill in the interior of the square.

Some Propositions from the Model

Several propositions emerge from this model, even in its present crude state. Examining a few of them will serve to illuminate the model, show its usefulness, and begin the process of applying it to the preceding history of drug utilization and regulation.

(1) Transitions between modes of behavior can be caused either by changes in the context—including changes in knowledge about an existing situation—or by changes in taste. For example, an existing pattern of customary behavior might be changed into instrumental behavior by an increase in personal autonomy or into command behavior by a rise in the rate of perceived contextual change. In terms of figure 2, people and groups can move either horizontally or vertically.

The growth in the use of drug prescriptions over the past half-century can be understood in the context of this proposition. The growth was the result both of legal changes and of the increased interest in prescriptions on the part of sick people. The greater interest resulted from changes in the nature of available drugs. Before the Depression, most people seeking drugs were quite healthy—since the available drugs typically only relieved symptoms without affecting serious illness. Since then, drugs have assisted more and more in the treatment of serious diseases, and people using drugs consequently were increasingly ill, that is, increasingly in the midst of rapid, dangerous change. Consumers of drugs have thus moved to the right in figures 2 and 3 because the occasion for using medicinal drugs has changed.

(2) A return to customary (or command) behavior after a period in another mode does not mean a return to the same customs (or commands) as before. Indeed, we would expect customs and commands to be different after they had been interrupted by another type of behavior.

Consider a person or group acting in a customary fashion. If the environment changes in an unexpected but perceptible manner, this person or group may become dissatisfied with the existing customs and replace them by instrumental or command behavior. This new behavior will permit adaptation to the new conditions; that is their attraction. But if the changes in the external environment slow and cease after a while, behavior will drift back into the customary mode. Even though this change represents a return to a familiar mode of behavior, the patterns of actions that get transformed into customs will not be the old customs. The temporary use of instrumental or command behavior will have shattered the old customs and replaced them by new actions designed to meet the new conditions. These new actions will become the new customs.

A firm that institutes cost-cutting practices in response to a rise in its costs may lose its crusading zeal after a while, but will not simply return to its old, wasteful ways. The innovations of the cost-cutting campaign typically will be embodied in new rules of thumb instead. A doctor who searches the drug literature in response to the appearance of new symptoms or new therapies may tire of his inquiry in short order, but he will not in general forget or fail to use what he has learned.

(3) Modes of behavior cannot be sustained in conditions or among populations unsuitable for them. In other words, actual behavior will tend toward the pattern shown in figure 2. Attempts to alter or maintain modes of behavior, consequently, will be unsuccessful or short-lived under predictable circumstances. In particular:

(3a) Customary behavior cannot be sustained under conditions of great change or in populations with high autonomy. Custom and tradition cannot coexist with rapid movement and the expectation of continued movement in the future. Large changes in drug prices or in people's need for drugs will induce them to look around at pharmacies and reevaluate existing drug purchasing patterns.

(3b) Command behavior cannot be sustained under constant conditions or those of easy predictability. There is no justification for the hierarchical control, and it will tend to erode one way or the other, that is, into instrumental or customary behavior. The current decline in new drug introductions, for example, has made doctors restive with controls imposed by the Food and Drug Administration.

(3c) Instrumental behavior cannot be sustained in populations that have relatively little autonomy or in conditions of too much or too little change. Doctors, we may imagine, begin their careers aspiring to make instrumental choices among drugs and then lapse into customary behavior as they become aware of the limitations of medical knowledge and integrated into a medical community.

(4) It follows from the third corollary that perfect efficiency may be unattainable. It may require a degree of autonomy that the population lacks, and it may require a speed of change that is incompatible with the maintenance of instrumental behavior. Command and customary behaviors, of course, lack the optimizing properties of instrumental behavior, even under the restrictive assumptions in which competition leads to efficiency.[11]

Going further, attempts to reach perfectly efficient points may be self-defeating. If the attempts require an increase in the rapidity of change and the unpredictability of a situation, then the results of optimizing efforts may be to foster command behavior, rather than instrumental. Efforts to "shake up" an existing customary pattern may result in so much unexpected variation that instrumental behavior as well as customary behavior is avoided. This could happen if the population is socially oriented, as in the movement from A to B in figure 4, but it could also happen with a more autonomous population if the increase in change

Figure 4

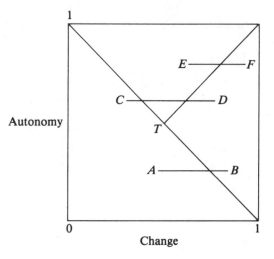

were large enough, as shown by the movement from *C* to *D*. And while the command behavior might result in efficiency, there is no reason why it has to. It may instead lead to an expansion of bureaucracies that moves the group away from the efficient point. If point *E* in figure 4 showed the original position, an increase in the rate of change in the pursuit of efficiency could lead to a movement to *F* with an increase in bureaucratization and a probable decrease in efficiency.

(5) Providing additional information to consumers will be useful only in certain contexts. Only in the instrumental mode will new information necessarily affect decison making, and the instrumental mode is only maintainable under certain conditions. Under other conditions, the information will be ignored much of the time as people fall back on customary and command modes of behavior. The 1906 Pure Food Act and its subsequent extensions may have simply provided information without moving people out of a customary mode. The information may have been useful, but it did not come close to fulfilling its intended purpose if this was the case. The extensive drug inserts mandated under the 1962 Drug Amendments may have been limited in their impact for similar reasons. And the package inserts for patients being introduced now may also be of only limited use.

(6) Finally, groups and nations may differ in their approach to similar problems. Doctors may be spread out along a line like *AB* in figure 5, which extends across a modal boundary. While most doctors act custom-

Figure 5

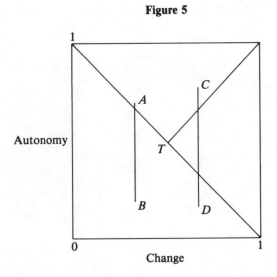

arily, some doctors would act instrumentally in this case. The instrumental minority could then serve as a conduit through which new information could affect the customs of the majority. Nations may be spread out along a line like *CD* as they contemplate policies to control the sale of medicine. Depending on where they are on the line, they could opt for any of the three modes of behavior in response to the same degree of uncertainty. The two-dimensional nature of the model allows for the common observation that responses to similar conditions differ among individuals, groups, and nations.[12]

If some of these propositions sound familiar, it is no wonder. This model summarizes a body of existing thought as much as it breaks new conceptual ground. But while the elements of this model are in the literature, they have not been brought together in a systematic way. They remain, therefore, on the fringes of knowledge, often mentioned, but never developed. One aim of the current inquiry is to bring them onto center stage. These propositions about behavior can, if they are connected with propositions about institutional structure, be useful in the analysis of policy shifts.

The analysis of institutional structures begins by distinguishing three distinct types. A *hierarchy* exists when people are arranged in well-defined power relationships, so that one person or group is in a position to give orders to other people with a reasonable expectation that they will be carried out. A *market* exists when people come together on an equal basis and exchange resources (money, services, commodities) in explicit, mutually acceptable bargains. The equality of the participants does not refer to equality of their resources but to the necessity to gain mutual agreement for the exchange to take place. A *community* exists when people interact informally and continually on a more or less equal footing. Communities are distinguished from hierarchies by the absence of a well-defined set of status or power relationships and from markets by the absence of explicit exchanges. Communities depend for their operation on the presence of continuing affective relationships, which may or may not be present in hierarchies and markets. The presence of these relationships is a poor index of the existence of a community, however, both because they sometimes exist in other structures and because they often are hard to observe from outside the community. They are very important in the functioning of any community, but they are not a defining or distinguishing characteristic of community structures.

The structures can be combined with the modes of behavior as shown in figure 6. We can imagine each mode of behavior existing in each structure, but it is clear on the face of it that not all modes of behavior fit easily into all structures. Consequently, it is necessary to specify which cells in figure 6 are "stable," that is, which cells have a comfortable fit between behavior and structure, and how the uncomfortable fits in other cells are expressed in actions. These specifications can be made in a further series of propositions. Amitai Etzioni has explored the fit between behavior and organizational structure in a model parallel to, but less formal than, the one presented here. The propositions to follow therefore both reformulate and extend Etzioni's analysis.[13]

(7) The diagonal cells in figure 6 are stable. That is, once a mode of behavior is imbedded in the structure corresponding to it, there is no pressure for change. Customary behavior fits comfortably into communities, which allow affective relationships and reciprocal actions to reinforce both the relationships and customary behavior. Instrumental behavior functions well in market settings. And command behavior is appropriate in hierarchies.

(8) One off-diagonal cell is stable as well. Customary behavior can exist in hierarchies without tension. People may obey the commands of traditional authority figures in conformity with the community traditions, not out of any desire to have decisions centrally made. It follows that the presence of conditions that promote customary behavior—no unanticipated important changes in the environment—need not threaten the existence of some hierarchies. Those hierarchies based on the continued exercise of power may be subject to stress in the absence of events calling for the use of that power, but hierarchies maintained by a continuing tradition of authority may not feel stress under those circumstances. Phrased

Figure 6

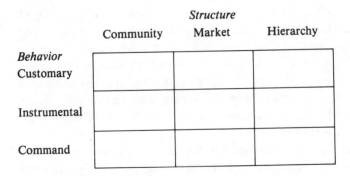

	Structure		
	Community	Market	Hierarchy
Behavior			
Customary			
Instrumental			
Command			

differently, it may be hard to distinguish between customary and command behavior and between community and hierarchical structures in some traditional settings.

(9) The tensions present in other cells come out in pressures to change the institutional structure, not in pressures to change the mode of behavior. According to propositions (1) through (3), modes of behavior are determined by the extent of unanticipated change in the environment and the degree of autonomy of the person or persons involved. This proposition says that the existence of a particular mode of behavior then creates pressure for the structure of personal interactions to conform with that mode.

In other words, the logical structure of the model is as follows. The interaction of personal characteristics and unanticipated changes in the environment creates forces pushing the pattern of behavior toward a particular mode. Then the existence of this mode of behavior creates forces that push the institutional structure toward a structure that is compatible with it. To a first approximation, then, the institutional structure within which behavior takes place does not influence the mode of behavior used.[14]

This proposition implies severe limitations to any drug policy. Public policies can change the institutional setting by which people obtain drugs, but they cannot directly alter the mode of behavior by which drugs are chosen. (Of course, if public policies reduce the flow of new drugs, then the reduction in the speed of change can affect doctors' and consumers' mode of behavior in choosing drugs.) Attempts to determine drug choices completely by means of hierarchical controls cannot be successful, just as attempts to get everyone making choices to think instrumentally about them can only achieve partial realization. For example, only about two-thirds of doctors' orders are obeyed, judging from available imperfect information on "compliance rates." There is considerable slippage in this hierarchical system.[15]

Looking more closely, we can identify at least two avenues by which the institutional structure might affect the mode of behavior. First, the structure may affect the extent of unpredictable change in the environment, which will in turn affect the mode of behavior. Use of a market may increase the rapidity of change, for example, while some community structures may reduce it. The rise in hierarchical control over new drug introductions, as just noted, has reduced the pace of change in drug therapy (albeit to an uncertain extent).

Second, the existence of a given institutional structure may create incentives for people to act in a mode that fits well with it. In market settings, for example, there are more incentives to act instrumentally than in rigid hierarchies. But these forces are less compelling than those that go in the opposite direction, from modes of behavior to the institutional structure. While they should not be ignored, they will seldom be dominant.

In terms of figure 6, this proposition asserts that the forces that operate when groups find themselves off the diagonal move horizontally, not vertically. The proposition is summarized in figure 7, where shaded areas represent stable cells and arrows show the direction in which groups in other cells may be expected to move.

(10) The existence of the forces to change the institutional structure does not mean that groups cannot remain in any of the cells of figures 6 and 7 for a long time. Altering institutional structures is a difficult job. It requires time and resources, and it will not be undertaken lightly. The forces making for change may not be strong enough in some cases to induce people to commit the time and energy needed to change the institutional structure within which they act.

Changing the institutional structure is analogous to making an investment in a new factory or signing a long-term contract. The process of building a factory or negotiating a contract is itself costly and will not be undertaken for trivial or transient gains. After the factory is built or the contract signed, the builder or signer is in a different position from before. This new position has its advantages, or course, but it also has drawbacks. The person involved presumably sees advantages to having the factory or the contract, but it also restricts his options for the near future. If he decides not to operate the factory, then it must be sold or abandoned at a loss. If he decides not to fulfill the contract, damages must be paid. In

Figure 7

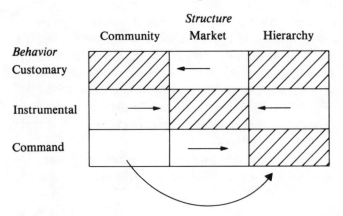

each case, the presumed benefits are obtained at the cost of losing some options. Similarly, changing an institutional structure may offer the benefit of relieving disharmony between a mode of behavior and its institutional setting, but the change requires effort and, once effected, imposes new costs on the people involved. Only if the disharmony is acute or the transition easy will the forces shown in figure 7 work themselves out quickly.

The model therefore describes long-run tendencies. In the long run, the extent of unanticipated change and personal autonomy will determine the mode of behavior which in turn will then determine the institutional structure of personal interactions. In the short run, however, myriad forces may impede the progress toward a long-run equilibrium. And if the conditions in the underlying environment change or if the nature of the population alters, then the tendency to move to the diagonal cells in figure 7 may never be realized. The direction of the forces may change before the forces become manifest in action.

In the short run, therefore, we may observe groups anywhere in figure 7. But if groups are observed in one of the unshaded cells, we would expect to find evidence of forces for change and, further, to find that any observed movement goes more often than not in the direction of the arrows.

These propositions, like the first half-dozen, summarize and codify ideas scattered through the literature. Their novelty is in their systematic presentation of these ideas and their formulation into a model. For, like those above, these ideas have been often stated, but seldom developed.

Connections with Other Theories

One reason for the lack of intellectual development in this area is that the types of behavior have been studied by a variety of different academic disciplines. Economists study instrumental behavior; lawyers and political scientists study command behavior; sociologists and social psychologists concentrate on customary behavior. Each of these disciplines has accumulated a body of knowledge about the mode of behavior and the institutional structure dominant in its chosen domain by specializing both its mode of inquiry and its subject matter. But a result of specialization is that the boundaries and transition points between the different modes of behavior and different institutional structures have been neglected. Within each separate discipline, material about the boundaries of the discipline are "interesting" but not "professional."

A few examples from the literatures of the different fields show how these disciplines fit into the model just presented. And examples also can identify places where the academic boundaries already have been breached and the transitions between different modes of behavior recognized. Examples of this phenomenon will be drawn primarily from economics, both because I am an economist by training and because specialization has gone further in economics than in other social science disciplines, making holes in its protective walls more apparent.

The first example of work at the boundary of economics concerns the theory of consumption. Stimulated by Keynes's ideas on the determinants of consumption, economists collected data on the relation between consumption and income at different times. The data exposed an apparent contradiction. If one compared different people at any one time, the proportion of income consumed fell as income rose; but if one compared the national ratio of consumption to income over time, it had not fallen as national income, and therefore the incomes of individuals within the national aggregate, had risen. The first result indicated that consumption rose less rapidly than income; the second, that they rose at the same rate.

The contradiction arose out of Keynes's theory, which predicted that consumption was a simple function of income and which did not recognize any difference between comparisons between people at a given time and between national aggregates at different times. The way out of the contradiction, therefore, was to revise the theory. James Duesenberry suggested in the late 1940s that the theory be revised by abandoning the assumption of independent preferences. In the terms used here, he denied that people were completely autonomous and introduced social elements into his theory. In his words:

There are strong psychological and sociological reasons for supposing that preferences are in fact interdependent . . . For any given relative income distribution, the percentage of income saved by a family will tend to be a unique, invariant, and increasing function of its percentile position in the income distribution. The percentage saved will be independent of the absolute level of income. It follows that the aggregate savings ratio will be independent of the absolute level of income.[16]

Appealing across disciplinary lines, Duesenberry asserted that the two bodies of data were the products of two entirely different processes. The comparison of different people at a single point in time showed what happened to the ratio of consumption to income as position within the income distribution, and therefore the social structure, varied. The comparison of national aggregates at different times showed the effects of shifting the whole distribution in time without changing it. Variations in the ratio of consumption to income are the results of moving within the social structure, of changing relative position. They are not to be expected when looking at the aggregate itself.

Economists did not flock to the interdisciplinary standard raised by Duesenberry. Instead, they continued to seek an explanation for the apparent contradiction consistent with the assumption of completely autonomous behavior. Such an explanation was found in the 1950s. It has two variants, referred to as the "life-cycle" and "permanent-income" hypotheses.[17] Differing in details, the two variants make the same assumption: that people make consumption plans for a long period—for their whole lives according to the life-cycle variant. Their consumption at any moment is determined by the plan, not by their current income.

Current incomes vary, and people experiencing high income for the moment will show low ratios of consumption to income, while people with temporarily low income will show a high ratio. At any moment in time, a disproportionate number of people with high incomes will be above their average or planned income, while a disproportionately large proportion of people with low incomes will be below this level (which is different for each person). Comparing different groups within the population, therefore, shows that people with higher incomes consume less of their income than people with lower incomes, as expected. But comparing national aggregates at different times does not show a similar result because the proportion of people experiencing temporarily high income is balanced by the proportion receiving temporarily low income. As in Duesenberry's theory, the apparent contradiction vanishes.

Once the contradiction was eliminated, it ceased to be more than a historiographic curiosity. The new theories found their place in the explanation of the short-period stability of consumption when income fell during recessions. And here both types of theories gave much the same explanation. They both appealed to the durability of consumption plans and the time needed to change them. Duesenberry emphasized the difficulty of reducing consumption expenditures, in part because of the implied loss in social standing, which he compared with the ease of raising them and advancing in the social structure. The later theorists simply noted that the proportion of people with income below their long-run expectations is larger in recessions than the proportion of people earning more than this level. It follows that the proportion of people with relatively high consumption-income ratios is higher than the proportion with relatively low ratios, and the aggregate ratio is high. The ratio of consumption to income therefore rises during recessions. Equivalently, the level of consumption falls less than the level of income.

This brief discussion shows that—at least to a first approximation—the two types of theories explain the same previously puzzling phenomena. Yet the life-cycle and permanent-income theories have been incorporated into the mainstream of economic analysis, while the relative-income hypothesis of Duesenberry has been left to languish as a historical curiosity, like the one it was formulated to explain.[18]

The reasons are clear. The later theories resolved the empirical puzzle within the confines of traditional economic theory. They explained the apparent contradiction without abandoning the assumption of continuous instrumental behavior. They therefore preserved the integrity of economic theory. It is like a geometry class, where the problem is to subdivide an angle without using a protractor. To perform the required task with the aid of a protractor—sociological theory in Duesenberry's case—earns disapproval or worse, not the high marks attainable by efforts with traditional tools.

The life-cycle and permanent-income theories have been refined and extended in the years since their original publication, while the relative-income theory has not. But this heterodox theory has not vanished. It exists on the fringes of economics where it has recently received renewed attention. Several authors have expressed their growing disenchantment with the goal of continuous economic growth in terms of the relative-income hypothesis. The argument, with variations, goes like this: Any individual wants to increase his income in order to make progress within the social structure. But when everyone increases his income, no one has risen relative to others, and everyone's aspirations to rise in a stable social hierarchy are frustrated. Even though everyone desires economic growth, everyone is disappointed by the result. The parallel with Duesenberry's explanation of the anomolous consumption behavior is obvious, as is the reliance of this view on his resolution of the consumption puzzle.[19]

This reference to economic growth reveals the policy implications in the choice of behavioral model. The relative-income theory, by admitting the existence of social attitudes and aspirations, allows consideration of factors excluded from orthodox economics. Any model that explicitly recognizes different attitudes and diverse modes of behavior may be expected to lead to policy conclusions different from the traditional economic ones.

Another illuminating example of work at the boundary of economics concerns uncertainty. The theory of pure competition assumes that information is costless and that all consumers and producers know all information relevant to the decisions they make. This clearly is false, and two models to deal with the costs of information were put forward around

1960. One stayed within the conventional boundaries of economics and has been incorporated into the mainstream of the discipline. The other breached the intellectual walls and has been neglected by economists as a result.

As with consumption, the earlier theory was the heterodox one. Herbert Simon proposed, in the terms introduced here, that the assumption of continuous instrumental behavior be replaced by assumed customary behavior. In his terms, maximizing behavior was replaced by "satisficing" behavior. This new term described behavior that did not ceaselessly strive for efficiency, but rather followed tradition or habit if the results—measured in some crude way—were not too bad. When the result of this customary behavior diverged too far from the goals of the person or organization acting, search behavior was instituted to find a better way of operating. As described by Simon, searching is an example of instrumental behavior, and the transition from satisficing to searching in his model is precisely the change from customary to instrumental behavior in the model presented here. Going further, Simon noted that if the divergence between experience and goals was too great, "emotional" behavior might result. Simon clearly had in mind a third mode of action, although the parallel between "emotional" and command behavior may be strained. Nevertheless, Simon articulated a theory based on discrete modes of behavior in which people did not maintain instrumental behavior continuously over their careers.[20]

The motivation for this theory was Simon's contention that it was too costly for people or for organizations to process continuously the information needed for even moderately complex decisions. To avoid these costs, people switched from instrumental to customary, satisficing, behavior. In contrast to Duesenberry's argument, the social aspects of personality play no role. Instead, the noise in the environment and the lack of simple connections between actions and results promote the use of customary behavior. In terms of figure 3, economic theory locates people in the instrumental area. Duesenberry located people below that area, while Simon put them to the left of it. Although quite different, the two theories can be seen as diverse expressions of the same underlying model.

George Stigler, writing shortly after Simon, looked at the other side of the information problem. Retaining the assumption of continuous instrumental behavior, Stigler asked how much costly information a firm would supply or a person acquire. The answer was that the firm would provide information up to the point where the expected gain of issuing the last scrap of information equaled the cost of issuing it, and that the person would accumulate information up to the point where the value of the last unit of information gathered equaled the cost of obtaining it. In economic language, they would issue and gather information until the marginal value of the information equaled its marginal cost.[21] On this foundation, Stigler and later writers constructed a theory of economic search, investigating the costs and gains from different stopping rules, the responses to different costs of information, the price structures compatible with costly information, and the role of costly information in explaining unemployment.[22]

As with the consumption function, the orthodox theory of Stigler has been extended and elaborated by economists until it has become an integral part of economic theory, while the heterodox theory of Simon has not. Fortunately, neglect by economists does not mean total neglect. Simon's ideas have been widely used outside of economics, where they do not rupture the boundaries of an academic discipline, and they have recently received some attention from economists as well. Attempts have been made to formalize the concept of satisficing behavior and to draw implications from these formulations about economic behavior.[23]

Both these examples show that certain problems within economics have stimulated work on the edges of the discipline. They also show that the discipline itself is very conservative, preferring an orthodox solution—that is, one that maintains traditional assumptions—to a more eclectic one.

Two terms in common use within economics today reveal this conservatism from a different vantage point, while showing also that the effort to combine elements from distinct academic disciplines still continues. The terms are *internal labor markets* and *implicit contracts.*[24] Both are noteworthy for their paradoxical nature. Internal labor markets are not markets, and implicit contracts are not contracts. They are both terms for noninstrumental behavior, but the words disguise the behavior as instrumental to locate it within economics.

Peter Doeringer and Michael Piore's well-known book on internal labor markets showed that labor was not allocated within firms by means of a market. They described and analyzed the mix of customary and command behavior used within firms in order to describe it and to distinguish it from the way labor is allocated among firms. To distinguish it from what is normally called a labor market, they had to coin a new term. But instead of selecting a totally different phrase, they chose to modify the usual term instead.

This is a curious phenomenon. It is as if green were to be called "proto-red" or "near blue." It identifies the behavior within firms in terms of the behavior among firms. It both affirms the difference by drawing explicit attention to it and denies it by approaching the internal behavior as a type of external behavior. It is as if there are several types of labor markets, internal and external, but all forms of labor organization are markets. Since Doeringer and Piore wanted explicitly to introduce into the economics literature a consideration of administrative and customary behavior, they did not want to be rejected by the discipline as "foreign." The noninstrumental behavior consequently was smuggled in in disguise.

The same analysis holds for implicit contracts. The dominant characteristic of implicit contracts is that they are not contracts at all, not conscious agreements by two parties that are communicated in some explicit way. Implicit contracts are customs, yet economists almost universally refer to them as implicit contracts. As with internal labor markets, the terms appears to be designed to retain the discussion within economics. Contracts are willful actions by consenting individuals or groups. They fit easily within the instrumental model of behavior. But custom, for obvious reasons, does not. Labeling customs as implicit contracts allows the inference that people have "implicitly" agreed to them. Their implicit agreement can be analyzed as if it were explicit, and the existence of custom can be more or less forgotten.

This appears clearly in an important article by Arthur Okun. He discussed inflation in two different kinds of markets, which he called auction and customer markets. An auction market is the traditional economic market. A customer market, by contrast, is one with "an established customer-supplier relationship" where the customer's and supplier's "interdependence puts a premium on maintaining the relationship." It is not a market based on exchange so much as a customary pattern of action based on a reciprocal relationship. In Okun's words: "The supplier obviously cannot promise the customer that he will offer the same deal forevermore. In particular, he may have to raise his price if his costs rise. But he can promise to treat the customer 'fairly' on all the dimensions of their transactions, thus offering the customer an implicit contract. It remains implicit because of the high cost of spelling out and negotiating the terms of an explicit, formal contract."[25] The key words in this passage are *promise* and *offer,* which are metaphors rather than descriptions. Okun did not imagine a supplier making a verbal or written promise to each customer to treat him "fairly." Nor did he have a vision of this supplier physically offering an implicit contract—"Here is an implicit contract!"—to the customer. The language is the language of exchange, but the process being described here is a reciprocal relationship.

Once we recognize that reciprocity rather than exchange is at issue and that there is no precise agreement on and calculation of "fairness" in the relationship, we can see that the preservation of the relationship itself becomes an important part of the interaction. Okun said that an explicit contract is not used because of its high cost. This implies that both parties want a formal contract and would have one if it were cheaper. But a formal contract would destroy the reciprocal relationship by eliminating the expectation of reciprocity. It would substitute market transactions for the expectation of "fair" dealing. It might not be desired—even if available—by either party. Okun's reliance on the economic metaphors led him into the implicit assumption that people strive always to exhibit instrumental behavior and are frustrated only by high costs. This will be true in some cases, but there clearly are others where the parties involved would rather use customary behavior and reciprocal relationships than instrumental behavior and explicit bargains.[26]

The characteristics of Okun's article pervade the economics literature on implicit contracts. There is an underlying assumption that instrumental behavior is preferred by all parties. In any long-term arrangements, this assumption leads to the inference that explicit contracts are desired. Only the cost of drawing up such contracts prevents their universal use. And whenever they cannot be used, implicit contracts—containing everything except actual agreement—are used instead. The literature describes customary behavior without ever admitting its existence.[27]

The works just discussed focus on the mode of behavior being used, but they also discuss the institutional structure within which the actions take place. Doeringer and Piore, in particular, explore the relationship between behavior and institutional arrangements.

To the extent that there is a theory of institutional change within economics, however, it conflicts with the model presented here. This theory starts from the work of James Buchanan and Gordon Tullock, and it regards all institutional change as the result of decisions made in the instrumental mode. In its dominant example, a governmental hierarchy is imposed over part of the economy to reach a well-defined goal. The model presented here allows that behavior as one case, but argues that many institutional changes take place in response to a change in the mode of behavior.[28]

Since economists concentrate on the description of instrumental behavior, it is natural that work on the edges of economics deals with the boundaries between instrumental and other behavior and between markets and other institutions. To find work on the other boundaries, those between customary and command behavior and between communal and hierarchical structures, we need to turn to sociology. A book by Peter Blau provides an elegant introduction to this problem. Without exploring in detail the reasons for a change in behavior, Blau analyzes the process by which deviations from normal customary behavior can lead to an institutional change from a community to a hierarchy.[29]

Blau's work can be considered as an answer to the question, What happens when a social exchange is not completed? This is a question outside the scope of economics, which assumes that exchanges are completed. One might even think of economics as the study of completed transactions. Aside from the subject matter—social as opposed to economic exchange—Blau's basic conceptualization of the problem is drawn from outside of economics. The frequent references in Blau's book and in the discussion here to economic concepts should not disguise this important fact.

Since the nature of communication in the three modes of behavior differs, the implications of uncompleted interactions should be considered for each. The basic form of interaction for instrumental behavior is an explicit trade, purchase, sale, or barter. If these trades are sanctioned by law, then failure of one party to pay or to deliver his side of the bargain will result in some kind of legal (command) action to compel completion of the trade or make restitution for deviations from the anticipated exchange. If the trades are not covered by law or are too small to invoke the costly procedures of the law, failure to complete a transaction will result in an unwillingness on the part of the injured party to enter into future bargains—a loss of business. Interaction in command behavior consists of orders, and refusal to obey orders leads typically to punishment—financial, physical, or other—of the recalcitrant. As in instrumental behavior, inability to impose these sanctions erodes the command relationship.

The simplest form of personal interaction in the customary mode is reciprocity. People help one another or provide services for one another and expect to receive help or services in return. There is no formal accounting, and no one—outside of a few status-seeking hostesses—keeps careful track of what is owed. But there is a clear sense of obligation when a favor has been received and a clear expectation that a hand extended will be reciprocated in some way.

Within this framework, Blau lists five options open to a person desiring some kind of service or help from another. He can supply services in return, that is, reciprocate. He can seek an alternate source for the desired service. He can, if he has the means, coerce the supplier. He can do without. Or, if he has no alternative, he can indicate that he will comply with the supplier's wishes in some other unspecified matter, that is, he can give the person supplying him authority over him. In Blau's words, "The absence of the first four alternatives defines the conditions of power in general."[30]

Blau does not dwell on the reasons a person might find himself in the position of wanting something for which he cannot pay immediately, but which he cannot do without. His prose seems to imply that the person has fallen into this position by mistake or inadvertence. If so, Blau is guilty of the same kind of solipsism as economists who assume that people always want to act in the behavior mode that they study—and adopt others only under stress. Economists assume that all people want to act instrumentally in market settings; Blau appears to be assuming that all people want to act customarily in community settings. The contrast between these two statements shows immediately that neither can be true. It is possible, therefore, that Blau's apparently hapless individual may instead be someone who wants to change from customary to command behavior in response, say, to an increase in the possibility of loss from unpredictable changes in the environment.

To recapitulate the argument so far: reciprocal interactions create or continue social bonds between peers. Interactions that are not reciprocated (for whatever reason) create status differentials. The person doing something for another without immediate return has a claim on the other. It is this claim that comprises his power. It follows that a major reason for reciprocating favors of all sorts is the desire to avoid becoming subordinate to another person.

The power to command compliance with your wishes is like credit. It is accumulated by doing things for others, and it is diminished by use, although people with enough power can have their wishes carried out without losing a great deal. Carrying the analogy with capital further, it is as if they are spending only the "interest" from their stock of power.[31]

The analogy with credit cannot be taken too far, however. In contrast to economic exchanges, social exchanges entail unspecified obligations. There is no way to bargain over the "price" of an activity, that is, over the size of the reciprocal obligation. Nevertheless, it is present, and there are a variety of sanctions that can be used against people who neither reciprocate nor acknowledge the obligation for the future they have incurred: termination of the possibility of future social interactions, termination of trust, loss of reputation, and guilt (if the sense of obligation has been internalized). And it is possible to detect gross changes in the rate of exchange of different services, which are caused by changes in the supply and demand for the services in question.

The power gained by assymmetric interactions becomes institutionalized when the simple exchange of benefit for obligation becomes transformed into two exchanges. The transformation is initiated when a person or organization delays gratification, that is, allows unreciprocated services to accumulate. Individuals benefiting from these services exchange compliance with the directives of the powerful person or institution for the approval of their peer group. The group exchanges group compliance for the benefit to the common welfare. The authority is institutionalized when the second of these exchanges becomes part of the group's culture. Power then derives from the institutional forms of the power, that is, from a hierarchical institution, not from current exchanges. And as long as these institutions retain enough compliance from the majority of people to be viable, they can impose their power on dissident minorities.[32] The shift from community to hierarchy is complete. Unreciprocated customary actions create the setting for command behavior. As the command behavior becomes institutionalized, the link to the original customary behavior fades into the background.

Within communities, a similar process extends the scope for social interactions beyond the immediate acquaintances of an individual. The existence of social norms provides a substitute for direct reciprocity between individuals. Instead of performing an action in the expectation of reciprocity from the person affected, people act to get social approval. And the group as a whole cooperates in the maintenance of the social structure because of the mutual benefits it confers. The direct interaction between individuals then is mediated through the group. People give charity without expectation of direct return. They vote in full knowledge that a single vote will not sway the election. They act in conformity with social norms, both imposed by the group they belong to and internalized as a result of past associations. Doctors, for example, refrain in general from excessive social contact with patients, lest the reciprocal needs of these individual contacts overwhelm the social obligations of their profession and lead them to deviate from their professional norms. The hierarchical institution is stable since the society's norms lead to customary behavior consistent with it. The shaded off-diagonal cell in figure 7 therefore is stable.[33]

This brief review of a varied literature shows that components of the model just presented have been discussed from different points of view by authors starting with different questions and often from different disciplinary backgrounds. But none of these authors has tried to mold these components into a single model, presumably because they were working on questions that did not suggest the need for a comprehensive model.[34]

The model just presented therefore should be thought of as synthetic, as drawing together strands from different traditions, rather than as hypothesizing the existence of a new form of action. It provides a tool for thinking about which form of behavior will be used in various settings and about the relative merits and stability of different institutional structures when faced with different modes of behavior. It must now be used to think about the nature of public policy toward medicinal drugs.

NINE

The Role of Government
in the Drug Market

THE VARIOUS THREADS running through the preceding discussion can be drawn together and woven into a set of proposals for public policy toward medicinal drugs. Several steps are needed to produce this fabric. First, an intellectual justification for government intervention in the drug market should be provided. Second, the development of actual government policy can be reviewed in light of both the model presented above and the justification for government policy derived from it. And finally, the analysis of previous policies leads naturally toward recommendations for future policy. Such recommendations can be compared with the provisions of the proposed Drug Regulation Reform Act of 1979, still pending in Congress, to reveal consistencies and differences between alternative recommendations for government policy.

A Justification for Drug Policy

The products sold in many markets change relatively slowly over time, giving rise to little change in the environment. These markets operate somewhere to the left of point T in the modal-choice box. Behavior in these markets consequently is a mixture of instrumental and customary behavior: This is shown by the circle in figure 8, which indicates the position of consumers in a fairly stable market. (People, we can assume, differ among themselves and are best represented in any spatial model by an area rather than a single point.) Customary behavior is more preva-

Figure 8

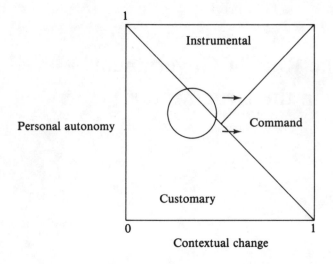

lent for the more static markets, and instrumental behavior—while never universal—is more common in less static ones. There is no demand for command behavior, and government policy is directed elsewhere.

Some markets, however, exhibit enough change and uncertainty to be found to the right of point *T*. Then there exists a demand for some kind of authoritative direction, which may be translated into government intervention, to change the institutional environment. As people move into the region of command behavior, markets appear less appropriate than hierarchical direction. There are many reasons, some better than others, why the government is active in different markets. Change and uncertainty form only one set, but it is a peculiarly important one for the history of drug regulation.

This can be demonstrated by reference to a relevant example introduced in the previous chapter. Under normal circumstances, a person's body more or less takes care of itself. Given the usual inputs and outputs, the internal mechanisms of the body maintain a rough equilibrium. Illness, however, destabilizes a person's environment; almost by definition, it represents increased change and uncertainty. If the illness is not a chronic one, the person becoming ill is subject to changes that are considerably harder to predict than usual. Given a store of knowledge in society that allows these changes to be seen as something other than acts of God, people tend to shift to the right in figure 8. They—or many of them— move into the region of command behavior. Being sick, they are not seeking to take charge. They are looking for someone else to do so. Indeed, one definition of illness is freedom from the obligation to act independently.[1] Sick people go to see doctors.

People have always gotten sick, but other, vast transformations have made the process today particularly disconcerting. Part of this uneasiness rests in the pace of unexplained change in the economy itself, which since the turn of the century has puzzled more than the common man. The "residual," that part of economic growth left unexplained by growth in the recognizable factors of production, increased sharply around 1900. At about the same time, the size of business firms rose and the scope of their activities expanded. The "Second Thirty Years War," including the two World Wars and the Great Depression, added to the sense of unexplained variation.

For most of the time since 1900, economic change in drugs has not been recognizably different from the average experience in other industries. After World War II, however, this changed dramatically. The drug industry became a center of technological change, of changes both in the way drugs were produced and in what drugs could be made.

The increasing awareness of general economic change gave rise to a general demand for command behavior, for some administrative control over the economy. This demand grew over time, with major additions during the World Wars and the Depression. After the conclusion of those troubles and conflicts, the special experience of the drug industry carried the impulse toward command behavior further in the drug area than in many other parts of the economy.

The two aspects of change—coming in turn from a person's illness and from the unpredictability of the economy and the drug industry—joined together in the postwar years as new drugs became increasingly effective against illness. The result was a multilayered command system. In its simplest form, the government stood at the top and the sick people at the bottom, with doctors in the middle. As the postwar period wore on, the unitary thrust of government policy as expressed through the Food and Drug Administration was replaced by a multifaceted policy originating at several levels of government. One result of this increasingly complex policy was to add to the intermediate—medical—levels of control as well. Another result was to create strains within the commanding hierarchy, some of which I have described.

In sum: The characteristics of the drug market today create demands for active intervention by some authoritative body. The combination of rapid change in the industry and the uncertainty felt by sick people locates this industry or area of choice to the right of point T in figure 8. It also places it further to the right than most other industries, giving rise to an unusually strong demand for active government policy.

Demands for a vigorous medicinal drug policy rose to a peak during the 1950s as the pace of discovery peaked. They resulted in a major extension of government jurisdiction over drugs during the 1960s, reflected in new legislative and regulatory mandates as well as in the expansion of the FDA. As the pace of technological change slowed and as people became more accustomed to the new drugs introduced in the 1950s, perceptions of how drugs are supplied changed. The supply of drugs was no longer seen by some people as more than usually subject to uncertainty and change. Some of the same people who had worked to get more regulation in the 1950s now argue for a relaxation of government intervention and a retreat from command behavior to instrumental and customary modes. Not everyone agrees with the perceptions or the recommendations of this vocal group—hence the current debate on drug regulation.

The debate is about control. This is a fundamental liberal dilemma. Recognizing that people left to their own devices are not able to solve all problems in an optimal way, how much control over them is justified? In terms of the model used here, how much command behavior is justified by the acknowledgment that not all unregulated behavior is instrumental? The answer to this question depends critically on people's perception of the political process. In particular, it rests on how much they value an open society. Since people cannot or will not always act instrumentally, increased openness implies costs in the form of inappropriate decisions made in a customary mode.

There is no assurance that command behavior will be closer to an optimum than customary, of course, although it is better adapted to situations of rapid change. The relevant costs of looser regulation are the additional ones imposed by relying on customary behavior—and any instrumental behavior that also exists—rather than command behavior. To the extent that instrumental and customary behavior are better than commands at allocating resources, these costs may be small or nonexistent. But assuming that they are present, the question involves weighing them against the gains of openness: flexibility, diversity, serendipity.

An Analytic Narrative

With these general considerations in mind, the history of drug revolution can be reviewed in terms of the model. The first part of the story is illus-

Figure 9

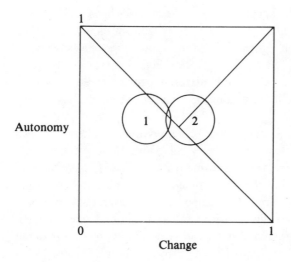

Figure 9

trated in figures 9 and 10. The first of these diagrams shows the mode of action used by drug consumers at two different times. The circles allow for diversity among people in their tastes and their perceptions; they are to be interpreted as a contiguous area of arbitrary shape. Similarly, the arrows in figure 10 show changes in either behavior or in structure that have taken place at different times.

Circle 1 in figure 9 represents the location of people at the turn of the century with respect to their purchases of drugs. Most people bought according to customary patterns, lacking the knowledge or inclination to do otherwise. Some people, as shown in the figure, undoubtedly made an ef-

Figure 10

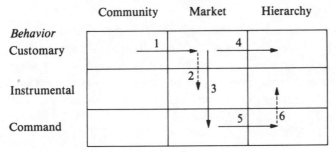

fort to act instrumentally againt all odds. The changes in the economy at that time pushed people out of a community organization into a market, as shown in arrow 1 in figure 10. This movement was not specific to drugs, but affected that market along with others. Instead of relying on locally formulated compounds and mixtures, people increasingly consumed medicines made by companies known only through their advertisements and products.

In this context, the 1906 Pure Food Act represented an attempt to deal with the disharmony between customary behavior and market structure. The Bureau of Chemistry, which became the FDA, would have liked to go further than it did, but it was restricted to informing the consumer about the composition of drugs. This knowledge was useful only if people took it into account in making decisions; it was an aid and an encouragement to the use of instrumental behavior. Accordingly, it is represented by the vertical arrow 2 in figure 10. The arrow is dashed, however, because the movement from customary to instrumental behavior never took place. Structure adapts to behavior more easily than behavior adapts to structure.

In the two decades after 1930, events combined to move people to the right in figure 9, indicated by a movement from circle 1 to circle 2. Some events were general. The Depression and the war induced a desire for more directed behavior. Most people did not understand these shattering events and did not see them as providing scope for more instrumental behavior. Instead, they preferred command behavior. Other contemporary events were specifically related to drugs. The discovery of new drugs, starting with the sulfa drugs in the 1930s and continuing with the antibiotics and other drugs after the war, changed people's behavior in two ways. The sheer number of new drugs made guidance more attractive. And as more powerful drugs began to appear, they began to be used for increasingly ill patients. People taking drugs, consequently, were in a more dependent position than before—they were more sick. The more general changes in society and the changes in drugs combined to move people to the right in figure 9.

This movement, a change in behavior, appears in figure 10 as arrow 3. This change created pressure for a sympathetic change in the institutional structure through which drugs are supplied. The FDA responded by articulating a hierarchical arrangement in the provision of drugs that became increasingly important as the therapeutic revolution advanced. The growing dominance of this new structure is shown by the horizontal arrows 4 and 5, both of which lead from unstable into stable cells.

The 1938 Federal Food, Drug, and Cosmetic Act was the primary vehicle through which a hierarchical structure was put together. While the act continued the trend of encouraging instrumental behavior by insisting that drug suppliers furnish accurate and increasingly extensive information with their products, it also introduced hierarchical elements into the purchase of drugs. (The information requirements of the 1906 and 1938 laws, of course, represented commands from the government to the drug firms, but these commands did not specify either what could be sold or how it could be sold. The latter elements were new to the 1938 law.)

Two hierarchical arrangements, one in the law and one in the regulations implementing the law, are particularly important. First, all new drugs had to be proven safe before they were placed on the market. In order to avoid a repetition of the Elixir Sulfanilamide disaster, caveat emptor was abandoned. Instead of allowing drugs to prove themselves on the market, they had to meet a minimal quality standard before being sold. The burden of assuring safety was shifted from the consumer and the discipline of the market to the companies and the FDA.

Second, the FDA insisted that some drugs be sold only by prescription. Just as the FDA assumed discretion over which drugs could appear on the market, it gave to doctors discretion over which drugs could be used on any specific occasion. This requirement appears to have been introduced to permit an intermediate class of drugs to be sold. Not safe enough to be purchased unaided, not dangerous enough to be banned, these drugs would be purchased by prescription. From the vantage point of 1938, it is likely that this intermediate class of drugs looked quite small. The regulation served to soften the distinction introduced by the law; the doctor-patient hierarchy softened the impact of the FDA-consumer hierarchy.

From the consumer's point of view, this is almost the end of the story. Each person desirous of getting a potent drug now must seek out a doctor and follow his recommendations, and the pharmacist who actually supplies the drug is constrained to act only on the orders of a licensed physician. (Recall that arrows 4 and 5 in figure 10 point into stable cells.) But conditions have not remained as they were in the immediate postwar years. The rate of discovery of new drugs has slowed dramatically, and some people have begun to acquire confidence that they can choose them on their own.

In terms of figure 9, the reduced rate of introduction of new drugs has moved people back to the left, partway back again from circle 2 to circle 1. This has increased the proportion of people falling in the instrumental zone, which in turn has increased the demand for a market rather than a hierarchical structure. This demand is shown at the dashed vertical arrow 6, representing a minority demand for more consumer discretion in the use of drugs. Only very small changes in the environment, such as package inserts for patients, reflect this desire in practice.

This is just part of the story because it treats only the bottom of the hierarchical system initiated by the 1938 regulations of the FDA. We need also to examine the behavior of doctors and the structures within which they operated to complete the narrative.

The legal changes of the 1930s were followed by the therapeutic revolution of the 1940s and 1950s, which introduced many new and powerful drugs. Given the legal structure created in 1938, these drugs were introduced as prescription drugs. Instead of being a small intermediate class of drugs in between "safe" and "unsafe," prescription drugs became the dominant class of medicines available. The way in which drugs were marketed was totally transformed. People were no longer able to make customary or instrumental choices for most drugs; they could buy them only with prescriptions. The command hierarchy consequently acquired a pervasive second level. The FDA designated which drugs could be placed on the market, and individual doctors directed consumers to purchase specific drugs.

The effect of the legal and technological changes was to remove the choice among drugs from the consumer to the doctor. How did doctors make their selections? They appear to have relied on custom as much as consumers did previously. There was not enough information around to indicate a unique choice in many cases, and most doctors did not have the training or time to evaluate the alternatives in others. Prescribing habits were taught informally through clinical experience, and they varied over time in response to changes in the medical customs referred to as "good medical practice" and to personal contacts between drug company representatives (detail men) and physicians. Some doctors continued to use instrumental behavior as much as possible, and their views were important in shaping good medical practice and the FDA's legislative mandate.

In short, some doctors use the available drug information instrumentally, but most do not; the uncertainty surrounding drug prescribing is so large that most prescribing is done in the customary mode. The two circles in figure 11, unlike the analogous circles in figure 9, do not represent the same group of people at different times. Instead, they reveal the location of two subsets of doctors. Most doctors are at the location indicated by circle 1, while academic doctors appear to have been located around 1960 in the region indicated by circle 2. They were far more impressed by

Figure 11

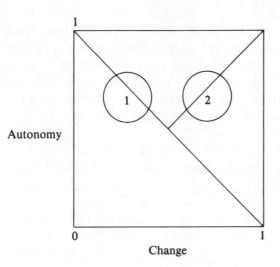

Autonomy

Change

the rapidity of change in the therapeutic arsenal than their nonacademic colleagues and far more interested in command behavior as a result. While few in number, their testimony before Congress in favor of the 1962 amendments to the 1938 act had far-reaching effects.

The 1962 amendments drew support from both groups of doctors. Neither customary nor command behavior fits comfortably into a market structure; a hierarchical structure is the only one into which both types fit without strain. This movement toward stable cells is shown as arrows 1 and 2 in figure 12. A hierarchical system was created within the medical establishment after 1962.

Figure 12

	Community	*Structure* Market	Hierarchy
Behavior Customary		1	→
Instrumental			↑ 3
Command		2	→

The Drug Amendments recognized the customary nature of prescribing habits. Doctors were seen in 1962 in the same light as consumers had been in 1938. Previous legislation had attempted to increase the extent of instrumental behavior by insisting that drugs carry full and accurate labels, but instrumental behavior never became dominant in the drug market. The alternative response to increased change in the environment was to introduce command behavior and hierarchical institutions; these were imposed by legislation and regulation.

Consumers were made subordinate to the choices of doctors in 1938, and practicing physicians were made subordinate to academic experts in 1962. The amendments of the latter year specified that drugs could only be sold if, in addition to being safe, there was substantial evidence of their effectiveness. The decision whether the existing evidence was substantial enough was delegated to academic experts in a series of measures introduced throughout the 1960s. Since the definition of effectiveness was interpreted to mean efficacy in treating illnesses specified on the drug's label, decisions about which drugs could be prescribed at all and about which drugs could be prescribed in specific cases were delegated increasingly to experts.

The post-1962 command hierarchy consequently has several levels. At the bottom are consumers, most often called patients to emphasize their subordinate role. They are subject to the commands of practicing doctors in their choice of drugs. (A few drugs, to be sure, can be bought without a doctor's prescription, but they represent a small proportion of the market and an even smaller proportion of the curative power of the modern pharmacopoeia.) With the consumers at the bottom of this pyramid are pharmacists, who are as constrained in what they can sell as the consumers are in what they can buy.

Above the consumers and pharmacists are practicing doctors, but they are subject in turn to the directives of the FDA. These directives, which specify what drugs can be prescribed and sometimes when they can be prescribed, originate either within the FDA or in councils of academic experts. These experts therefore are neither subordinate to the FDA nor above the agency. They are constrained by the FDA, as are clinical doctors, but the FDA also implements their directives as expressed in the reports of advisory committees and other quasi-official bodies.

The current command hierarchy thus has three distinct levels. Consumers and pharmacists occupy the bottom level. Clinical doctors occupy the second level. And the FDA and medical experts share the top level in a somewhat uneasy relationship.

As the hierarchy was being constructed, the conditions that gave rise to it began to change. Most importantly, the pace at which new drugs were introduced declined sharply after 1960. The new hierarchy itself was partly responsible for the fall. Its procedures sharply increased the cost of introducing new drugs and so discouraged some drug research. But this is not the whole story. Part of the decline in drug innovation was a reflection of events that were independent of the new command hierarchy. In addition, there was a general turning away from many aspects of government control of the economy. The changes that had seemed so dramatic and indicative of the need for command behavior became less unsettling over time, and people—losing faith with the confident predictions of the early 1960s—interpreted more of them as incomprehensible noise.[2] For both reasons, that is, because of developments within the drug industry and in the economy as a whole, the existing command hierarchy began to seem burdensome.

At the same time as consumers were reacting, doctors also perceived a reduction in the rate of change, which decreased the proportion of doctors in the command zone of behavior and increased it in the instrumental mode. This change altered the relative importance of circles 1 and 2 in figure 11 in favor of the former. It also is shown as the vertical arrow 3 in figure 12, which is dashed because it represents a shift of only some doctors. Those doctors are in an unstable cell. They are the medical critics of the 1962 Drug Amendments and of the regulatory interpretations of this law.

The existence of these medical critics of current drug policy and of a critical group of consumers (figure 10, arrow 6) highlights the central problem raised by these regulations. How much control there should be and whether the present amount exceeds or falls short of an optimum point are the pertinent questions.

Current Policy Alternatives

The amount and level of drug regulation can be assessed in relation to the risks of taking drugs described at the opening of this study. First, how can patients be protected from taking unsafe drugs? If anything, the press of congressional and public opinion has made the FDA overzealous in pursuit of drug safety, but increased safety is better sought at the level of prescribing—the doctors' level—than at the level of drug approvals. Doctors' prescribing habits do not follow the safest therapy very closely.

Good medical practice approximates the recommendations of academic medicine, but the approximation is quite loose and changes only slowly.

The second risk, that of not getting well through not being able to use a potent drug, is at the center of controversy over drug policy in academic medicine centers. Many doctors think that the FDA is restricting the supply of potent drugs. The FDA has maintained that this is not the case, but its figures have been contested. A more informed representation of FDA policy is that the supply of potent drugs is restricted in order to reduce other risks. To the extent that the debate has been within the medical community, this risk of harm from a drug has been emphasized, but the history of FDA policy suggests strongly that another risk is at least as important as determining this policy.

This third risk is that of not receiving value when purchasing a drug. The less important aspect of the risk relates to prices. It has received attention as a reflection of concern over the rising costs of medical care and as the locus of an attempt to get at the most visible—even if not the largest—part of medical costs. Drugs account for just under 10 percent of personal medical costs in the United States. But since other parts of medical costs are more extensively covered by insurance, the share of drugs in out-of-pocket medical payments by consumers is close to one quarter (table 25). Drug expenditures therefore loom larger in any individual's medical budget than they do in the national cost of medical care, and public concern over drug prices exceeds that warranted by their share of total medical costs.

Table 25. Components of personal health care expenditures, 1978 (dollars in millions).

Component	Total	Direct payment	Percentage of total	Percentage of total direct payment
Total	167,911	55,317	100	100
Hospital care	76,025	7,534	45	14
Physicians' services	35,250	12,013	21	22
Dentists' services	13,300	16,213	8	18
Other professional services	4,275	2,233	3	4
Drugs and drug sundries	15,098	12,667	9	23
Eyeglasses	3,879	3,478	2	6
Nursing home care	15,751	7,179	9	13
Other health services	4,333	—	3	0

Source: Robert W. Gibson, "National Health Expenditures, 1978," *Health Care Financing Review,* 1 (Summer 1979): 25.

Both state and federal governments recently have undertaken policies to reduce drug prices. These policies are still too new to show much effect, and they may be overshadowed by other changes in the supply of drugs. For example, the increased severity of drug regulation following the 1962 Drug Amendments and its attendant regulations have slowed the pace of drug introduction. According to the argument made earlier, this change will act to lower drug prices, simply because more drugs will be produced without patent protection. This effect may be more important than the government programs directly aimed at lowering drug prices.

The more important aspect of the risk of not getting value for money in drug purchases is the risk of buying an "innocuous" drug. Part of the cost is the price of the ineffective drug, and part is the foregone benefit that might have been obtained from a more effective drug. To the extent that the placebo effect is operating, so that a drug has an effect independent of its pharmacological action, these costs are reduced. But the net cost that results from these various influences has not been calculated in any but a few situations.

One such situation is presented by Laetrile, the "anticancer" drug widely believed to be ineffective and not currently approved as a drug by the FDA. The predominant medical opinion is that the cost of forgoing more effective treatment is very large, dwarfing both the cost of Laetrile itself and the placebo effect of taking it. Regulatory policy is designed to avoid that cost in the case of Laetrile. And it generalizes the case of Laetrile to other drugs, resulting in a regulatory policy that denies people the option of taking "innocuous" drugs to the maximum extent possible.[3]

Regulatory policy threfore confronts the consumer with the choice of not seeking medical care at all or using treatment that the FDA thinks efficacious. If, as in the case of much anticancer therapy, the treatment is painful or even disfiguring, people may elect to refuse it by not seeing a doctor. But they are not offered the choice of getting some benefit from being in the care of someone they trust without receiving the approved, burdensome treatment. They cannot opt for command behavior in time of confusion and stress without also getting a particular onerous program of therapy.

Why not? There would be little danger if the people who would opt for such an intermediate treatment would otherwise have avoided treatment altogether. But if the people who would seek such an intermediate position were those who would otherwise have received effective medical treatment, then there is a cost in terms of greater morbidity or mortality. Since these people would choose this less effective treatment, we must assume that they would rather have the less effective, but less painful, treatment than the approved one. This may be an informed or an uninformed choice, but it should not be ignored.

Current drug policy ignores it. By denying this choice, the policy restricts people more than it should. I would favor allowing people to choose this intermediate treatment position, although I would try to make sure that their choice was an informed one. But whether or not people are capable of understanding the relevant information, I still would favor giving people more choice for their own well-being than the current system allows.[4]

This conclusion assumes that people can make choices for themselves. To some extent this is a practical argument; people can and do make lots of important choices for themselves. And in part it is a moral argument; people should be allowed to make as many choices about their own lives as possible. There are, of course, common-sense exceptions to the moral argument. For example, Chad Green, a preschooler who died after Laetrile treatments for leukemia, clearly should not have been expected to choose and was not making choices of this magnitude for himself. The question in his case was who should make the choice for him: his parents, the courts, or a regulatory commission. But the question for adults is whether they should allow themselves to be regarded—as was Chad Green—as irresponsible, or whether they should be seen as responsible for their own treatment. Given the fallible nature of people, this is a liberal dilemma in our society.

The question of responsibility underlies the current debate about consumer product legislation in general and medicinal drug regulation in particular. But the literature on this legislation and regulation often diverts attention from the problem of individual choice. For example, institutional structures responsible for the containment of choice can be criticized on two grounds. They may be inefficient in accomplishing the goals set for them. They may be inappropriate mechanisms, or applied in an inconsistent way, or conflict with other institutions. But quite separately, people may criticize institutional arrangements because they disagree with the aims the institutions were designed to further or that they set themselves after the fact. The two types of criticism often overlap in the analysis of medicinal drug policy, since people with different goals may also analyze the efficiency of institutions differently, but these criticisms need to be distinguished conceptually to reduce the risk of discussing differences in goals under the guise of discussing the methods of achieving these goals.

In a prominent example of this confusion, the literature on the "drug lag" purports to be concerned with means, asserting that the FDA is keeping helpful drugs off the American market. Seeing no offsetting loss from having access to these drugs, the FDA's critics have accused it of inefficiency in pursuing known ends. This criticism, however, misses its mark because the difference is not one of procedure, but one of goals. The approval process in the United States is slow because the FDA is anxious to deny "innocuous" drugs access to the market. These drugs by definition do not have harmful side effects. Their availability consequently does not appear as a problem in the "drug-lag" literature. But it is a severe problem to the FDA.

One way to visualize the difference is to note that the FDA's critics focus on the drugs themselves, while the FDA is concerned with the choice among drugs. (As with any abstraction, this one distorts at the same time that it clarifies. The argument certainly should not be taken to imply that the FDA is not concerned with the drugs themselves.) The critics quote the medical literature on the effects of the drugs they want to have available in the United States. They do not discuss who would use them or whether the procedures that would clear these drugs would clear other drugs as well. Wardell argued recently, for example, that "if practolol [a beta-blocker currently unavailable in this country] were available and used optimally, . . . it would save at least 10,000 lives a year."[5] His use of the qualifying phrase, "if used optimally," reveals his lack of concern for how this drug might actually be used in ordinary practice. The FDA, by contrast, thinks that the procedures that would clear more potent new drugs would also clear some innocuous drugs. The presence of these drugs would lead to their use when more potent drugs would be appropriate, in the FDA's view, and this cost of forgone aid—this opportunity cost, in the jargon of economics—weighs heavily on the agency.

Peeling off another layer of the argument exposes another way of seeing the conflict. The FDA's critics do not worry about the opportunity costs of drug misuse because they assume that drug prescribers and (to a lesser extent) users act instrumentally. While the presence of innocuous drugs on the market imposes a cost on these people—they have to learn that they are innocuous—the costs are not major. The FDA assumes that doctors act customarily and that they are quite likely to use an innocuous drug if it is available. The expected costs of having innocuous drugs are larger with the assumption of instrumental behavior.

The argument about behavior is empirical and should be amenable to resolution by empirical evidence. Some evidence along that line was presented above, where it was argued that physicians' drug choices were by necessity largely customary. Some of the present critics of the FDA argued in a similar vein when the 1962 Drug Amendments were being considered by Congress. It is hard to know whether their views or the world has changed in the interim to produce their disagreements with current FDA policy.

Despite the relevance of empirical data on doctors' behavior, we are not yet at the underlying problem. For even if their behavior is customary, the costs of their prescribing innocuous drugs may not appear as large to critics as they appear to the FDA. There are two reasons for this. First, the critics simply may not think that the costs of using innocuous drugs—the opportunity costs—are as large as the FDA implicitly asserts. Second, and more importantly, the critics may argue that the freedom of choice implied by the looser FDA policy that would allow the foreign drugs to be introduced in the United States is a value in itself. With this change in focus from drugs to choices and from medicine to political theory, we come to the center of the problem. It is the problem of drug regulation as a whole, not just of the drug lag.

Taking your medicine is a risky business. It is one risk among many in an uncertain world. There are ways to reduce the risk from taking medicine, but each reduction has a cost. The risk can never be eliminated entirely, and the pursuit of riskless therapy will become ever more costly without reaching its goal. Any other, more realistic goal implies the acceptance of some risks. The question, then, is how risky this aspect of life should be, or, conversely, how many choices should be reserved to the people?

The pace of drug discovery has slackened considerably since the last major revision of drug regulation in the 1960s (table 2). In fact, the change in regulatory posture has helped to decrease the rate of innovation as we have seen. But whatever the cause, the decrease itself has changed the context of drug regulation. As the number of new drugs put on the market each year has fallen, the average age of drugs on the market has risen. Doctors and consumers consequently have more opportunity to acquire information about the drugs they are using. In other words drugs have become less mysterious over the last decade.

Some people, the more autonomous ones, have switched from command to instrumental behavior in their choice of which drug to take in any specific instance. They have moved to the left in the behavioral diagrams (figures 9 and 11). The result is to produce the broken arrows in figures 10 and 12, showing a movement into the cell with instrumental behavior and hierarchical structure.

This is an unstable situation. The disharmony between behavior and institutional structure creates pressure for change in the institutional structure, which is apparent in the literature on drug regulation today. Since the people who have moved into the region where instrumental behavior is indicated also tend to be articulate and vocal, the debate over drug policy is likely to increase in intensity. If regulation continues along its present path, more and more people will shift into the instrumental mode, generating more and more criticism of current policy.

Two questions arise as a result of this view. First, the pressure for a revision of drug regulation has already resulted in a bill before Congress, the Drug Regulation Reform Act of 1979. How responsive is that bill to the considerations noted here? Second, leaving aside the current proposals for change, are there any statements one might make about the desirable nature of change in drug regulation?

In response to the first question, the Drug Regulation Reform Act of 1979 could either promote or impede granting doctors and consumers more choices about the drugs they use. On the one hand, the particular provisions of the proposed law appear to encourage more choices. On the other, the bill as a whole appears to restrict them. To start with the particular, the bill contains provisions to speed the appearance of new drugs onto the market. Two channels are proposed. The FDA would be empowered to approve a drug provisionally for up to three years. This would allow a drug to be sold on the American market before the FDA was willing to commit itself to a firm position on its safety and effectiveness. In addition, a "drug treatment investigation" would be introduced to allow drugs not yet approved to be used therapeutically under investigational new drug (IND) status. The distribution of these new drugs would be monitored under the IND program, which maintains more FDA control than the provisional approval.[6]

In addition, the distribution of newly approved drugs could be restricted for three years and surveillance required for five. This would allow the FDA to approve new drugs about which it was still unsure more quickly than it does now, since it would not lose control over their distribution with its approval.[7]

The bill also contains provisions to speed the flow of generic drugs to the market. When a new drug is approved, information about it would be collected into a "monograph." This monograph would be available publicly within four months, and it would be distinct from a license to produce the drug. The license would be granted only to the firm submitting the information in the monograph for the first five years, but available to any firm meeting good manufacturing practices after that. In other words, the legal status of generic producers would be clarified, and the FDA would not stand in the way of the production of generic drugs—as long as control of their quality was assured. Of course this change in regulation would not in any way alter the status of drug patents. To the extent that patents were still valid after the initial five-year period of drug approval, they still would restrict competing production of a drug.[8]

Each of these measures can be criticized. The public monograph system may undercut the profitability of drug companies by revealing trade secrets. And the possibility of restricting distribution could be used by the FDA to restrict the availability of drugs that would otherwise have been generally available, rather than to make partially available drugs that would not otherwise have been available at all. These are real problems, and they should be investigated.[9] But they should not be allowed to obscure the purpose of these measures: to make more drugs available in America.

These provisions of the 1979 bill also must be seen in the context of the proposed legislation as a whole. They must be weighed against the many other provisions and against the combined thrust of the bill's directives. While the provisions I have cited move in the direction of looser controls over drug approval, the bill as a whole would give the FDA tighter control, if only by its ability to write regulations interpreting the bill's myriad provisions. This raises the possibility that the legislation, by its structure and complexity rather than its particular provisions, would result in tighter FDA control over the flow of new drugs to the market. Certainly, the history of the FDA and drug regulation makes this outcome more likely than not. And to the extent that this is the probable result of the proposed legislation, it suggests that the bill, if passed, would result in fewer, not more, choices being available to drug consumers.

That outcome would represent a step backward. It would intensify the existing debate about drug regulation, place the FDA in an even more embattled position than it is now, and blur once more the central issue of how much drug risk is acceptable. It would fail to take account of recent changes in the drug industry. And it would—unnecessarily in my view—restrict the scope of individual choices.

Moving in the opposite direction of widening drug choices would be hard. The difficulties do not reside in the legislation; the Drug Regulation Reform Act could easily be interpreted to allow for looser drug regulation, if only by emphasizing the provisions just noted over others in the bill. There are two barriers to a freer market for drugs, one of which is in the FDA itself.

The FDA has been monitoring the supply of medical drugs for three-quarters of a century. As the preceding narrative has demonstrated, the agency has followed and developed certain regulatory themes in the course of this long history, and these aspects of drug regulation are by now built into the very structure of the FDA. We cannot identify all the ways in which the traditions or customs of the FDA are maintained, whether through the longevity of employees, promotion policies, the socialization of new employees, or whatever, but we can be sure that they are there.

For purposes of this discussion, the most important facet of FDA regulation is the agency's expression of its conviction that individuals—both doctors and consumers—cannot make reasonable choices among drugs. As a result the FDA has undertaken to control the decision of which drug to use, beginning in 1906 with the listing of ingredients, progressing to keeping some drugs off the market, and then to shaping drug labeling. In addition, the agency tried with increasing success to deny drug prescribers and users the option of taking "innocuous" drugs, that is, to force them to use the drugs the FDA regards as appropriate for their condition.

It would be hard for the FDA to reverse field and work to loosen its hold on drug choices. If there were sufficient legislative and popular pressure on the agency to do so, it might slowly move in that direction, but the political pressures do not push in that direction. They push toward more, not less, control because of the difficulty people have in dealing with low-probability events. The second barrier to looser controls comes from the public response to drug tragedies.

Both the theoretical work on the perception of probability and the reactions to drug tragedies chronicled above support the conclusion that people have great difficulty understanding the nature of low-probability events. It is one thing to say that a certain unpleasant event has a probability of one in 50,000, or, equivalently, that it can be expected to happen randomly once in each 50,000 trials. It is quite another to contemplate this unlikely event after it has happened and acknowledge that it is an unfortunate outcome of a random process. People are much more likely to try to explain why this event happened on this trial rather than some other or to attempt to discover how it might have been avoided.

These questions surely have their uses. It is through efforts like these that scientific progress is made and public policy developed. But they also cloud the stochastic nature of the events in question. Society cannot embrace a public policy embodying risks unless it can also acknowledge the existence of these risks. Adverse drug reactions—however much they may be seen as true risks in the abstract—always appear to be deterministic events after the fact. For better or for worse, adverse drug reactions do not fit into the category of acts of God, like hurricanes, earthquakes, and floods.

A change in thinking, therefore, is an essential prerequisite to a change in the direction of drug regulation. People must be able to acknowledge the stochastic component of taking drugs and to live with bad throws of the dice when they come up. This does not mean that some drugs are not better than others or more appropriate than others in specific cases. There are choices to be made, and we should try to make the best choices possible. But even after these best choices are made, there is still some unreduceable risk in taking drugs.

Letting more drugs onto the American market would increase both the chance of having adverse drug reactions and the chance of finding a drug appropriate to any given condition. Stated differently, it would increase both the chance of getting sick from taking a drug and of getting well from taking a drug. It is not possible at the current moment to say which chance is increased more, but the literature on the "drug lag" is full of implicit assertions that the risk of getting well would be increased by the larger amount. More work on this question would be exceedingly useful.

Even if research shows that more drugs are better, in the sense that more people gain from having the additional drugs available than are harmed by adverse reactions from them—another question still remains. The people who will be helped by the new drugs are not the same as the people who will be hurt. What can we do for the people who are hurt?

These people clearly can be compensated for their medical costs and the income they might have lost by being sick. The more comprehensive our medical insurance is, the more likely they are to be covered in any case. But this compensation by its nature must be incomplete. There is no way to compensate suffering people for their suffering, or their relatives and associates for any related problems. To make the point dramatically, there is no adequate compensation for death.

It follows that people must be willing to accept some uncompensated risk. People do this all the time in other areas. They drive cars, they smoke, they do not fully insure themselves even when it is possible. In order for the direction of drug regulation to be changed, people would have to be willing to bear more risks with drugs. This does not mean that the monetary compensation or the drug firms' liability for drug reactions should be reduced, but rather that people should not try to go beyond these partial redresses or try to get full "redress" by avoiding the risk altogether. Their "redress" must be that the social policy under which they were harmed is a beneficial one, or phrased negatively, that the attempt to eliminate the risk under which they suffered would do more harm than good.

In terms of the framework used by Blau to explain the growth of hierarchies, people would have to accept the added drug risk as a social obligation. Just as people vote or give charity to support an institutional structure that provides general benefits to society, they would have to accept the possibility of severe discomfort or disability to sustain a beneficial drug policy. It is easy to demonstrate that the probability of a severe accident is small, but that does not seem to be the key to popular acceptance. Instead, people have to identify their personal misfortune as a randomly distributed "cost" of a policy that has in the aggregate more benefits than costs.

It is hard for people to think this way, partly because it is a difficult way to think and partly because the line between avoidable and unavoidable risks in medicine is neither obvious nor static. We are constantly being told that previously incurable conditions can now be treated and that previously approved activities are now thought harmful. In such a context, it is hard to separate out the things that must be endured for the common good from those that could and should be avoided.

Granted the difficulty of implementing a program allowing more drugs to be available, how would such a program look? It is quite easy to outline one such program. The one I have in mind combines less surveillance at the premarket level and more surveillance, of a particular kind, at the prescription level.

Reduced premarket surveillance can be gained by implementation of the sections of the Drug Regulation Reform Act of 1979 already discussed. They empower the FDA to make tentative, limited decisions about drugs before all the information is in. They provide the agency with the opportunity to change its mind about the conditional release of a drug or to restrict the availability of an experimental new drug by use of the therapeutic IND. If the FDA used these various provisions for tentative release of drugs that would otherwise not be released or would be released only more slowly—as opposed to using them to tie up drugs that would have been released for sale in any case—that would go far toward changing drug policy in the direction recommended.

This policy shift, if undertaken, needs to be complemented by other actions. With more new and experimental drugs on the market, consumers would need to be assured that doctors will not prescribe them wantonly. The attempt to monitor each and every prescription is self-defeating. It is prohibitively expensive, and it is probably actively harmful as well. Detailed surveillance would have to be codified. These rules would change slowly, and medical practice would lose a valuable element of flexibility. It would serve no purpose to reduce the impact of command behavior at the FDA level only to reimpose it at the doctor level.

Instead of trying to evaluate each prescription, public policy could assure that each physician licensed to prescribe drugs is qualified to make the choices that the expansive FDA policy would present to them. Rather than evaluating each prescription, this policy would evaluate the basic conditions under which the prescription was written. Physicians' qualifications could be tested by a periodic recertification program, similar to that adopted by several states.

Existing recertification programs for doctors, however, have a serious flaw. They do not examine the qualifications of the doctor; they inquire into the doctors' activities. Instead of measuring the output of the doctors' education, they measure the inputs. This is an indication of customary behavior: doctors are being recertified on the basis of their adherence to the customs of medical education.

Customary behavior is appropriate and even inevitable in many situations in medicine, but this is not one of them. There are many conclusions about drug therapy that are well-known and that should be known by any practitioner prescribing drugs. Doctors should periodically demonstrate that they have this knowledge in order to renew their license to prescribe drugs. In other words, recertification should be done through a test of some sort, rather than through accounting for hours spent in a classroom.

A recertification test need not be extensive. In fact, it cannot be esoteric by its very nature. The attempt is not to see if doctors know of the latest discoveries in some arcane field; it is to see if they have the basic knowledge of existing drugs in order to make comparisons with the claims for new ones. The test should be composed of basic questions that every doctor should be able to answer without thinking about them in order to find those doctors whose knowledge of drugs has been allowed to atrophy through disuse or other cause to the point where informed choices are not possible.

There could even be grades of licensing. Doctors who wanted to take a more stringent test might be in a category to make use of the therapeutic INDs or other experimentally released drugs. Special legislation might be introduced to allow the FDA to release drugs to a restricted set of doctors before general release, with admission to this set open to all doctors on the basis of their knowledge of drugs. In addition, there might be a simpler test for nurses or physicians' assistants that would let them prescribe a limited set of drugs. These drugs would be well-known drugs without serious side effects that could exist in an intermediate status between prescription and over-the-counter drugs.

This proposed plan is simply a prototype. It is designed to show the kind of system that might be used to provide for more choices in the taking of drugs, without simply allowing people to do as they please. Medicinal drugs are designed to be taken by sick people. Sick people by and large are desirous of opting out of decisions, of using command behavior. Given this peculiar aspect of the drug market, it would be inappropriate simply to sell the drugs to consumers. Aside from any other reasons why this policy would be bad, no one seems to want it. (Even if people want it in the abstract, chances are that they delegate their decision-making powers when they are sick.) The problem for policy, therefore, is to allow as much scope for individual choice and as much flexibility to take account of changing drug availability as is consistent with the dependent nature of sick people. We cannot and should not return to Holmes's 1911 dictum that therapeutic claims for drugs are protected by constitutional guarantees of the freedom of speech, but we can try to allow people and their chosen agents as much freedom of choice as is consistent with the care of sick people.

Notes

1. Introduction

1. Roger J. Traynor, "The Ways and Meanings of Defective Products and Strict Liability," *Tennessee Law Review,* 32 (Spring 1965): 368.

2. David F. Cavers, "The Evolution of the Contemporary System of Drug Regulation under the 1938 Act," in John B. Blake ed., *Safeguarding the Public: Historical Aspects of Medicinal Drug Control* (Baltimore: Johns Hopkins University Press, 1970), p. 170.

3. U.S. Department of Health, Education, and Welfare, *Task Force on Prescription Drugs: Report and Recommendations,* Committee Print of U.S. Congress, Senate, Subcommittee on Monopoly of the Select Committee on Small Business, 90th Cong., 2nd sess., 1968, p. 17.

4. Kenneth Arrow, "Uncertainty and the Welfare Economics of Medical Care," *American Economic Review,* 53 (December 1963): 941–973, separated the last two of these risks in his classic treatment of the economics of medical care.

5. U.S. Congress, Senate, Hearings before the Subcommittee on Health of the Committee on Labor and Public Welfare, *Examination of the Pharmaceutical Industry,* 93rd Cong., 1st and 2nd sess., 1973–1974.

6. As the term is used here, *drugs* are roughly the same as medicines. Narcotic regulation is largely distinct from the regulation of medicines, and it enters this study only tangentially. *Pharmaceuticals* is a more precise term than *drugs,* since it excludes illegal narcotics, but it has come to be too restrictive. It refers now to products used in the course of organized medicinal care. But the supply of drugs has changed greatly in the twentieth century, and pharmaceuticals (in this restricted sense) have risen in relative importance. Any history of regulation in this area cannot ignore the existence of nonpharmaceutical medicines in earlier years.

7. Morris Fishbein, *A History of the American Medical Association, 1847–1947* (Philadelphia: Saunders, 1947), pp. 35–37.

8. Thomas McKeown, *The Modern Rise of Population* (London: Edward Arnold, 1976), esp. p. 160; see also Victor R. Fuchs, *Who Shall Live? Health, Economics, and Social Choice* (New York: Basic Books, 1974).

9. U.S. Congress, Senate, Hearings before the Subcommittee on Antitrust and Monopoly of the Committee on the Judiciary, *Administered Prices in the Drug Industry,* 86th Cong., 1st and 2nd sess., 1960–1961; U.S. Congress, Senate, *Administered Prices: Drugs,* Senate Report 448, 87th Cong., 1st sess., 1961; U.S. Congress, Senate, Hearings before the Subcommittee on Monopoly of the Select Committee on Small Business, *Competitive Problems in the Drug Industry,* 90th Cong., 1st sess., to 94th Cong., 2nd sess., 1967–1977; U.S. Congress, Senate, Committee Print of Subcommittee on Monopoly of the Select Committee on Small Business, *Competitive Problems in the Drug Industry: Summary and Analysis,* 92nd Cong., 2nd sess., 1972; Richard Harris, *The Real Voice* (New York: Macmillan, 1964).

10. For the academic economic literature, see Henry Steele, "Monopoly and Competition in the Ethical Drugs Market," *Journal of Law and Economics,* 5 (October 1962): 131–164; Michael H. Cooper, *Prices and Profits in the Pharmaceutical Industry* (Oxford: Pergamon Press, 1966); Peter Costello, "The Tetracycline Conspiracy: Structure, Conduct and Performance in the Drug Industry," *Antitrust Law and Economic Review,* 1 (Summer 1968): 13–44; Harold Clymer, "The Changing Costs of Pharmaceutical Innovation," in Joseph D. Cooper, ed., *The Economics of Drug Innovation* (Washington, D.C.: American University Center for Study of Private Enterprise, 1970); Fred M. Scherer, "Discussion," in Cooper, *The Economics of Drug Innovation;* Hugh D. Walker, *Market Power and Price Levels in the Ethical Drug Industry* (Bloomington: Indiana University Press, 1971); Martin N. Baily, "Research and Development Costs and Returns: The U.S. Pharmaceutical Industry," *Journal of Political Economy,* 80 (January 1972): 70–85; Sam Peltzman, "An Evaluation of Consumer Protection Legislation: The 1962 Drug Amendments," *Journal of Political Economy,* 81 (September 1973): 1046–91; Robert Ayanian, "The Profit Rates and Economic Performance of Drug Firms," in Robert B. Helms, ed., *Drug Development and Marketing* (Washington, D.C.: American Enterprise Institute, 1975); Lester G. Telser et al., "The Theory of Supply with Applications to the Ethical Pharmaceutical Industry," *Journal of Law and Economics,* 18 (October 1975): 449–478; Erol Caglarcan et al., "Resource Allocation in Pharmaceutical Research and Development," in Samuel A. Mitchell and Emery A. Link, *Impact of Public Policy on Drug Innovation and Pricing* (Washington, D.C.: American University, 1976); David Schwartzman, *Innovation in the Pharmaceutical Industry* (Baltimore: Johns Hopkins, 1976); Kenneth W. Clarkson, *Intangible Capital and Rates of Return: Effects of Research and Promotion on Profitability* (Washington, D.C.: American Enterprise Institute, 1977); Henry G. Grabowski and Dennis G. Mueller, "Industrial Research and Development, Intangible Capital Stocks, and Firm Profit Rates," *Bell Journal of Economics,* 9 (Autumn 1978): 328–343; Henry G. Grabowski, John M. Vernon, and Lacy Glenn Thomas, "The Effects of Regulatory Policy on the Incentives to Innovate: An International Comparative Analysis," in Mitchell and Link, *Impact of*

Public Policy; Henry G. Grabowski, John M. Vernon, and Lacy G. Thomas, "Estimating the Effects of Regulation on Innovation: An International Comparative Analysis of the Pharmaceutical Industry," *Journal of Law and Economics,* 21 (April 1978): 133–164.

For the popular literature, see Morton Mintz, *By Prescription Only* (Boston: Beacon Press, 1967, rev. ed. of *The Therapeutic Nightmare,* 1965); James S. Turner, *The Chemical Feast* (New York: Grossman, 1970); Walter S. Measday, "The Pharmaceutical Industry" in Walter Adams, ed. *The Structure of American Industry,* 5th ed. (New York: Macmillan, 1977); John M. Blair, *Economic Concentration* (New York: Harcourt Brace Jovanovich, 1972); Milton Silverman and Philip R. Lee, *Pills, Profits, and Politics* (Berkeley and Los Angeles: University of California Press, 1974).

11. Richard Lyons, "Demoralized F.D.A. Struggles to Cope," *New York Times,* March 14, 1977, pp. 1, 49.

12. U.S. Congress, House, Citizens Advisory Committee on the Food and Drug Administration, *Report to the Secretary of H.E.W.,* 84th Cong., 1st sess., 1955; U.S. Department of Health, Education, and Welfare, *Task Force on Prescription Drugs;* U.S. Department of Health, Education, and Welfare, Review Panel on New Drug Regulation, *Final Report* (Washington, D.C.: Department of Health, Education, and Welfare, May 1977).

13. *The U.S. Generic Drug Market* (New York: Frost and Sullivan, 1976), p. 35.

14. For a recent FDA statement, see Donald Kennedy, "Generic Drugs," Address to the Annual Convention, House of Delegates, New York Medical Society, October 23, 1978. For an account of the industry's reaction to FDA policy, see Lynne M. Pauls and Baldwin E. Kloer, *FDA Enforcement Activities within the Pharmaceutical Industry: Analysis of Relative Incidence* (Indianapolis: Eli Lilly, 1978).

15. *Drug Topics Red Book* (Oradell, N.J.: Medical Economics Co., annual).

16. In cases like ampicillin and tetracycline where both generic and brand-name preparations exist, the former group is occasionally called commodity or unbranded generics and the latter, branded generics.

17. S. E. Berki et al., "The Mysteries of Prescription Pricing in Retail Pharmacies," *Medical Care,* 15 (March 1977): 241–250.

18. U.S. Food and Drug Administration, Drug Listing Branch, Bureau of Drugs, *National Drug Code Directory* (Washington, D.C.: Department of Health, Education, and Welfare, 1969–); *Physicians' Desk Reference* 33rd ed. (Oradell, N.J.: Medical Economics Co., 1979); *Drug Topics Red Book* (1979); Richard Burack, *The New Handbook of Prescription Drugs* (New York: Ballantine Books, 1975).

19. Sissela Bok, "The Ethics of Giving Placebos," *Scientific American,* 231 (November 1974): 17–23.

20. Norman Cousins, "Anatomy of an Illness (as Perceived by the Patient)," *New England Journal of Medicine,* 295 (December 23, 1976): 1458–63; or Norman Cousins, *Anatomy of an Illness as Perceived by the Patient* (New York: Norton, 1979).

21. Erik Juhl et al., "The Epidemiology of the Gastrointestinal Randomized Clinical Trial," *New England Journal of Medicine,* 296 (January 6, 1977):

20–22. The proportion of articles on gastroenterological therapy that reported the results of randomized clinical trials rose from 0.3 percent in 1964 to 1.7 percent in 1973, illustrating both the current avoidance and the growing attention to statistical trials.

22. Raymond A. Bauer, "Risk Handling in Drug Adoption: The Role of Company Preference," *Public Opinion Quarterly,* 25 (Winter 1961): 546–555; Theodore Caplow, "Marketing Attitudes: A Research Report from the Medical Field," *Harvard Business Review,* 30 (November–December 1952): 105–112; Theodore Caplow and John J. Raymond, "Factors Influencing the Selection of Pharmaceutical Products," *Journal of Marketing,* 19 (July 1954): 18–23; Robert Ferber and Hugh G. Wales, "The Effectiveness of Pharmaceutical Advertising: A Case Study," *Journal of Marketing,* 22 (1958): 395–407; Robert Ferber and Hugh G. Wales, *The Effectiveness of Pharmaceutical Promotion* (Urbana: University of Illinois Press, 1958); Ben Gaffin and Associates, *Report on a Study of Advertising and the American Physician* (Chicago: American Medical Association, 1953); Ben Gaffin and Associates, *The Fond du Lac Study: An Intensive Study of the Marketing of Five New Ethical Pharmaceutical Products in a Single Market, Resulting in Some Theory of Scientific Marketing and Service Programs for Action* (Chicago: American Medical Association, 1956).

23. Richard E. Nisbett and T. D. Wilson, "Telling More Than We Can Know: Verbal Reports on Mental Processes," *Psychological Review,* 84 (May 1977): 247. According to these authors, people do not have access to their own thought processes; they have no more insight into their own decision making than into the decision making of others. People answer questions about their motivation by making plausible inferences about factors that could have influenced the behavior in question, not by recalling their actual thoughts. They tell the investigator what *should* have caused the actions, according to their understanding, not what actually did.

One classic sociological study avoided this pitfall by observing doctors' actions directly through the examination of prescription records in addition to asking them to describe what they thought they were doing. See James S. Coleman, E. Katz, and H. Menzel, *Medical Innovation: A Diffusion Study* (Indianapolis: Bobbs-Merrill, 1966).

24. Marc Bloch, *Feudal Society* (Chicago: University of Chicago Press, 1961), pp. 113–116; Hans H. Gerth and C. Wright Mills, *From Max Weber: Essays in Sociology* (New York: Oxford University Press, 1946), pp. 51–55.

25. Richard M. Cyert and James G. March, *A Behavioral Theory of the Firm* (Englewood Cliffs, N.J.: Prentice-Hall, 1963).

26. The terms *custom* and *command* are taken from John Hicks, *A Theory of Economic History* (Oxford: Oxford University Press, 1969). In contrast to Hicks, who sees history in the Whig tradition of progress toward the goal of instrumental behavior, I see the three modes of behavior as coexisting or as supplanting one another from time to time.

27. Eliot Freidson, *Doctoring Together: A Study of Professional Social Control* (New York: Elsevier, 1975), pp. 8–11, 90–94, 240–259.

28. George Homans, "Social Behavior As Exchange," *American Journal of Sociology,* 63 (1958): 597–606; A. W. Gouldner, "The Norm of Reciprocity: A

Preliminary Statement," *American Sociological Review*, 25 (1960): 161–178. See Harold K. Schneider, *Economic Man: The Anthropology of Economics* (New York: Free Press, 1974), for a survey of the sociological and anthropological uses of this concept.

29. See William E. McAuliffe, "Measuring the Quality of Medical Care: Process versus Outcome," *Milbank Memorial Fund Quarterly: Health and Society*, 57 (Winter 1979): 118–152, for an argument that medical care as a whole should be evaluated by its inputs, not its outputs.

30. See Amitai Etzioni, *A Comparative Analysis of Complex Organizations*, rev. ed. (New York: Free Press, 1975), chap. 5, for a parallel categorization of behavior and institutions without this important second hypothesis.

2. Drug Regulation in the Progressive Era

1. The phrase is taken from the title of Morton White's classic study, *Social Thought in America: The Revolt Against Formalism* (London: Oxford University Press, 1976; first published in 1949).

2. A modern business organization can be defined as a firm that has many different operating units and which is managed by a hierarchy of salaried executives. Alfred Chandler, *The Visible Hand: The Managerial Revolution in American Business* (Cambridge, Mass.: Harvard University Press, 1977), p. 1.

3. This story is told in detail by Chandler, ibid.

4. Samuel P. Hayes, *The Response to Industrialism, 1885–1914* (Chicago: University of Chicago Press, 1957), p. 48; Robert H. Wiebe, *The Search for Order, 1877–1920* (New York: Hill and Wang, 1967), pp. 44–52. See William H. Becker, "The Wholesalers of Hardware and Drugs, 1870–1900," Ph.D. dissertation, Johns Hopkins University, 1969, for a description of the changing distribution network for drugs in the late nineteenth century.

5. *The Age of Reform* (New York: Random House, 1955), p. 149.

6. Sidney Fine, *Laissez-Faire and General Welfare State* (Ann Arbor: University of Michigan Press, 1956); Hayes, *The Response to Industrialism;* Wiebe, *The Search for Order;* David Noble, *The Progressive Mind, 1890–1917* (Chicago: Rand-McNally, 1970); Jerry Israel, ed., *Building the Organization Society* (New York: Free Press, 1972); White, *Social Thought in America.*

7. This discussion of licensing is based on Lawrence Friedman, "Freedom of Contract and Occupational Licensing, 1890–1910: A Legal and Social Study," *California Law Review*, 53 (1965): 487–534. The case referred to is *Dent* v. *West Virginia*, 129 U.S. 114 (1888). See also Walter Gellhorn, *Individual Freedom and Governmental Restraints* (Baton Rouge: Louisiana State University Press, 1956), for an account opposing the present extension of licensing laws.

8. Joseph F. Kett, *Formation of the American Medical Profession, 1780–1860* (New Haven: Yale University Press, 1968); Richard H. Shryock, *Medical Licensing in America* (Baltimore: Johns Hopkins, 1967); Paul Starr, The *Social Transformation of American Medicine* (New York: Basic Books, forthcoming), chap. 4. See *Journal of the American Medical Association*, 37 (November 16, 1901): 1304–18, for a survey of state licensing laws as of that date.

9. Edward Kremers and George Urdang, *History of Pharmacy: A Guide and*

Survey, rev. by Glenn Sonnedecker (Philadelphia: Lippincott, 1976), pp. 215–217, 381–382. Retail druggists also joined with (unlicensed) wholesale druggists and patent medicine manufacturers to maintain prices, but their "Tripartite Agreement" was ruled an illegal "drug trust" in 1907. Becker, "The Wholesalers of Hardware and Drugs," p. 280.

10. In some states, a few narcotics or poisons were unobtainable over the druggist's counter. U.S. Congress, Senate, *Digest of the Pure Food and Drug Laws of the United States and Foreign Countries,* by William E. Mason, Senate Report 3, 57th Cong., 1st sess., 1901.

11. J. W. Jervey, "Common Law Rights and the Physician's Prescription," *New York Medical Journal,* 74 (July 20, 1901): 112.

12. D. L. Dykstra, "Patent and Proprietary Medicines: Regulation Control Prior to 1906," Ph.D. dissertation, University of Wisconsin, 1951, p. 129; Kremers and Urdang, *History of Pharmacy,* p. 266; Kett, *Formation of the American Medical Profession,* pp. 2–6, shows that this overlap of function was traditional.

13. See Starr, *The Social Transformation of American Medicine,* chap. 4.

14. Glenn Sonnedecker, "Contribution of the Pharmaceutical Profession toward Controlling the Quality of Drugs in the Nineteenth Century," in John B. Blake, ed., *Safeguarding the Public: Historical Aspects of Medicinal Drug Control* (Baltimore: Johns Hopkins University Press, 1970), pp. 103–109.

15. Torald Sollmann, "The Pharmacopoeia as the Standard for Medical Prescribing," *Journal of the American Medical Association,* 51 (December 12, 1908): 2013–18.

16. Sherman M. Mellinkoff, "Chemical Intervention," *Scientific American,* 229 (September 1973): 103; Harry F. Dowling, *Medicines for Man* (New York: Knopf, 1970), p. 18.

17. Erwin Ackerknecht, *Therapeutics from the Primitives to the Twentieth Century* (New York: Hafner Press, 1973), pp. 114–115; W. R. Houston, "The Doctor Himself as a Therapeutic Agent," *Annals of Internal Medicine,* 11 (February 1938): 1418.

18. James H. Young, *The Toadstool Millionaires: A Social History of Patent Medicines in America before Federal Regulation* (Princeton: Princeton University Press, 1961), surveys the world of patent medicines from a hostile viewpoint. See his p. 68 for his attitude on their dangers.

19. See Adelaide Hechtlinger, *The Great Patent Medicine Era* (New York: Grosset & Dunlap, 1970), for reproductions of advertisements for patent medicines. The newspapers' attitudes sometimes are linked to "red clauses" in the advertising contracts canceling them in the event of restrictive legislation. But the newspapers would have had the same interest in preserving patent medicine advertising without the red clauses as they did with them. The only effect of the red clauses was to speed the cancellation of advertising contracts after unfavorable legislation. See Dykstra, "Patent and Proprietary Medicines."

20. Henry L. Swain, "The Attitude of the Profession toward Patent Medicines and Appliances," *Yale Medical Journal,* 8 (December 1901): 169–176.

21. H.C. Wood, "Nostrums," *Journal of the American Medical Association,* 32 (April 29, 1899): 908–911; Dykstra, "Patent and Proprietary Medicines," p. 46; Young, *The Toadstool Millionaires,* pp. 103, 157; U.S. Bureau of the Census,

Thirteenth Census of the United States, vol. VIII, *Manufacturers, 1909: General Report and Analysis* (Washington, D.C.: Government Printing Office, 1913), p. 40. There were 3,642 establishments making patent medicines and compounds and druggists' preparations in 1909. They employed an average of six people and averaged $40,000 in sales.

22. Young, *The Toadstool Millionaires,* pp. 107–108, 206.

23. 34 Stat. 768 (1906).

24. U.S. Congress, Senate, *Digest of the Pure Food and Drug Laws.*

25. Oscar E. Anderson, *The Health of a Nation: Harvey W. Wiley and the Fight for Pure Food* (Chicago: University of Chicago Press, 1958), p. 120. See also A. Hunter Dupree, *Science in the Federal Government: A History of Policies and Activities to 1940* (Cambridge, Mass.: Harvard University Press, 1957), pp. 176–177.

26. Thomas A. Bailey, "Congressional Opposition to Pure Food Legislation, 1879–1906," *American Journal of Sociology,* 36 (July 1930): 52–64; Anderson, *The Health of a Nation,* pp. 78–80, 131ff.; Young, *The Toadstool Millionaires,* pp. 226–233; Stephen Wilson, *Food and Drug Regulation* (Washington, D.C.: American Council on Public Affairs, 1942), p. 28.

27. The Division of Chemistry also published a variety of bulletins showing the extent of food adulteration. We may infer that these rather dense publications had little effect relative to the more colorful Poison Squad. Wilson, *Food and Drug Regulation,* pp. 21–22; Young, *The Toadstool Millionaires,* pp. 71–75. Harvey M. Wiley, in his *The History of a Crime against the Food Law* (Washington, D.C.: Harvey Wiley, 1929), pp. 57–77, gives his version of the activities of the Poison Squad, which continued until 1907.

28. Upton Sinclair, *The Jungle* (New York: Doubleday, Page, 1906), pp. 117, 143; Young, *The Toadstool Millionaires,* p. 205; Wilson, *Food and Drug Regulation,* p. 28.

29. 34 Stat. 674 (1906).

30. James G. Burrow, *AMA: Voice of American Medicine* (Baltimore: Johns Hopkins University Press, 1963), pp. 71–83.

31. Anderson, *The Health of a Nation,* pp. 133–143, 166; Morton Keller, *Affairs of State: Public Life in Late Nineteenth Century America* (Cambridge, Mass.: Harvard University Press, 1977), pp. 413–414.

32. 34 Stat. 768–772 (1906).

33. M. Clayton Thrush, "The U.S. Pharmacopoeia and the National Formulary," *Journal of the American Medical Association,* 54 (February 5, 1910): 437–441; Sollmann, "The Pharmacopoeia as the Standard for Medial Prescribing," p. 2017.

34. Dupree, *Science in the Federal Government,* p. 179. The bureau's employees rose from 110 in 1906 to 425 in 1908. Its name was changed in 1901.

35. Wiley, *The History of a Crime against the Food Law;* Anderson, *The Health of a Nation,* pp. 249–252; James H. Young, *The Medical Messiahs* (Princeton: Princeton University Press, 1967), p.44.

36. James C. Munch and James C. Munch, Jr., "Notices of Judgment: The First Thousand," *Food, Drug and Cosmetic Law Journal,* 10 (April 1955): 219–242.

37. Young, *The Medical Messiahs,* pp. 44–45; 38 Stat. 785 (1914).

38. *U.S.* v. *Johnson,* 221 U.S. 488 (1911); *American School of Magnetic Healing* v. *McAnnulty,* 187 U.S. 94 (1902).

39. 37 Stat. 416 (1912).

40. Paul B. Dunbar, "Memories of Early Days of Federal Food and Drug Law Enforcement," *Food, Drug and Cosmetic Law Journal,* 14 (February 1959): 123.

41. Young, *The Toadstool Millionaires,* p. 248; Young, *The Medical Messiahs,* pp. 57, 65, 93. The Proprietary Association adopted a code of ethics of its own in 1915.

42. *American School of Magnetic Healing* v. *McAnnulty,* 187 U.S. 94 (1902); Young, *The Medical Messiahs,* pp. 67–87.

43. *Federal Trade Commission* v. *Raladam Co.,* 283 U.S. 643 (1931).

44. Burrow, *AMA: Voice of American Medicine,* pp. 107–131; James G. Burrow, "The Prescription Drug Policies of the American Medical Association in the Progressive Era," in John B. Blake, ed. *Safeguarding the Public: Historical Aspects of Medicinal Drug Control* (Baltimore: Johns Hopkins University Press, 1970).

45. This conclusion does not extend to narcotics, which were regulated separately after 1915.

3. The Legacy of the New Deal

1. H. C. Wood, "Nostrums," *Journal of the American Medical Association,* 32 (April 29, 1899): 908–911; C. Rufus Rorem and Robert P. Fischelis, *The Costs of Medicines,* pub. no. 14 of the Committee on the Cost of Medical Care (Chicago: University of Chicago Press, 1932).

2. See Paul B. Dunbar, "Memories of Early Days," pp. 134–135; Stephen Wilson, *Food and Drug Regulation* (Washington, D.C.: American Council on Public Affairs, 1942), pp. 78–79; Fred B. Linten, "Leaders in Food and Drug Law, Part Five," *Food, Drug and Cosmetic Law Journal,* 5 (November 1950): 771–87; and Bernard Sternsher, *Rexford Tugwell and the New Deal* (New Brunswick, N.J.: Rutgers University Press, 1964), p. 225, for slightly different accounts. Dunbar claims the idea of revision arose within the FDA; others claim it came from Tugwell. Tugwell's biographer notes that he had listed the reorganization of the FDA as a major problem before his conversation with Campbell.

3. David F. Cavers, "The Food, Drug, and Cosmetic Act of 1938: Its Legislative History and Its Substantive Provisions," *Law and Contemporary Problems,* 6 (Winter 1939): 2–42; Charles O. Jackson, *Food and Drug Legislation in the New Deal* (Princeton: Princeton University Press, 1970), pp. 26–27.

4. Agricultural Department Appropriations, 34 Stat. 768–769 (1906).

5. Dunbar, "Memories of Early Days," p. 126; Henry Welch and Felix Marti-Ibañez, eds., *The Impact of the FDA on Our Society* (New York: MD Publications, 1956), p. 13.

6. Rexford Tugwell, *The Democratic Roosevelt* (Garden City, N.J.: Doubleday, 1957), p. 466.

7. Ibid., p. 464.

8. Franklin Roosevelt sent a special message to Congress supporting the re-

vision of the food and drug laws in 1935. Wilson, *Food and Drug Regulation*, p. 113.

9. Burrow, *AMA: Voice of American Medicine*, pp. 273–278; Jackson, *Food and Drug Legislation*, p. 211.

10. Ruth deForest Lamb, *American Chamber of Horrors: The Truth about Food and Drugs* (New York: Farrar and Rinehart, 1936); Cavers, "The Food, Drug, and Cosmetic Act of 1938," pp. 6–8; Jackson, *Food and Drug Legislation*, pp. 209–213.

11. Cavers, "The Food, Drug, and Cosmetic Act of 1938," pp. 3–5; Sternsher, *Rexford Tugwell and the New Deal*, pp. 223–237.

12. Federal Trade Commission Act, Wheeler-Lea Amendment, 52 Stat. 111 (1938); Milton Handler, "The Control of False Advertising under the Wheeler-Lea Act," *Law and Contemporary Problems*, 6 (Winter 1939): 91–110; Charles A. Sweeney, "Federal Trade Commission in Control of False Advertising of Foods, Drugs, and Cosmetics," *Food, Drug and Cosmetics Law Journal*, 12 (September 1957): 606–616; Otis Pease, *The Responsibilities of American Advertising: Private Control and Public Influence, 1920–1940* (New Haven: Yale University Press, 1958), pp. 121–125.

13. Young, *The Medical Messiahs*, pp. 298–301.

14. Jackson, *Food and Drug Legislation*, chap. 7; Young, *The Medical Messiahs*, p. 186. A member of the Massengill family published a history of pharmacy and his family's involvement with it in 1943. He did not mention Elixir Sulfanilamide. Samuel Evans Massengill, *A Sketch of Medicine and Pharmacy* (Bristol, Tenn.: S. E. Massengill Co., 1943).

15. Cavers, "The Food, Drug, and Cosmetic Act of 1938," pp. 20, 40.

16. Federal Food, Drug, and Cosmetic Act, 52 Stat. 1040 (1938) at 1049–53.

17. Tugwell, *The Democratic Roosevelt*, p. 465; quoted in Sternsher, *Rexford Tugwell and the New Deal*, p. 122.

18. U.S. Congress, Senate, Hearings before a Subcommittee of the Committee on Commerce, *Food, Drug, and Cosmetic Act* (S. 1944), 73rd Cong., 2nd sess., 1934, p. 59; reprinted in Charles W. Dunn, *Federal Food, Drug and Cosmetic Act: A Statement of its Legislative Record* (New York: Stechert, 1938), p. 1083.

19. U.S. Congress, Senate, Hearings before the Committee on Commerce, *Food, Drug, and Cosmetic Act* (S. 2800), 73rd Cong., 2nd sess., 1934, p. 590; reprinted in Dunn, *Federal Food, Drug and Cosmetic Act*, p. 1195, and quoted in Edward B. Williams, "Exemption for the Requirement of Adequate Directions for Use in the Labelling of Drugs," *Food, Drug and Cosmetics Law Journal*, 2 (June 1947): 164.

20. U.S. Congress, House, *Food, Drug, and Cosmetic Act*, House Report 2139, 75th Cong., 3rd sess., 1938, p. 8; reprinted in Dunn, *Federal Food, Drug and Cosmetic Act*, p. 822, and quoted in Williams, "Exemption from the Requirement," p. 163.

21. Rorem and Fischelis, *The Costs of Medicines*, p. 153.

22. U.S. Food and Drug Administration, "Promulgation of Regulations under the Federal Food, Drug, and Cosmetic Act," 3 Fed. Reg. 3168 (December 28, 1938). The regulation was reworded in 1941, but its thrust was not al-

tered. U.S. Food and Drug Administration, "Regulations for the Enforcement of the Federal Food, Drug, and Cosmetic Act," 6 Fed. Reg. 1920 (April 15, 1941).

23. U.S. Food and Drug Administration, *Annual Report* (Washington, D.C.: Government Printing Office, 1939), p. 5; reprinted in Food Law Institute, *Federal Food, Drug, and Cosmetic Law: Administrative Reports, 1907–1949* (Chicago: Commerce Clearing House, 1951), p. 929.

24. No internal records of the FDA's procedures in formulating the regulation have survived. A public hearing on the regulations as a whole largely ignored this one, as most witnesses were interested primarily in the labeling of food. The few who commented on this regulation spoke only to the issue of whether the drug manufacturer would be liable if the druggist failed to follow his label. The issue of self-medication did not arise. U.S. Food and Drug Administration, "Public Hearing to Consider Regulations for the Enforcement of Federal Food, Drug and Cosmetic Act," November 17–18, 1938. Copy available at the National Records Center, Suitland, Md., file 603, box 145, accession number 52–A89, location 20/43: 43–2–0.

25. U.S. Congress, House, Hearings before the Committee on Interstate and Foreign Commerce, *A Bill to Amend Section 503 (b) of the Federal Food, Drug, and Cosmetic Act* (H.R. 3298), 82nd Cong., 1st sess., 1951, pp. 97–105. Two violations were at issue: the selling of drugs over the counter without adequate labeling and the unauthorized refilling of prescriptions, which was the subject of another part of the regulation.

26. Charles W. Dunn, "The Durham-Humphrey Bill," *Food, Drug and Cosmetic Law Journal,* 5 (December 1950); 856–857.

27. 62 Stat. 582 (1948).

28. *U.S.* v. *Sullivan,* 332 U.S. 689 (1948). The district court opinion said: "This regulation as it affects the present case would require the drug to be sold on a physician's prescription and to bear the direction for use specified in the prescription." The first clause was included for accuracy, but only the second was being litigated. The United States brief to the Supreme Court relegated to a footnote the comment that adequate directions for use by laymen of dangerous drugs could not be written.

29. U.S. Congress, House, *A Bill to Amend Section 503(b)* (H.R. 3298), p. 16.

30. Richard J. Hopkins, "Medical Prescriptions and the Law: A Study of the Enactment of the Durham-Humphrey Amendment to the FDC Act," M.A. thesis, Emory University, 1965; Young, *The Medical Messiahs,* pp. 273–274.

31. U.S. Congress, House, *Amending Section 503(b) of the Federal Food, Drug, and Cosmetic Act,* House Report 700, 82nd Cong., 1st sess., 1951. The regulations as they existed at the time are reproduced in U.S. Congress, House, *A Bill to Amend Section 503 (b)* (H.R. 3298), pp. 16–17.

32. U.S. Congress, Senate, *Amending Sections 303 (c) and 503 (b) of the Federal Food, Drug, and Cosmetic Act,* Senate Report 946, 82nd Cong., 1st sess., 1951, pp. 2–4; Federal Food, Drug, and Cosmetic Act, Humphrey-Durham Amendment, 65 Stat. 648 (1951); Hopkins, "Medical Prescriptions and the Law," pp. 151–166.

33. Williams, "Exemption from the Requirement," pp. 157–158.

34. Ibid., pp. 163–172. See also Peter Barton Hutt, "Regulation of the Practice of Medicine under the Pure Food and Drug Laws," *Association of Food and Drug Officials of the United States,* 33 (January 1969): 9.

35. See Hopkins, "Medical Prescriptions and the Law," for the role of the AMA and drug manufacturers in 1951.

36. R. L. Grant, "The How and Why of the Certification of Insulin," in Welch and Marti-Ibañez, *The Impact of the FDA,* pp. 51–53.

37. Austin Smith and Arthur D. Herrick, eds., *Drug Research and Development* (New York: Revere Publishing, 1948), pp. 402–403; Welch and Ibañez, *The Impact of the FDA,* p. 53; 21 U.S. Code 357.

38. Smith and Herrick, *Drug Research and Development,* pp. 405–409. The statements in the text about antibiotics do not apply to chloramphenicol, which is substantially more toxic than the other antibiotics discovered in the 1940s. This difference was not discovered, however, until after 1951.

39. U.S. Congress, House, *Amending Section 503 (b),* pp. 1–2, 11. In the context, *efficacy* referred to whether a drug could be used efficaciously without a prescription rather than to the overall efficacy of the drug, but the language in the House bill nevertheless foreshadows the language of the 1962 Drug Amendments.

4. The Therapeutic Revolution

1. Testimony of Henry Gadsden, U.S. Congress, Senate, *Examination of the Pharmaceutical Industry,* Hearings before the Subcommittee on Health of the Committee on Labor and Public Welfare, 93rd Cong., 1st and 2nd sess., 1973–1974, pt. 3, p. 867.

2. Rorem and Fischelis, *The Costs of Medicines,* pp. 5–6, 120, 127. Another explanation offered was that drug expenditures were spread evenly across the population, so that no small group bore the burden.

3. Ibid. pp. 83, 149, 208. "Proprietary vs. Non-Proprietary," *Journal of the American Medical Association,* 97 (October 24, 1931): 1226, contains a reproduction of the poster.

4. John C. Krantz, Jr., ed., *Fighting Disease with Drugs* (Baltimore: National Council of Pharmaceutical Research, 1931), pp. 7–9.

5. Krantz, *Fighting Disease with Drugs,* pp. 7, 99–141. Martha Marquardt, *Paul Ehrlich* (New York: Henry Schuman, 1951), pp. 119–120. The seven diseases that were only partially controlled were treatable by more antitoxins, by a synthetic arsenical drug chemically related to Salversan, and by drugs derived from plants. Curiously, diabetes is not listed.

6. Marquardt, *Paul Ehrlich,* p. 91.

7. Marquardt, *Paul Ehrlich;* M. P. Earles, "Salversan and the Concept of Chemotherapy," *Pharmaceutical Journal,* 204 (April 18, 1970): 400–402. Ehrlich received the Nobel Prize in 1908 for his ideas, not for the discovery of Salversan.

8. Dickinson W. Richards, "A Clinician's View of Advances in Therapeutics," in Paul Talalay, ed., *Drugs in Our Society* (Baltimore: Johns Hopkins University Press, 1964).

9. Appropriations for Sundry Civil Expenses, 31 Stat. 1133 (1901); Krantz, *Fighting Disease with Drugs,* pp. 105, 115; Smith and Herrick, eds., *Drug Research and Development,* p. 383.

10. Krantz, *Fighting Disease with Drugs,* pp. 116–17; Cooper, *The Economics of Drug Innovation,* p. 44; Richards, "A Clinician's View," p. 30.

11. Cooper, *The Economics of Drug Innovation,* p. 42. The account that follows draws heavily on Cooper's clear exposition of this story, pp. 41–54. For references to and excerpts from the classic papers, see Bo Holmstedt and Goren Liljestrand, eds., *Readings in Pharmacology* (New York: Macmillan, 1963), pp. 296–304.

12. Louis S. Goodman and Alfred Gilman, *Pharmacological Basis of Therapeutics,* 5th ed. (New York: Macmillan, 1975), pp. 1113–24; Cooper, *The Economics of Drug Innovation,* pp. 42–45.

13. James Grier, *A History of Pharmacy* (London: Pharmaceutical Press, 1937); Bernard J. Stern, *American Medical Practice in the Perspective of a Century* (New York: Commonwealth Fund, 1945), p. 43; Iago Galdson, *Progress in Medicine: A Critical Review of the Last Hundred Years* (New York: Knopf, 1940), pp. 297–304.

14. In the opinion of at least some contemporary observers, the sulfanilamide compounds were relatively nontoxic as well and not the source of new dangers. Galdston, *Progress in Medicine,* p. 302.

15. Cooper, *The Economics of Drug Innovation,* pp. 45–48; Holmstedt and Liljestrand, *Readings in Pharmacology,* pp. 305–309.

16. Cooper, *The Economics of Drug Innovation,* pp. 48–50; Holmstedt and Liljestrand, *Readings in Pharmacology,* pp. 309–315.

17. U.S. Federal Trade Commission, *Economic Report on Antibiotics Manufacture* (Washington, D.C.: Government Printing Office, June 1958), pp. 47–49, 245–257, contains a full account of wartime penicillin production.

18. See Max Tishler, "Role of the Drug House in Biological and Medical Research," *Bulletin of the New York Academy of Medicine,* 35 (September 1959): 590–600, for a brief account of the organization of this research.

19. The account here draws extensively on the excellent treatment by Peter Costello, "The Tetracycline Conspiracy: Structure, Conduct and Performance in the Drug Industry," *Antitrust Law and Economic Review,* 1 (Summer 1968): 13–44.

20. U.S. Federal Trade Commission, *Economic Report on Antibiotics Manufacture,* pp. 94–95. These are shares of penicillin production, not of total antibiotics. Costello's "The Tetracycline Conspiracy" data occasionally confuse the two. They also show the relative decline of unintegrated producers. The top four integrated firms produced 82 percent of the penicillin made in 1956. U.S. Federal Trade Commission, *Economic Report on Antibiotics Manufacture,* p. 9.

21. Holmstedt and Liljestrand, *Readings in Pharmacology,* pp. 315–320. For a concise description of the technique, see U.S. Congress, Senate, *Administered Prices in the Drug Industry,* pt. 25, pp. 15304–305.

22. Patent no. 2,446,102 (July 27, 1948). Patents for new uses of existing substances were not granted before 1952. See Title 35, U.S. Code: Patents, 66 Stat. 792 (1952), sec. 100, for the new law; and Edmund W. Kitch, "The Patent System and the New Drug Research and Marketing," in R. L. Landau, ed.,

Regulating New Drugs (Chicago: Center for Policy Study, University of Chicago, 1973), pp. 81–107, for criticism of it.

23. Selman A. Waksman, *My Life with the Microbes* (New York: Simon & Schuster, 1954), p. 204; U.S. Federal Trade Commission *Economic Report on Antibiotics Manufacture*, pp. 24, 162–189; U.S. Congress, Senate, *Administered Prices in the Drug Industry*, pt. 24, pp. 13658, 13664.

24. Waksman, *My Life with the Microbes*, p. 204; Tom Mahoney, *The Merchants of Life* (New York: Harper & Bros., 1959), p. 198; Merck and Co., *Stock Application*, New York Stock Exchange no. A-12333, March 21, 1946.

25. Richard M. Cyert and James G. March, *A Behavioral Theory of the Firm* (Englewood Cliffs, N.J.: Prentice-Hall, 1963).

26. Harry F. Dowling, *Tetracycline* (New York: Medical Encyclopedia, 1955); C. L. Lewis et al., "Chloramphenicol (Chloromycetin) in Relation to Blood Dyscrasias with Observations on Other Drugs," *Antibiotics and Chemotherapy*, 2 (December 1952): 601–609. Chloromycetin causes fatal aplastic anemia in a small proportion of cases.

27. See William S. Comanor, "Research and Competitive Product Differentiation in the Pharmaceutical Industry in the U.S.," *Economica*, New Series 31 (November 1964): 372–384.

28. U.S. Federal Trade Commission, *Economic Report on Antibiotics Manufacture*, pp. 245–257, contains a detailed history of the patent litigation.

29. It also led to protracted court challenges of its legality. See Charles W. Wolfram, "The Antibiotics Class Actions," *American Bar Foundation Research Journal*, 1976 (1976): 253–363, for an account of extensive litigation on tetracycline, some of which continues today.

30. U.S. Federal Trade Commission, *Economic Report on Antibiotics Manufacture*, pp. 140–142.

31. U.S. Congress, Senate, *Administered Prices in the Drug Industry*, pt. 24, p. 13849.

32. Ibid., pp. 13663–64; Costello, "The Tetracycline Conspiracy," p. 39.

33. U.S. Federal Trade Commission and U.S. Securities and Exchange Commission, *Rates of Return for Identical Companies in Selected Manufacturing Industries* (Washington, D.C.: Government Printing Office, 1956). Profits for the drug industry are shown separately starting in the second quarter of 1956.

34. Costello, "The Tetracycline Conspiracy," p. 40.

35. This conclusion obviously depends on the allocation of costs shown in table 4. While Lederle's allocation method is not known, it is probable that the costs of joint activities, like research and marketing, were allocated in proportion to sales. Reallocation of these expenses to the most profitable lines (in terms of easily allocated costs) is possible, but problematical. It assumes that Lederle engaged in research and marketing solely to enhance its tetracycline sales and that the effects of these expenditures on the sales of other products was pure serendipity. It also assumes that Lederle overestimated its profits from tetracycline, which seems unlikely in the legal context.

36. Ben Gaffin and Associates, *The Fond du Lac Study*, pp. 783–789.

37. It is worth noting that the drug firms were not found to have violated the antitrust laws. Their initial conviction was reversed on appeal, and the reversal was sustained by the Supereme Court. See *U.S.* v. *Charles Pfizer and Co. et al.,*

426 F.2d 32 (1970), affirmed 404 U.S. 548 (1972). Nevertheless, the drug companies paid out almost $200 million in settlements of private damage suits brought while the criminal suit was in progress. See Wolfram, "The Antibiotics Class Actions."

38. Only three of the five firms selling tetracycline actually manufactured it, so the question of advertising another firm's products arose in any case. But this situation arose out of the legal maneuvering over the patent, not out of a single profit-maximizing calculation. The two firms advertising another firm's products were vouching for their supplier, not their licensees. The customer—the doctor—was ignorant of the interfirm transactions.

39. Testimony of Philip Bowman, U.S. Congress, Senate, *Administered Prices in the Drug Industry,* pt. 24, p. 13849; reproduced in Donald C. King, *Marketing Prescription Drugs* (Ann Arbor: Michigan Business Report no. 56, Bureau of Business Research, Graduate School of Business Administration, University of Michigan, 1968), p. 63. The data are from that quotation and from Costello, "The Tetracycline Conspiracy," p. 23.

40. Norman Applezweig, "Steroids," *Chemical Week,* 104 (May 17, 1969): 57–72.

41. The ranking of firms in the drug industry is hard for several reasons. There has been an extraordinary amount of merger activity in this industry, and the units of observation keep changing. This creates problems in itself, but it also means that the data for different firms are not comparable. Integrated firms seldom report drug sales in their annual reports or other generally available publications, and their size has to be estimated from more aggregated behavior. The statement in the text is based primarily on the firms' annual reports, on Moody's, and on scattered information about firms like Hoffman–La Roche, Ciba-Geigy, and Lilly that are not subject to Securities and Exchange Commission rules on disclosure of financial information.

42. The wholesale price of drugs did not rise over this time, and the rise in the average size of drug firms is not a statistical artifact (see table 24).

43. Mahoney, *The Merchants of Life,* p. 201.

44. Approximately twenty new drugs (new chemical entities) were introduced each year during the 1940s; this rate rose to about fifty new drugs a year in the 1950s (see table 2).

45. U.S. Congress, Senate, *Administered Prices in the Drug Industry,* pt. 24, pp. 13652, 13664. Mickey C. Smith, *Principles of Pharmaceutical Marketing* (Philadelphia: Lea and Febiger, 1968), pp. 271–274.

46. Mahoney, *The Merchants of Life,* p. 226.

47. Frank H. Clarke, ed., *How Modern Medicines Are Discovered* (Mt. Kisco, N.Y.: Future Publishing, 1973), pp. 44–45, 50–52; U.S. Food and Drug Administration, Drug Listing Branch, *National Drug Code Directory,* 1969–.

48. Clarke, *How Modern Medicines Are Discovered,* pp. 46–47. Oral antidiabetic drugs can only be used when the patient's pancreas is capable of responding to the stimulus. Patients without any pancreas function still need insulin.

49. Gaffin, *The Fond du Lac Study,* p. 749.

50. Henry Steels, "Monopoly and Competition in the Ethical Drugs Market," *Journal of Law and Economics,* 5 (October 1962): 131–164; Norman Taylor, *Plant Drugs That Changed the World* (New York: Dodd, Mead, 1965), pp.

24–31, 230–253; Clarke, *How Modern Medicines Are Discovered,* pp. 58–63; Judith Swazey, *Chlorpromazine in Psychiatry: A Study of Therapeutic Innovation* (Cambridge, Mass.: M.I.T. Press, 1974), pp. 85, 160–161.

51. Sales data are from Schwartzman, *Innovation in the Pharmaceutical Industry,* pp. 124–125. These firms were seven out of the top ten drug firms by sales in 1960, according to Schwartzman, p. 125. Of the other three firms, American Home Products had 28 percent of its sales in its brands of meprobamate, while Squibb and Abbott were more diversified. Hoffman–La Roche and Ciba-Geigy were not listed.

52. The discrepancy appears to come from the use of accelerated depreciation in the computation of the IRS data, but not in the FTC-SEC data, and the omission of nontaxable foreign income in the former but not in the latter. Heavy investment both at home and abroad in the early 1970s made the two series diverge sharply. I would like to thank Douglas Cocks for this information.

53. Kenneth W. Clarkson, *Intangible Capital and Rates of Return: Effects of Research and Promotion on Profitability* (Washington, D.C.: American Enterprise Institute, 1977), p. 64; Henry G. Grabowski and Dennis G. Mueller, "Industrial Research and Development, Intangible Capital Stocks, and Firm Profit Rates," *Bell Journal of Economics,* 9 (Autumn 1978): 332.

54. George J. Stigler, *Capital Rates of Return in Manufacturing Industries* (Princeton: Princeton University Press for the National Bureau of Economic Research, 1963), pp. 58–62, 152–226. The new SIC classification in 1947 separated drugs from toilet preparations. Profits for these two activities were almost identical in that year, but a divergence between them for earlier years would affect the comparison of Stigler's two subperiods.

55. U.S. Food and Drug Administration, "Promulgation of Regulations under the Federal Food, Drug and Cosmetic Act."

56. Milton Silverman, *The Drugging of the Americas* (Berkeley and Los Angeles: University of California Press, 1976), surveys drug marketing in South America.

57. Harold Clymer, "The Economic and Regulatory Climate: U.S. and Overseas Trends," in Helms, ed., *Drug Development and Marketing,* p. 139.

58. Becker, "The Wholesalers of Hardware and Drugs," pp. 247–266; Smith, *Principles of Pharmaceutical Marketing,* p. 299.

59. U.S. Federal Trade Commission, *Economic Report on Antibiotics Manufacture,* p. 128; King, *Marketing Prescription Drugs,* pp. 50, 96–97; Morton Mintz, *By Prescription Only* (Boston: Beacon Press, 1967; rev. ed. of *The Therapeutic Nightmare,* 1965), pp. 435–437; Smith, *Principles of Pharmaceutical Marketing,* p. 293. For detail-man impact, see Robert Ferber and Hugh G. Wales, "The Effectiveness of Pharmaceutical Advertising: A Case Study," *Journal of Marketing,* 22 (1958): 395–407; Gaffin, *Report on a Study of Advertising and the American Physician;* and Gaffin, *The Fond du Lac Study.*

60. Harry F. Dowling, "The American Medical Association's Policy on Drugs in Recent Decades," in John B. Blake, ed., *Safeguarding the Public: Historical Aspects of Medicinal Drug Control* (Baltimore: Johns Hopkins University Press, 1970), pp. 123–124.

61. Gaffin, *Report on A Study of Advertising and the American Physician,* pt.

I. This study is very hard to find, and I have taken my account from the report of it in a second study done by Ben Gaffin and Associates for the AMA, *The Fond du Lac Study*, p. 5816. For pages of drug advertising in *Journal of the American Medical Association*, see U.S. Congress, Senate, Hearings before the Subcommittee on Antitrust and Monopoly of the Committee on the Judiciary, *Drug Industry Antitrust Act* (S. 1552), 87th Cong., 1st and 2nd sess., (1961–1962), pt. 1, p. 131.

62. Estes Kefauver, *In a Few Hands: Monopoly Power in America* (New York: Pantheon Books, 1965), p. 75; Dowling, "The American Medical Association's Policy," pp. 126–127.

63. Dowling, "The American Medical Association's Policy," pp. 127–129.

64. Rorem and Fischelis, *The Costs of Medicines*, p. 231.

65. Alfred Chandler, *The Visible Hand: The Managerial Revolution in American Business* (Cambridge, Mass.: Harvard University Press, 1977), pp. 290–292; Reese V. Jenkins, *Images and Enterprises: Technology and the American Photographic Industry, 1839–1925* (Baltimore: Johns Hopkins University Press, 1975).

5. Doctors and Drugs

1. It will be become evident that only data limitations prevent me from making a similar argument about consumers' choice of drugs before World War II.

2. *Physicians' Desk Reference*, 1979, p. ii.

3. U.S. Congress, Senate, *Examination of the Pharmaceutical Industry*, pt. 5, pp. 1737–56, 1778–96. See pp. 1559–77 for a description of the survey.

4. Ibid., pp. 1778–79. General practitioners reported less than average use of Goodman and Gilman, *The Pharmacological Basis of Therapeutics*, while specialists in internal medicine reported more.

5. Goodman and Gilman, *The Pharmacological Basis of Therapeutics*, pp. 1096–1103, 1183. The antibiotic chapters were written by Louis Weinstein.

6. There are two anemias caused by chloramphenicol, a dose-related anemia that need not be fatal if monitored carefully and fatal aplastic anemia which comes after the drug therapy is concluded. Ibid., p. 1196; *Physicians' Desk Reference*, 1979, p. 1277.

7. David N. Holvey, ed., *The Merck Manual of Diagnosis and Therapy*, 12th ed. (Rahway, N.J.: Merck Sharp & Dohme, 1972); Walter Modell, ed., *Drugs of Choice, 1976–77* (St. Louis: C. V. Mosby, 1976); American Medical Association, Department of Drugs, *AMA Drug Evaluations*, 3rd ed. (Acton, Mass.: American Medical Association, 1977); U.S. Congress, Senate, *Examination of the Pharmaceutical Industry*, pt. 5, p. 1737.

8. Lewis et al., "Chloramphenicol (Chloromycetin)"; U.S. Congress, House, *Hearings on Drug Safety before the Subcommittee on Intergovernmental Relations of the Committee on Government Operations*, 88th Cong., 2nd sess., 1964, pt. 1, pp. 148–49. The question posed in the survey—comparative fatality rates of anemia victims—is odd. The issue is not whether some anemias are more likely to be fatal than others, but whether taking chloramphenicol increases the risk of dying. The survey should have compared fatality rates from this disease for everyone.

9. Henry Welch et al., "Blood Dyscrasias: A Nationwide Survey," *Antiobiotics and Chemotherapy*, 4 (June 1954); American Medical Association, Council on Drugs, "Registry on Blood Dyscrasias: Report to the Council," *Journal of the American Medical Association*, 179 (March 17, 1962): 888–890; William R. Best, "Chloramphenicol-Associated Blood Dyscrasias: A Review of Cases Submitted to the AMA Registry," *Journal of the American Medical Association*, 201 (July 17, 1967): 181–188.

10. S. L. Leikin et al., "Aplastic Anemia Due to Chloramphenicol," *Clinical Proceedings of the Children's Hospital of Washington*, 17 (July 1961): 171–181. No source was given for the number of people with aplastic anemia, but the format of the data follows the AMA registry's. Since no other source was apparent, I assumed this source was used.

11. K. M. Smick et al., "Fatal Aplastic Anemia: An Epidemiological Study of its Relationship to the Drug Chloramphenicol," *Journal of Chronic Disease*, 17 (October 1964): 899–914.

12. Ralph O. Wallerstein et al., "Statewide Study of Chloramphenicol Therapy and Fatal Aplastic Anemia," *Journal of the American Medical Association*, 208 (June 16, 1969): 2045–50. Note that this research is not capable of showing whether the incidence of aplastic anemia is dose-related.

13. These are the 95 percent confidence limits of the binomial distribution.

14. Wallerstein et al., "Statewide Study."

15. Wallerstein, ibid., compares the risk of getting fatal aplastic anemia from chloramphenicol with the risk of getting this disease from phenylbutazone and quinacrine, but neither of these drugs competes with chloramphenicol in therapy. The former is an anti-inflammatory drug, the latter is not listed in the *PDR*.

16. O. Idsøe et al., "Nature and Extent of Penicillin Side-Reactions, with Particular Reference to Fatalities from Anaphylactic Shock," *Bulletin of World Health Organization*, 38 (1968): 160.

17. *The Pharmacological Basis of Therapy*, pp. 1147,1149. Note the technical distinction between toxic and allergic drug reactions which has to do with the existence of identifiable proclivities toward adverse reactions in the population at risk.

18. As with chloramphenicol, there is a literature on the epidemiology of penicillin risk. Since the penicillin reaction is much quicker than the chloramphenicol reaction, investigators have been able to compile data on fatalities among clinic patients treated—typically for venereal disease—with penicillin. R. R. Willcox, "Influence of Penicillin Allergic Reactions on V.D. Control Programmes," *British Journal of Venereal Disease*, 40 (September 1964): 200–209, amassed data from a variety of places for an overall proportion of one fatality for each 78,000 therapies. P. F. Frank et al., "Protection of a Military Population from Rheumatic Fever," *Journal of the American Medical Association*, 193 (September 6, 1965): 775–783, reported no deaths among 315,000 uses. Idsøe et al., "Nature and Extent," the classic source for data on allergic penicillin reactions, estimated the risk of fatality to be in the range of .0015 to .002 percent. Andrew H. Rudolph and Eleanor V. Price, "Penicillin Reactions among Patients in Venereal Disease Clinics: A National Survey," *Journal of the American Medical Association*, 223 (January 29, 1973): 499–501, reported on

deaths in four three-month periods spread over fifteen years, finding one fatality in 95,000 cases. The former report is based on eleven fatalities; the latter, on one. All these estimates except Frank's are well within the confidence interval for fatal chloramphenicol risk found by Wallerstein et al., "Statewide Study." See Louis Lasagna, "Discussion," in Joseph D. Cooper, ed., *The Philosophy of Evidence,* vol. 3 of *Philosophy and Technology of Drug Assessment* (Washington, D.C.: Interdisciplinary Communication Association, 1972), p. 49, for recogntion of the similarity between chloramphenicol and penicillin risk.

19. Note, for example, the following words from the second edition of *AMA Drug Evaluations:* "Blood dyscrasias, including aplastic anemia, have occurred following therapy with chloramphenicol. Despite the seriousness of these reactions, including some fatalities, the incidence of blood dyscrasias probably compares favorably with the incidence of severe anaphylactic reactions caused by penicillin or *fatal hepatic toxicity and severe staphylococci diarrhea associated with tetracycline therapy"* (emphasis added). American Medical Association, Department of Drugs, *AMA Drug Evaluations,* 2nd ed. (Acton, Mass.: AMA, 1973), pp. 551–552. This comparison is missing in the third edition of the *AMA Drug Evaluations,* 1979.

20. *Motor Vehicle Facts and Figures, 1977* (Detroit: Motor Vehicle Manufacturers' Association, 1977), p. 57. There were 3.38 motor vehicle traffic deaths for each 100 million vehicle-miles traveled in 1976.

21. "Editorial," *New England Journal of Medicine,* 258 (January 9, 1958): 97; Charles D. May, "Gilded Antibiotics" [Editorial], *Pediatrics,* 22 (September 1958): 415; Maxwell Finland, "Antibiotic Blood Level Enhancement: Editorial," *Antibiotic Medical and Clinical Therapeutics,* 5 (June 1958): 359–363; "Buffered Tetracycline and Antibiotic Blood Levels," *The Medical Letter,* 1 (January 23, 1959): 2–3. The editorials contain full citations of the earlier literature.

22. William P. Boger and John J. Gavin, "An Evaluation of Tetracycline Preparations," *New England Journal of Medicine,* 261 (October 22, 1959): 832. See Calvin M. Kunin et al., "Enhancement of Tetracycline Blood Levels," *New England Journal of Medicine,* 259 (July 24, 1958): 147–156, for similar experimental results; and Charles D. May, "Selling Drugs by 'Educating' Physicians," *The Journal of Medical Education,* 36 (January 1961): 1–23, for further commentary.

23. Donald C. Blair et al., "Biological Availability of Oxytetracycline HC1 Capsule: A Comparison of All Manufacturing Sources Supplying the United States Market," *Journal of the American Medical Association,* 215 (January 11, 1971): 251–254.

24. For example, one study reported that the comparison between two brands of tetracycline was affected by whether the subjects were ambulatory or sleeping. J. Adir and W. H. Barr, "Effect of Sleep on Bioavailability of Tetracycline," *Journal of Pharmaceutical Science,* 66 (July 1977): 1000–04.

25. A California regulation required drug distributors to identify the source of their final dosage forms. *The California Pharmacist* collected and published some of the resulting data, which were reproduced in the Kennedy Hearings.

U.S. Congress, Senate, *Examination of the Pharmaceutical Industry,* pt. 2, pp. 470–474.

26. W. H. Barr et al., "Assessment of the Biologic Availability of Tetracycline Products in Man," *Clinical Pharmacology and Therapeutics,* 13 (January-February 1972): 97–108.

27. The FDA has maintained continuously that there is no reason to distinguish among antibiotics from different sources because the agency individually certifies each batch. The following statement by the chief of the FDA's Bureau of Drugs is entirely typical: "Based on many years of experience with this program [of antibiotic certification] we are confident there is no significant difference between so-called generic and brand name antibiotic products on the American market." Henry E. Simmons, "Assuring Total Drug Quality," *Journal of the American Pharmaceutical Association,* New Series 13 (February 1973): 97.

28. The articles were drawn from *International Pharmacy Abstracts, Abstracts on Drug Equivalence: Bioavailability and Drug Equivalence,* vol. 7 (1970) to vol. 12, nos. 1–12 (January-June 1975) (Washington, D.C.: American Society of Hospital Pharmacists, 1975), a computer search of the medical literature, and combing the back issues of selected journals. Articles, editorials, and letters that did not present experimental evidence from living subjects were excluded from the sample, as were articles not obtainable in the library of the Harvard Medical School and articles that drew only methodological conclusions.

29. "Digitalis . . . has the lowest margin of safety [of common drugs] . . . Physicians would be well advised to prescribe the digoxin product with which they are familiar and to indicate the commercial source of the drug to be dispensed if it is prescribed by generic name." Goodman and Gilman, *The Pharmacological Basis of Therapeutics,* pp. 667–668, 671. See also B. F. Johnson, "Biological Availability of Digoxin from Lanoxin Produced in the United Kingdom," *British Medical Journal,* 4 (November 10, 1975): 323–326; John L. Colaizzi and John G. Wagner, "Digoxin (bioavailability monograph)," *Journal of the American Pharmaceutical Association,* New Series 15 (January 1975): 43–46.

30. See J. Koch-Weser, "Bioavailability of Drugs, Parts I and II," *New England Journal of Medicine,* 291 (August 1 and September 5, 1974): 233–237, 503–506, for a summary of the debate as it then existed, including a clear distinction between bioequivalence and therapeutic equivalence and lists of unequal drugs according to both standards. The article lists thirty-four bioinequivalent drugs, but only thirteen therapeutically inequivalent drugs.

31. Alvin Feinstein, "Clinical Biostatistics IX: How Do We Measure 'Safety' and 'Efficacy'?" *Clinical Pharmacy and Therapeutics,* 12 (May-June 1971): 544.

32. Louis S. Goodman, "The Problem of Drug Efficacy: an Exercise in Dissection," in Paul Talalay, ed., *Drugs in Our Society* (Baltimore: Johns Hopkins University Press, 1964), pp. 49–54.

33. Juhl et al., "The Epidemiology." Only 0.2 percent of gastroenterological articles on other (nondrug) treatments were randomized clinical trials. On the other hand, the proportion of articles reporting the results of randomized clinical trials rose over time.

34. U.S. Department of Health, Education and Welfare, *Task Force on Pre-*

scription Drugs, pp. 27–29. See Finland, "Antibiotic Blood Level Enhancement," p. 62, for a clear statement that this assumption is invalid.

35. U.S. Office of Technology Assessment, Drug Bioequivalence Study Panel, *Drug Bioequivalence* (Washington, D.C.: Government Printing Office, 1974), pp. 3, 23, 57–58.

36. The annual *Drug Topics Red Book* gives wholesale prices and often suggested retail prices for all drugs.

37. U.S. Congress, Senate, *Examination of the Pharmaceutical Industry,* pt. 5, pp. 1548–1859, contains a full report of the survey including the questionnaire and extensive tables of the replies. The data represented here come from the replies themselves, which were obtained from the FDA under the Freedom of Information Act.

38. In addition, some doctors said they looked for cost information in certain sources but—elsewhere on the questionnaire—reported that they never consulted the sources in question (see Table 11). Other doctors checked all the boxes for different types of information, suggesting that they did not consider which kind of information they looked for in filling out the questionnaire. If doctors who answered in these ways and who did not list alternative sources of cost information as well are included in the number who lack all cost information, the estimated proportion in this category rises to 40 percent. Of these, 88 percent listed patient care as their primary activity; 35 percent, as their sole activity.

39. The same conclusion is reported in U.S. Congress, Senate, *Examination of the Pharmaceutical Industry,* pt. 5, p. 1645.

40. The frequency of use by doctors as a whole differs from the frequency of use by those doctors who said they sought cost information in the listed sources. For example, half of all doctors reported no contact with pharmacists, but 29 percent of those who said they got cost information from pharmacists also reported no contact with them. Similarly, almost 40 percent of doctors denied any contact with detail men, but 18 percent of doctors getting cost information from detail men also denied the existence of this contact. Inconsistencies like these are troublesome; they suggest that the numbers in table 10 are overestimates. Ibid., pp. 1771, 1776; table 11.

41. D. R. Lowy, L. Lowy, and R. S. Warner, "A Survey of Physicians' Awareness of Drug Costs," *Journal of Medical Education,* 47 (May 1972): 349–351. Unfortunately, the authors reported only the median response in the binary comparisons. If they had reported the mean response instead, then a model analogous to the one underlying the chloramphenicol research reported above could have been constructed. On the assumption that doctors know a fixed proportion of relative prices correctly and guess randomly at all others, the mean provides enough information to calculate an estimate of this fixed proportion (taking account of random successes on the unknown comparisons) and confidence limits around it (from the variance of the underlying binomial distribution). If the mean were ten correct answers, then the estimated proportion of known comparisons would be five, or one-third of the fifteen asked about. Since large binomial probabilities make for small variances, appropriate confidence limits would bracket this value quite closely.

42. A survey of sixty Canadian doctors reported that few of them even knew

the active ingredients in fixed drug combinations that they prescribed. See Pierre Biron, "A Hopefully Biased Pilot Survey of Physicians' Knowledge of the Content of Drug Combinations," *Canadian Medical Association Journal*, 109 (July 7, 1973): 35–39.

43. U.S. Department of Health, Education and Welfare, *Task Force on Prescription Drugs*, p. 17. See also U.S. Congress, Senate, *Competitive Problems in the Drug Industry*, pp. 3–4, for similar views.

44. For example, Smith, *Principles of Pharmaceutical Marketing*, p. 74; Russel R. Miller, "Prescribing Habits of Physicians: A Review of Studies on Prescribing of Drugs, Parts I–VIII," *Drug Intelligence and Clinical Pharmacy*, 7, 8 (November 1973–February 1974): 492–500, 557–564 (vol. 7), 81–91 (vol. 8); reprinted in U.S. Congress, Senate, *Examination of the Pharmaceutical Industry*, pt. 4, pp. 1369–96.

45. M. H. Becker et al., "Correlates of Physicians' Prescribing Behavior," *Inquiry*, 9 (September 1972): 30–42, reported that a sample of doctors prescribed more different drugs for both fatigue and the common cold than there were doctors in the sample, but did not calculate how many drugs were used by each doctor.

46. Charlotte Muller, "Medical Review of Prescribing," *Journal of Chronic Disease*, 18 (July 1965): 689–696; T. W. Meade, "Prescribing of Chloramphenicol in General Practice," *British Medical Journal*, 1 (March 18, 1967): 671–674; Pual D. Stolley et al., "The Relationship between Physician Characteristics and Prescribing Appropriateness," *Medical Care*, 10 (January-February 1972): 17–28; M. H. Becker et al., "Characteristics and Attitudes of Physicians Associated with the Prescribing of Chloramphenicol," *HSMHA Health Reports* (formerly *Public Health Reports*), 86 (November 1971): 993–1003; M. H. Becker et al., "Differential Education Concerning Therapeutics and Resultant Physician Prescribing Patterns," *Journal of Medical Education*, 47 (February 1972): 118–127; M. H. Becker et al., "Correlates of Physicians' Prescribing Behavior." The first study concluded that its approach had only limited value because "disagreement among reviewers . . . was considerable." The last study used chloramphenicol as a measure because of the extensive publicity it had received. The test was doctors' *receptivity* to the literature, not the efficacy of the treatment.

47. R. F. Maronde et al., "A Study of Prescribing Patterns," *Medical Care*, 9 (September-October 1971): 383–395; Gregory R. Mundy et al., "Current Medical Practice and the Food and Drug Administration," *Journal of the American Medical Association*, 229 (September 23, 1974): 1744–78; McAuliffe, "Measuring the Quality of Medical Care."

48. Coleman, Katz, and Menzel, *Medical Innovation*. From internal evidence, it appears probable that Coleman and his colleagues were studying the diffusion of Achromycin, which competed most closely with the previous tetracycline compounds, Aureomycin and Terramycin. No comparative evidence on the relative effectiveness of these closely related compounds existed at the time of their study.

49. Miller, "Prescribing Habits of Physicians"; Caplow and Raymond, "Factors Influencing the Selection of Pharmaceutical Products."

50. See U.S. Food and Drug Administration, "Legal Status of Approved

Labelling for Prescription Drugs: Prescribing for Uses Unapproved by the FDA," 37 Fed. Reg. 16503 (August 15, 1972).

51. Coleman, Katz, and Menzel, *Medical Innovation,* pp. 111–112.

52. Miller, "Prescribing Habits of Physicians," emphasized the role of the medical community in his review of the literature on drug adoptions. He noted at the outset of his review that he devoted little attention to the results of drug prescribing; he did not give reasons for this limitation of his reviews, and he assumed that he could review the literature on drug prescribing without reference to results.

53. A glance at any major medical journal will show this bias. Most seminars on therapeutic choices are organized this way also.

54. If the hypothetical doctor uses fewer drugs and writes fewer new prescriptions, the contrast between the average utilization of his 30 once-a-week drugs and the average utilization of other drugs is greater than in the example calculated in the text. If the hypothetical doctor uses more drugs and writes more prescriptions, the contrast is less.

55. Since seeing detail men is disapproved of by many doctors, the self-reported figure of three-fifths probably is an underestimate. The allegation that detail men were performing surgery came from a malpractice suit involving alleged actions in 1975. U.S. Congress, Senate, *Examinaton of the Pharmaceutical Industry,* pt. 5, p. 1771; *New York Times,* February 9, 1978, sec. 4, p. 14; February 15, 1978, sec. 2, p. 10.

56. U.S. Congress, Senate, *Examination of the Pharmaceutical Industry,* pt. 4, pp. 1418–24. The data were furnished to the subcommitteee by the drug companies.

57. Robert Richard Rehder, "The Role of the Detail Man in the Diffusion and Adoption of an Ethical Pharmaceutical Innovation within a Single Medical Community," Ph.D. dissertation, Stanford University, 1961, pp. 195–196. Rehder accompanied four detail men in the Palo Alto area and observed doctors apologizing to detail men for not using their products.

58. Bauer, "Risk Handling in Drop Adoption." Unfortunately, the statistical results of this suggestive study were not reported in any detail.

59. Drug sales (within therapeutic classes) are highly correlated with promotion expenditures, but these expenditures are only one of many factors explaining drug sales. The data are consistent with the model without showing that drug sales are the results of advertising expenditures. See Ronald S. Bond and David F. Lean, *Sales, Promotion and Product Differentiation in Two Prescription Drug Markets* (Washington, D.C.: Federal Trade Commission, 1977), for an analysis of the sales and promotion of two types of drugs; and Richard Schmalensee, *The Economics of Advertising* (Amsterdam: North-Holland Publishing, 1972), for a general discussion of the statistical problems in such an investigation.

60. Mickey C. Smith, "Social Barriers to Rational Drug Therapy," *American Journal of Hospital Pharmacy,* 29 (February 1972): 125.

61. Steven N. Wiggins, "Product Quality Regulation and Innovation in the

Pharmaceutical Industry," Ph.D. dissertation, Massachusetts Institute of Technology, 1979.

6. The Postwar Expansion of Regulation

1. U.S. Congress, House, *Report to the Secretary of H.E.W.* The FDA's appropriation rose rapidly after the war, but the increase was more apparent than real because all prices rose in the late 1940s. The personnel data, therefore, give a more accurate picture of the FDA's growth. The committee's data differ slightly from those in table 18, since the committee reported the total size of the FDA as 829 in fiscal 1955.

2. U.S. Office of Management and Budget, *The Budget of the U.S. Government, and Appendix* (Washington, D.C.: Government Printing Office, 1966), appendix, p. 407; U.S. Congress, House, *Report to the Secretary of H.E.W.*, p. 39.

3. U.S. Congress, Senate, *Administered Prices: Drugs*, p. 3; Harris, *The Real Voice*, pp. 55-65; Kefauver, *In a Few Hands*, p. 8.

4. U.S. Congress, Senate, Hearings, *Drug Industry Antitrust Act*, pp. 1-20; Frank Cacciapaglia, Jr., and Howard B. Rockman, "The Proposed Drug Industry Antitrust Act: Patents, Pricing and the Public," *George Washington Law Review*, 30 (June 1962): 899; Harris, *The Real Voice*, pp. 121-123.

5. U.S. Congress, Senate, Hearings, *Drug Industry Antitrust Act*, pp. 23, 195-451.

6. Morton Mintz, " 'Heroine' of FDA Keeps Bad Drug Off Market," *Washington Post*, July 15, 1962, p. A1. The reporter who broke the story later wrote a book about drugs and the FDA. See Mintz, *By Prescription Only*.

7. U.S. Congress, Senate, *Drug Industry Act of 1962*, Senate Report 1744, 87th Cong., 2nd sess., 1962, pt. 2, pp. 5-6; *Brief for the Petitioners, Weinberger et al. v. Hynson, Wescott and Dunning*, 72-394 (1972), pp. 15-17.

8. There were also private suits against Merrell for damages sustained during the adverse drug reactions. Despite their success, these suits led to no discernible breaks in either the total sales or net worth of the firm. The suits were not followed in the medical press, and Merrell had insurance covering much of the damages. Kefauver, *In a Few Hands*, pp. 60-64; Paul D. Rheingold, "The MER/29 Story: An Instance of Successful Mass Disaster Litigation," *California Law Review*, 56 (January 1968): 116-148; Silverman and Lee, *Pills, Profits and Politics*, p. 92. For a general discussion of drug firm liability for adverse drug reactions, see Richard A. Merrill, "Compensation for Prescription Drug Injuries," *Virginia Law Review*, 59 (January 1973): 1-120.

9. 76 Stat. 780 (1962). The law also extended the FDA's time limit for acting on an NDA from 60 to 180 days; it required drug manufacturers to register with the FDA and keep certain records of their production; and it extended the FDA's antibiotic certification activities to all antibiotics.

10. For similar views, see William M. Wardell and Louis Lasagna, *Regulation and Drug Development* (Washington, D.C.: American Enterprise Institute, 1975), p. 1.

11. "Where a drug is essentially innocuous, it [the FDA] must clear the drug despite the fact that its claim of effectiveness is not borne out by the evidence."

U.S. Congress, Senate, Senate Report, *Drug Industry Act of 1962*, pp. 15–16.

12. 76 Stat. 780 (1962) at 781.

13. Herbert L. Ley, "Discussion," in Joseph D. Cooper, ed., *The Quality of Advice*, vol. 2 of *Philosophy and Technology of Drug Assessment* (Washington, D.C.: Interdisciplinary Communication Associates, 1971), p. 100.

14. National Research Council, Division of Medical Science, *Drug Efficacy Study: Final Report to the Commissioner of Food and Drugs, FDA* (Washington, D.C.: National Academy of Sciences, 1969), pp. 1–2. For a summary of the report, see Cooper, *The Quality of Advice*, pp. 269–282.

15. National Research Council, *Drug Efficacy Study*, p. 3.

16. Daniel X. Freedman, "Discussion," in Joseph D. Cooper, *Decision Making on the Efficacy and Safety of Drugs*, vol. 1 of *Philosophy and Technology of Drug Assessment* (Washington, D.C.: Interdisciplinary Communication Associates, 1971), p. 108.

17. National Research Council, *Drug Efficacy Study*, pp. 7–9. HEW Secretary Abraham Ribicoff had stated during the hearings for the 1962 law that "relative efficacy" was not involved. U.S. Congress, Senate, Hearings, *Drug Industry Antitrust Act*, pt. 5, p. 2585; U.S. Congress, Senate, Senate Report, *Drug Industry Act of 1962*, p. 16.

18. National Research Council, *Drug Efficacy Study*, p. 11. The quoted phrase appears in quotation marks in the report. It is adapted from the council's guidelines for the study. Ibid., p. 42.

19. Ibid., p. 9.

20. See Cooper, *The Quality of Advice*, p. 277, for a similar, but less sympathetic, view.

21. U.S. Food and Drug Administration, "Combination Drugs for Human Use," 36 Fed. Reg. 3127 (February 18, 1971); U.S. Food and Drug Administration, "Fixed-Combination Prescription Drugs for Humans," 36 Fed. Reg. 20037 (October 15, 1971); Richard J. Crout, "Fixed-Combination Prescription Drugs: FDA Policy," in Louis Lasagna, ed., *Combination Drugs: Their Use and Regulation* (New York: Stratton Intercontinental Medical Book Corp., 1975), p. 2; John H. Budd, "Combination Drugs in Medical Practice," in Lasagna, *Combination Drugs*, pp. 47–48.

22. U.S. Food and Drug Administration, "Drug Efficacy Study Implementation Notices," 37 Fed. Reg. 2969 (February 10, 1972). See also U.S. Food and Drug Administration, "New Drugs," 37 Fed. Reg. 23185 (October 31, 1972), for comments on the initial announcement and the FDA's replies to them. Information on "old drug determination letters" comes from oral communication with William H. Goodrich, former general counsel to the FDA, and William Vodra, former assistant general counsel to the FDA for drugs.

23. U.S. Food and Drug Administration, "Over-the-Counter Drugs," 37 Fed. Reg. 85 (January 5, 1968). See also U.S. Food and Drug Administration, "Procedures for Classification of Over-the-Counter Drugs," 37 Fed. Reg. 9464 (May 1, 1968), for comments on the January announcement and the FDA's reply to them.

24. National Research Council, *Drug Efficacy Study*, pp. 4, 6; *A Chronology and Review of the National Academy of Sciences–National Research Council*

Drug Efficacy Study (Philadelphia: Smith, Kline & French Laboratories, 1971), pp. 14–15.

25. This history is summarized, with citation in *Upjohn Co.* v. *Finch*, 422 F.2d 944 (1970), and in Charles C. Ames and Steven C. McCracken, "Framing Regulatory Standards to Avoid Formal Adjudication: The FDA as a Case Study," *California Law Review*, 64 (January 1976): 14–73. The new regulations were delayed by procedural objections; they only became effective with their reissue in 1970.

26. *Upjohn Co.* v. *Finch*, 422 F.2d 944 (1970) at 954–955.

27. See Ames and McCracken, "Framing Regulatory Standards," for an extensive discussion of this procedural view of the changes taking place around the time of the Panalba case.

28. National Research Council, *Drug Efficacy Study*, p. 9.

29. Ames and McCracken, "Framing Regulatory Standards," p. 21; U.S. Food and Drug Administration, "Hearing Regulations and Regulations Describing Scientific Content of Adequate and Well-Controlled Clinical Investigations," 35 Fed. Reg. 7250 (May 8, 1970).

30. U.S. Food and Drug Administration, "Hearing Regulations."

31. *A Chronology and Review*, pp. iii, 17.

32. *Weinberger* v. *Hynson, Westcott and Dunning*, 412 U.S. 609 (1973) at 621, 626. The court cited an earlier decision involving the Federal Communications Commission where it had restricted the right of claimants to an agency hearing in the following terms: "We do not think Congress intended the Commission to waste time on applications that do not state a valid basis for a hearing." *U.S.* v. *Storer Broadcasting Co.*, 351 U.S. 192 (1956) at 205.

33. *Weinberger* v. *Hynson, Wescott and Dunning*, 412 U.S. 609 (1973) at 632. The other related cases decided at the same time were *Ciba Corp.* v. *Weinberger*, 412 U.S. 640 (1973); *Weinberger* v. *Bentex Pharmaceuticals et al.*, 412 U.S. 695 (1973); *USV Pharmaceuticals Corp.* v. *Weinberger* 412 U.S. 655 (1973).

34. *USV Pharmaceuticals Corp.* v. *Weinberger*, 412 U.S. 655 (1973).

35. The court battles just chronicled concerned the FDA's actions on previously approved drugs. Because more rigorous standards for new drugs did not threaten existing sources of income, as these same standards did when applied to drugs already on the market, the new standards were applied to new drugs earlier than to old drugs. Indeed, the law itself mandated a two-year delay in the application of the new standards to old drugs.

36. *Alpha* v. *Matthews*, 530 F.2d 1054 (1976) at 1055.

37. Ibid. at 1056.

38. 84 Stat. 1242 (1970).

7. Recent Changes in the Drug Industry

1. Henry Grabowski, *Drug Regulation and Innovation: Empirical Evidence and Policy Options* (Washington, D.C.: American Enterprise Institute, 1976), p. 37. See Grabowski for references to the literature summarized.

2. Grabowski, Vernon, and Thomas, "The Effects of Regulatory Policy"; Grabowski, Vernon, and Thomas, "Estimating the Effects of Regulation."

3. Wiggins, "Product Quality Regulation." The reasons for the decline in FDA processing time in the 1970s is unclear.

4. Ronald W. Hansen, "The Pharmaceutical Development Process: Estimates of Development Costs and Times and the Effects of Proposed Regulatory Changes," in Robert I. Chien, ed., *Issues in Pharmaceutical Economics* (Lexington, Mass.: D. C. Heath, Lexington Books, 1979); Grabowski, Vernon, and Thomas, "Estimating the Effects of Regulation." The costs in question are *not* adjusted (discounted) to allow for the time pattern of expenditures. If the time pattern did not change, adding discounting will not affect the result.

5. Wiggins, "Product Quality Regulation," chap. 5.

6. As noted at several points so far, the proximate cause is an important part of the story, but by no means its entirety.

7. Sanjaya Lall, *Major Issues in the Transfer of Technology to Developing Countries: A Case Study of the Pharmaceutical Industry* (New York: United Nations Conference on Trade and Development, 1975), p. 8; Barrie G. James, *The Future of the Multinational Pharmaceutical Industry to 1990* (New York: Wiley, 1977), pp. 248–249. In addition to revealing the existence of the world outside the United States, these figures suggest caution in the use of international statistics. If the location of activity—whether sales, research and development, or new drug introductions—is given as the location of a firm's home office, the findings may tell us more about the national distribution of firms than about the actual location of the activity in question.

8. The foreign share was 9 percent in 1968 and 17 percent in 1978. *Annual Survey Reports* (Washington, D.C.: Pharmaceutical Manufacturers' Association, 1977), p. 19; *Annual Survey Reports,* 1978, p. 14.

9. James, *The Future of the Multinational Pharmaceutical Industry,* p. 204.

10. Peltzman, "An Evaluation of Consumer Protection Legislation."

11. Vincent A. Kleinfeld, "Commentary," in Blake, *Safeguarding the Public.*

12. There are problems with the statistical procedures used by Peltzman as well, but they are not relevant here. See Thomas McGuire, et al., " 'An Evaluation of Consumer Protection Legislation: The 1962 Drug Amendments': A Comment," *Journal of Political Economy,* 83 (May–June 1975): 655–661; Sam Peltzman, " 'An Evaluation of Consumer Protection Legislation: The 1962 Drug Amendments': A Reply," *Journal of Political Economy* 83 (May–June, 1975): 653–667.

13. The articles are cited and summarized in the monograph by Wardell and Lasagna, *Regulation and Drug Development.*

14. William M. Wardell, "Therapeutic Implications of the Drug Lag," *Clinical Pharmacy and Therapeutics,* 15 (January 1974): 73–96; Wardell and Lasagna, *Regulation and Drug Development,* chap. 9. The quoted passages are from Wardell and Lasagna, *Regulation and Drug Development,* pp. 95, 97, 103.

15. *Weinberger* v. *Hynson, Westcott and Dunning,* 412 U.S. 609 (1973) at 626.

16. Note that the question how well consumers could act on their own behalf does not even arise in this context. Given the terms of the current discussion, the only issue is who should be the consumer's agent.

17. Maurice F. Cuthbert, et al., "The United Kingdom," in William M. Wardell, ed., *Controlling the Use of Therapeutic Drugs: An International Comparison* (Washington, D.C.: American Enterprise Institute, 1978).

18. Wardell and Lasagna, *Regulation and Drug Development,* pp. 122–123.

19. Schwartzman, *Innovation in the Pharmaceutical Industry,* pp. 170–173, 274–278.

20. *The U.S. Generic Drug Market,* pp. 3–4, 8, 41–42; Schwartzman, *Innovation in the Pharmaceutical Industry,* p. 108. The estimates for 1972 are 61 percent (Frost and Sullivan) and 65 percent (Schwartzman). Schwartzman's use of the proportion of 1972 sales accounted for by drugs whose patents will have expired by 1980 as an estimate of the allocation of 1980 sales between patented and nonpatented drugs is biased since it ignores the sales of drugs introduced in the late 1970s.

21. *The U.S. Generic Drug Market,* pp. 3–4. The Pharmaceutical Manufacturers' Association reported that approximately 10 percent of all new prescriptions identified drugs only by the generic name at this time, but the apparent conflict may not be real. Generic drugs cost less than brand-name drugs, often considerably less. Consquently, it is entirely possible that while 10 percent of new prescriptions specified generic names, the dollar amount of these prescriptions represented less than 5 percent of total drug sales. *Prescription Drug Industry Fact Book,* p. 38.

22. *The U.S. Generic Drug Market,* p. 35; "How Pharmacists' Generic Preferences Have Changed," *American Druggist,* May 15, 1974, pp. 25–36; See also, "What Companies Do Pharmacists Prefer When Dispensing These 12 Generic Rx's?" *Pharmacy Times,* 40 (February 1974): 60–66, for similar data.

23. Bond and Lean, *Sales, Promotion and Product Differentiation,* p. 23.

24. Schwartzman, *Innovation in the Pharmaceutical Industry,* pp. 251, 276, 282. Schwartzman notes one exception to the uniform tetracycline price in 1960: Upjohn sold Panmycine for $35.70. See also table 3.

25. Schwartzman admits his perplexity on p. 274 (ibid.). He has an extensive discussion of price competition among antibiotics and a few other drugs on pp. 251–299.

26. See Douglas L. Cocks, "Product Innovation and the Dynamic Elements of Competition in the Ethical Pharmaceutical Industry," in Helms, *Drug Development and Marketing,* pp. 225–254, for the formal model; Douglas L. Cocks and John R. Virts, "Pricing Behavior of the Ethical Pharmaceutical Industry," *Journal of Business,* 47 (July 1974): 349–362, for evidence of falling prices; and W. Duncan Reekie, "Price and Quality Competition in the United States Drug Industry," *Journal of Industrial Economics,* 26 (March 1978): 223–237, for tentative evidence on increasing demand elasticities.

27. The role of pharmacists in drug price competition is increasing over time. The drug market of the 1960s can be discussed with only minimal reference to pharmacists, but this is far from true for the 1980s.

28. See table 7. Whatever the current trend of drug company profits, some uncertainty remains about the effect of regulation on the prices of new drugs. Fewer new drugs, according to another argument, mean more market power and consequently a higher price for each. Theoretically, this argument differs from the one in the text in the identification of competitors for new drugs. Empirically, it suggests that the market behavior of antibiotics is anomalous rather than typical.

29. See John M. Firestone, *Trends in Prescription Drug Prices* (Washington,

D.C.: American Enterprise Institute, 1970); *Prescription Drug Industry Fact Book.* Firestone's data are not available for the 1960s and 1970s in a single consistent series. Real producers (wholesale) and retail prices have remained below their 1967 level through mid-1979. *Monthly Labor Review,* September 1979, pp. 93, 98.

30. Theodore Marmor, *The Politics of Medicare* (Chicago: Aldine, 1973), provides a fine legislative history of Medicare and Medicaid in which surprises and "unexpected outcomes" (p. 88) abound. The data on health expenditures are from Robert W. Gibson, "National Health Expenditures, 1978," *Health Care Financing Review,* 1 (Summer 1979): 1–36. The share of health expenditures paid by private health insurance rose sharply in the two decades *before* 1965, when the federal government's share was stable.

31. Julian Pettingill, "Trends in Hospital Use by the Aged," *Social Security Bulletin,* 35 (July 1972): 3–14; Karen Davis and Roger Reynolds, "The Impact of Medicare and Medicaid on Access to Medical Care," in Richard N. Rosett, ed., *The Role of Health Insurance in the Health Services Sector* (New York: National Bureau of Economic Research, 1976), pp. 392–394.

32. *Annual Survey Reports,* p. iii. The share of drugs in total health expenditures is small enough—less than 10 percent—that the distortion in this rough calculation introduced by their exclusion from most health insurance is not important (see table 25).

33. *State Health News,* Health Policy Center, Georgetown University (September 1977). All but one state had antisubstitution laws in 1970.

34. G. B. Hastings and R. Kunnes, "Predicting Prescription Prices," *New England Journal of Medicine,* 277 (September 21, 1967): 625–627; Richard A. Horvitz et al., "Savings from Generic Prescriptions: A Study of 33 Pharmacies in Rochester, New York," *Annals of Internal Medicine,* 82 (May 1975): 601–607; S. E. Berki et al., "The Mysteries of Prescription Pricing in Retail Pharmacies," *Medical Care,* 15 (March 1977): 241–250. In contrast with the ambiguous reports on American drug pricing policy, the Canadian policy of compulsory drug patent licensing—along the lines proposed by Senator Kefauver—seems clearly capable of reducing drug prices. See Thomas K. Fulda and Paul F. Dickens III, "Controlling the Cost of Drugs: the Canadian Experience," *Health Care Financing Review,* 1 (Fall 1979): 55–64.

35. The program was first announced by the secretary of HEW in U.S. Congress, Senate, *Examination of the Pharmaceutical Industry,* pt. 1, p. 279. The regulations initiating the program were set out in U.S. Department of Health, Education, and Welfare, "Limitations on Payments or Reimbursement for Drugs," 40 Fed. Reg. 32284 (July 31, 1975). subsequent notices of the program and proposed MACs for various drugs have appeared in the Federal Register since then. *Hoffman–La Roche* v. *Califano,* civil no. 78–0467, in the U.S. District Court for the District of Columbia, is only one of several court challenges to the MAC program currently under litigation.

8. Uncertainty and Economic Behavior

1. For a similar view, see Peter Barton Hutt, "Balanced Government Regulation of Consumer Products," *Food Technology,* 31 (January 1977): 58–63.

2. U.S. District Court, Northern District of Ohio, Eastern Division, "Memorandum Opinion and Order," October 9, 1979.

3. Ian MacNeil, "The Two Futures of Contracts," *Southern California Law Review,* 47 (1974): 691–816.

4. Talcott Parsons, *The Social System* (Glencoe, Ill.: Free Press, 1951), pp. 439–447.

5. Walter Mischel, *Personality and Assessment* (New York: Wiley, 1968), pp. 73–101; Daryl J. Bem and Andrea Allen, "On Predicting Some of the People Some of the Time: The Search for Cross-Sectional Consistencies in Behavior," *Psychological Review,* 81 (November 1974): 506–520.

6. David Riesman, *The Lonely Crowd: A Study of the Changing American Character* (New Haven: Yale University Press, 1950).

7. Richard Christie and Florence L. Geis, *Studies in Machiavellianism* (New York: Academic Press, 1970), p. 285.

8. H. A. Witkin et al., *Psychological Differentiation* (New York: Wiley, 1962); Leopold W. Gruenfeld and Ann E. MacEachron, "A Cross-National Study of Cognitive Style among Managers and Technicians," *International Journal of Psychology,* 10 (1975): 28.

9. I assume that each boundary is monotonically increasing or decreasing.

10. The distinction between habit and custom corresponds roughly to Reisman's distinction between tradition-directed and other-directed behavior. In his framework the difference between them is in how fast they change over time, rather than in how far the rules of behavior are internalized.

11. See Paul A. Samuelson, *Economics,* 11th ed. (New York: McGraw-Hill, 1980), or any similar text for definition and discussion of economic efficiency.

12. See Craig D. Burrell, ed., *Drug Assessment in Ferment: Multinational Comparisons,* vol. 6 of *Philosophy and Technology of Drug Assessment* (Washington, D.C.: Interdisciplinary Communication Associates, 1976); or William M. Wardell, *Controlling the Use of Therapeutic Drugs,* for a survey of national differences in the approaches to drug policy.

13. Amitai Etzioni, *A Comparative Analysis of Complex Organizations,* rev. ed. (New York: Free Press, 1975), chap. 5, put together three modes of behavior and three types of institutions in a diagram very similar to figure 6. But while this model and his model are variations on a common theme, there are important differences between them. Etzioni was concerned with behavior within the organization, "compliance," and organizational goals. Behavior here is defined more broadly, and organizations are identified by their structure rather than by their goals. In addition, Etzioni identified three stable cells in the three-by-three array, but he did not specify how the tensions in unstable cells would be worked out. Since the present theory contains an explicit model of how behavior is determined, it has strong implications for the way in which these tensions will be expressed.

14. Compare with Etzioni, *A Comparative Analysis,* p. 119. "In the six ineffective types [cells] we would expect to find . . . *a strain toward an effective type.* We would expect to find some indication of pressure on goals, compliance, or both, to bring about an effective combination" (emphasis in original).

15. Milton S. Davis, "Variations in Patients' Compliance with Doctors'

Orders: Analysis of Congruence between Survey Responses and Results of Empirical Investigations," *Journal of Medical Education,* 41 (November 1966): 1037–48; M. V. Marston, "Compliance with Medical Regimens: A Review of the Literature," *Nursing Research,* 19 (July-August 1970): 312–323.

16. James S. Duesenberry, *Income, Saving and the Theory of Consumer Behavior* (Cambridge, Mass.: Harvard University Press, 1949), p. 3.

17. Franco Modigliani and R. E. Brumberg, "Utility Analysis and the Consumption Function: An Interpretation of Cross-section Data," in K. K. Kurihara, ed., *Post-Keynesian Economics* (New Brunswick, N.J.: Rutgers University Press, 1954); Milton Friedman, *A Theory of the Consumption Function* (Princeton: Princeton University Press, 1957).

18. An influential review of new theories of the consumption function in the late 1950s did not even mention Duesenberry. Similarly, a closely reasoned attack on the progressive income tax in the same decade did not take note of Duesenberry's demonstration that his behavioral assumptions implied a strong argument in favor of the progressive income tax. M. J. Farrell, "The New Theories of the Consumption Function," *The Economic Journal,* 69 (December 1959): 678–696; Walter J. Blum and Harry Kalven, Jr., *The Uneasy Case for Progressive Taxation* (Chicago: University of Chicago Press, 1953).

19. The most complete statement of this view is in Fred Hirsch, *Social Limits to Growth* (Cambridge, Mass.: Harvard University Press, 1976). See also Richard A. Easterlin, "Does Money Buy Happiness?" *The Public Interest,* 30 (Winter 1973): 3–10, for an interesting application.

20. Herbert A. Simon, *Models of Man* (New York: Wiley, 1957); Herbert A. Simon, "Theories of Decision-Making in Economics and Behavioral Science," *American Economic Review,* 49 (June 1959): 253–283.

21. George J. Stigler, "The Economics of Information," *Journal of Political Economy,* 69 (June 1961).

22. A good selection of the technical literature on uncertainty can be found in P. A. Diamond and Michael Rothschild, eds., *Uncertainty in Economics: Readings and Exercises* (New York: Academic Press, 1978).

23. Richard R. Nelson and Sidney G. Winter, "Toward an Evolutionary Theory of Economic Capabilities," *American Economic Review, Papers and Proceedings,* 63 (May 1973): 440–449; Richard R. Nelson and Sidney G. Winter, "Factor Price Changes and Factor Substitution in an Evolutionary Model," *Bell Journal of Economics,* 6 (Autumn 1975): 466–486; Roy Radner, "A Behavioral Model of Cost Reduction," *Bell Journal of Economics,* 6 (Spring 1975): 196–215; Roy Radner and Michael Rothschild, "Notes on the Allocation of Effort," *Journal of Economic Theory,* 10 (June 1975): 358–376; Oliver E. Williamson, *Markets and Hierarchies: Analysis and Antitrust Implications* (New York: Free Press, 1975).

24. The former was introduced by Peter Doeringer and Michael J. Piore, *Internal Labor Markets and Manpower Analysis* (Lexington, Mass.: D. C. Heath, 1971); the latter is common in the recent macroeconomic literature. It is worth noting that the term *implicit contracts* in economics does not refer to the unwritten but legally enforceable implicit contracts present in many commercial transactions.

25. Arthur M. Okun, "Inflation: Its Mechanics and Welfare Costs," *Brookings Papers on Economic Activity,* 2 (1975): 462.

26. Okun said later in his article, "Although I cannot prove that the prevalence of customer markets yields a net benefit, subjectively I think the system is worth saving." "Inflation," p. 384. The desired proof would be within the discipline of economics where only instrumental behavior is recognized. It consequently could not acknowledge the social desires of the people involved. So Okun was forced to fall back on his "subjective," nonprofessional judgment in an effort to acknowledge these desires.

27. Okun's partitionings of markets parallels McNeil's partitioning of contracts in "The Two Futures of Contracts." McNeil talked of "transactional" contracts when an isolated economic transaction was involved and of "relational" contracts when ongoing relations were involved. While the distinction is the same, McNeil was talking of actual contracts, whereas Okun was not.

28. James M. Buchanan and Gordon Tullock, *The Calculus of Consent: Logical Foundations of Constitutional Democracy* (Ann Arbor: University of Michigan Press, 1962). For applications of this style of reasoning to problems of economic policy, see George J. Stigler, "The Theory of Economic Regulation," *Bell Journal of Economics,* 2 (Spring 1978): 3–21; Sam Peltzman, "Toward a More General Theory of Regulation," *Journal of Law and Economics,* 19 (August 1976): 211–240. For an application to United States history, see Lance E. Davis and Douglass C. North, *Institutional Change and American Economic Growth* (Cambridge: Cambridge University Press, 1971).

29. Peter Blau, *Exchange and Power in Social Life* (New York: Wiley, 1964). See also Homans, "Social Behavior as Exchange"; and Gouldner, "The Norm of Reciprocity," for the theoretical background.

30. Blau, *Exchange and Power in Social Life,* pp. 118–119.

31. Ibid., pp. 22, 133–134.

32. Ibid., pp. 209–215.

33. Ibid., pp. 235, 253–261.

34. Etzioni, as noted earlier, is a partial exception to this statement. In addition, a recent book on societal decision making lists the three modes of behavior and one other as possible means of allocating scarce resources. The authors discuss the market, accountable political processes, and customary approaches as ideal types of resource allocation. They clearly refer to the three modes of behavior described in the model here, but they do not embody them in a formal model. They also add an additional decision mode: lotteries. This addition represents an additional way for societies to allocate resources; it does not describe a distinct mode of individual behavior. See Guido Calabresi and Philip Bobbitt, *Tragic Choices* (New York: Norton, 1978), pp. 31–50.

9. The Role of Government in the Drug Market

1. Parsons, *The Social System,* pp. 439–447.

2. Henry Aaron, *Politics and the Professors: The Great Society in Perspective* (Washington, D.C.: Brookings Institution, 1977).

3. Recent evidence suggests that Laetrile may contain enough cyanide to be

actively harmful, but this evidence has been generated to buttress a preexisting opposition. See Janardan Khandekar, "Studies of Amygdalin (Laetrile) Toxicity in Rodents," *Journal of the American Medical Association,* 242 (July 13, 1979): 169–171.

4. See Franz J. Ingelfinger, "Medicine: Meritorious or Meretricious," *Science,* 200 (May 26, 1978): 942–946, for a similar view on Laetrile.

5. William Wardell, "Rx: More Regulation or Better Therapies," *Regulation,* 3 (September-October 1979): 28.

6. U.S. Congress, Senate, *Drug Regulation Reform Act of 1979,* S. 1075, 96th Cong., 1st sess., 1979. secs. 109 (e), 129.

7. Ibid., sec. 108.

8. Ibid, secs. 111, 121.

9. On the public monograph system, see Fay Dworkin, "Impact of Disclosure of Safety and Efficacy Data on Expenditures for Pharmaceutical Research and Development," Paper delivered at the Seminar on the Economics of the Pharmaceutical Industry, Newark, N.J., October 14, 1978.

Bibliography

Aaron, Henry. *Politics and the Professors: The Great Society in Perspective.* Washington, D.C.: Brookings Institution, 1977.

Ackerknecht, Erwin. *Therapeutics from the Primitives to the Twentieth Century.* New York: Hafner Press, 1973.

Adams, Samuel Hopkins. "The Great American Fraud." *Collier's,* October 7, 1905.

Adams, Walter. *The Structure of American Industry,* 5th ed. New York: Macmillan, 1977.

Adir, J., and W. H. Barr. "Effect of Sleep on Bioavailability of Tetracycline." *Journal of Pharmaceutical Science,* 66: 1000–04 (July 1977).

American Medical Association, Council on Drugs. *New and Non-official Drugs.* Philadelphia: Lippincott, 1907–1964.

———. "Registry on Blood Dyscrasias: Report to the Council." *Journal of the American Medical Association,* 179: 888–890 (March 17, 1962).

American Medical Association, Council on Pharmacy and Chemistry. *Nostrums and Quackery.* Chicago: AMA Press, 1912.

American Medical Association, Department of Drugs. *AMA Drug Evaluations,* 2nd ed. Acton, Mass.: American Medical Association, 1973.

———. AMA *Drug Evaluations,* 3rd ed. Acton, Mass.: American Medical Association, 1977.

American Pharmaceutical Association, National Formulary Board. *The National Formulary.* Washington, D.C.: American Pharmaceutical Association, 1888–

Ames, Charles C., and Steven C. McCracken. "Framing Regulatory Standards to Avoid Formal Adjudication: The FDA as a Case Study." *California Law Review,* 64: 14–73 (January 1976).

Anderson, Oscar E. *The Health of a Nation: Harvey W. Wiley and the Fight for Pure Food.* Chicago: University of Chicago Press, 1958.

Annual Survey Reports. Washington, D.C.: Pharmaceutical Manufacturers' Association, annual.

Applezweig, Norman. "Steroids." *Chemical Week,* 104, no. 20: 57–72 (May 17, 1969).

Arrow, Kenneth. "Uncertainty and the Welfare Economics of Medical Care." *American Economic Review,* 53: 941–973 (December 1963).

Ayanian, Robert. "The Profit Rates and Economic Performance of Drug Firms." In Robert B. Helms, ed., *Drug Development and Marketing.* Washington, D.C.: American Enterprise Institute, 1975.

Bailey, Thomas A. "Congressional Opposition to Pure Food Legislation, 1879–1906." *American Journal of Sociology,* 36: 52–64 (July 1930).

Baily, Martin N. "Research and Development Costs and Returns: The U.S. Pharmaceutical Industry." *Journal of Political Economy,* 80: 70–85 (January 1972).

Barr, W. H., et al. "Assessment of the Biologic Availability of Tetracycline Products in Man." *Clinical Pharmacology and Therapeutics,* 13: 97–108 (January-February 1972).

Bauer, Raymond A. "Risk Handling in Drug Adoption: The Role of Company Preference." *Public Opinion Quarterly,* 25: 546–555 (Winter 1961).

Becker, M. H., et al. "Characteristics and Attitudes of Physicians Associated with the Prescribing of Chloramphenicol." *HSMHA Health Reports* (formerly *Public Health Reports*), 86: 993–1003 (November 1971).

———. "Differential Education Concerning Therapeutics and Resultant Physician Prescribing Patterns." *Journal of Medical Education,* 47: 118–127 (February 1972).

———. "Correlates of Physicians' Prescribing Behavior." *Inquiry,* 9: 30–42 (September 1972).

Becker, William H. "The Wholesalers of Hardware and Drugs, 1870–1900." Ph.D. dissertation, Johns Hopkins University, 1969.

Bem, Daryl J., and Andrea Allen. "On Predicting Some of the People Some of the Time: The Search for Cross-Sectional Consistencies in Behavior." *Psychological Review,* 81: 506–520 (November 1974).

Berger, Peter L. *Invitation to Sociology: A Humanistic Perspective.* Garden City, N.Y.: Doubleday, Anchor Books, 1963.

Berki, S. E., et al. "The Mysteries of Prescription Pricing in Retail Pharmacies." *Medical Care,* 15: 241–250 (March 1977).

Berliner, Joseph S. *Factory and Manager in the U.S.S.R.* Cambridge, Mass.: Harvard University Press, 1957.

Best, William R. "Chloramphenicol-Associated Blood Dyscrasias: A Review of Cases Submitted to the AMA Registry." *Journal of the American Medical Association,* 201: 181–188 (July 17, 1967).

Biron, Pierre. "A Hopefully Biased Pilot Survey of Physicians' Knowledge of the Content of Drug Combinations." *Canadian Medical Association Journal,* 109: 35–39 (July 7, 1973).

Blair, Donald C., et al. "Biological Availability of Oxytetracycline HC1 Capsules: A Comparison of All Manufacturing Sources Supplying the United States Market." *Journal of the American Medical Association,* 215: 251–254 (January 11, 1971).

Blair, John M. *Economic Concentration.* New York: Harcourt Brace Jovanovich, 1972.

Blake, John B., ed. *Safeguarding the Public: Historical Aspects of Medicinal Drug Control.* Baltimore: Johns Hopkins University Press, 1970.

Blau, Peter. *Exchange and Power in Social Life.* New York: Wiley, 1964.

Bloch, Marc. *Feudal Society.* Chicago: University of Chicago Press, 1961.

Blum, Walter J., and Harry Kalven, Jr. *The Uneasy Case for Progressive Taxation.* Chicago: University of Chicago Press, 1953.

Boger, William P., and John J. Gavin. "An Evaluation of Tetracycline Preparations." *New England Journal of Medicine,* 261: 827–832 (October 22, 1959).

Bok, Sissela. "The Ethics of Giving Placebos." *Scientific American,* 231, no. 5: 17–23 (November 1974).

Bond, Ronald S., and David F. Lean. *Sales, Promotion and Product Differentiation in Two Prescription Drug Markets.* Washington, D.C.: Federal Trade Commission, 1977.

Buchanan, James M., and Gordon Tullock. *The Calculus of Consent: Logical Foundations of Constitutional Democracy.* Ann Arbor: University of Michigan Press, 1962.

Budd, John H. "Combination Drugs in Medical Practice." In Louis Lasagna, ed., *Combination Drugs: Their Use and Regulation.* New York: Stratton Intercontinental Medical Book Corp., 1975.

"Buffered Tetracycline and Antibiotic Blood Levels." *The Medical Letter,* 1: 2–3 (January 23, 1959).

Burack, Richard. *The New Handbook of Prescription Drugs.* New York: Ballantine Books, 1976.

Burrell, Craig D., ed. *Drug Assessment in Ferment: Multinational Comparisons.* Vol. 6 of *Philosophy and Technology of Drug Assessment.* Washington, D.C.: Interdisciplinary Communication Associates, 1976.

Burrow, James G. "The Prescription-Drug Policies of the American Medical Association in the Progressive Era." In John B. Blake, ed., *Safeguarding the Public: Historical Aspects of Medicinal Drug Control.* Baltimore: Johns Hopkins University Press, 1970.

———. *AMA: Voice of American Medicine.* Baltimore: Johns Hopkins University Press, 1963.

Cacciapaglia, Frank, Jr., and Howard B. Rockman. "The Proposed Drug Industry Antitrust Act: Patents, Pricing and the Public." *George Washington Law Review,* 30: 875–949 (June 1962).

Caglarcan, Erol, et al. "Resource Allocation in Pharmaceutical Research and Development." In Samuel A. Mitchell and Emery A. Link, *Impact of Public Policy on Drug Innovation and Pricing.* Washington, D.C.: American University, 1976.

Calabresi, Guido, and Philip Bobbitt. *Tragic Choices.* New York: Norton, 1978.

Caplow, Theodore. "Marketing Attitudes: A Research Report from the Medical Field." *Harvard Business Review,* 30: 105–112 (November-December 1952).

——— and John J. Raymond. "Factors Influencing the Selection of Pharmaceutical Products." *Journal of Marketing,* 19: 18–23 (July 1954).

Cavers, David F. "The Evolution of the Contemporary System of Drug Regulation under the 1938 Act." In John B. Blake, ed., *Safeguarding the Public: Historical Aspects of Medicinal Drug Control.* Baltimore: Johns Hopkins University Press, 1970.

———. "The Food, Drug, and Cosmetic Act of 1938: Its Legislative History and Its Substantive Provisions." *Law and Contemporary Problems,* 6: 2–42 (Winter 1939).

Chandler, Alfred. *The Visible Hand: The Managerial Revolution in American Business.* Cambridge, Mass.: Harvard University Press, 1977.

Chien, Robert I., ed. *Issues in Pharmaceutical Economics.* Lexington, Mass.: D. C. Heath, Lexington Books, 1979.

Christie, Richard, and Florence L. Geis. *Studies in Machiavellianism.* New York: Academic Press, 1970.

A Chronology and Review of the National Academy of Sciences–National Research Council Drug Efficacy Study. Philadelphia: Smith Kline & French Laboratories, 1971.

Clarke, Frank H., ed. *How Modern Medicines Are Discovered.* Mt. Kisco, N.Y.: Future Publishing, 1973.

Clarkson, Kenneth W. *Intangible Capital and Rates of Return: Effects of Research and Promotion on Profitability.* Washington, D.C.: American Enterprise Institute, 1977.

Clymer, Harold. "The Changing Costs of Pharmaceutical Innovation." In Joseph D. Cooper, ed., *The Economics of Drug Innovation.* Washington, D.C.: American University Center for Private Enterprise, 1970.

———. "The Economic and Regulatory Climate: U.S. and Overseas Trends." In Robert B. Helms, ed., *Drug Development and Marketing.* Washington, D.C.: American Enterprise Institute, 1975.

Cocks, Douglas L. "Product Innovation and the Dynamic Elements of Competition in the Ethical Pharmaceutical Industry." In Robert B. Helms, ed., *Drug Development and Marketing.* Washington, D.C.: American Enterprise Institute, 1975.

——— and John R. Virts. "Pricing Behavior of the Ethical Pharmaceutical Industry." *Journal of Business,* 47: 349–362 (July 1974).

Colaizzi, John L., and John G. Wagner. "Digoxin (bioavailability monograph)." *Journal of the American Pharmaceutical Association,* New Series 15: 43–46 (January 1975).

Coleman, James S.; E. Katz; and H. Menzel. *Medical Innovation: A Diffusion Study.* Indianapolis: Bobbs-Merrill, 1966.

Comanor, William S. "Research and Competitive Product Differentiation in the Pharmaceutical Industry in the U.S." *Economica,* New Series 31: 372–384 (November 1964).

Cooper, Joseph D., ed. *The Economics of Drug Innovation.* Washington, D.C.: American University Center for Study of Private Enterprise, 1970.

———, ed. *Decision Making on the Efficacy and Safety of Drugs.* Vol. 1 of *Philosophy and Technology of Drug Assessment.* Washington, D.C.: Interdisciplinary Communication Associates, 1971.

———, *The Quality of Advice.* Vol. 2 of *Philosophy and Technology of Drug Assessment.* Washington, D.C.: Interdisciplinary Communication Associates, 1971.

————, *The Philosophy of Evidence*. Vol. 3 of *Philosophy and Technology of Drug Assessment*. Washington, D.C.: Interdisciplinary Communication Associates, 1972.

Cooper, Michael H. *Prices and Profits in the Pharmaceutical Industry*. Oxford: Pergamon Press, 1966.

Costello, Peter. "The Tetracycline Conspiracy: Structure, Conduct and Performance in the Drug Industry." *Antitrust Law and Economic Review,* 1: 13–44 (Summer 1968).

Cousins, Norman. "Anatomy of an Illness (as Perceived by the Patient)." *New England Journal of Medicine,* 295: 1458–63 (December 23, 1976).

————. *Anatomy of an Illness as Perceived by the Patient*. New York: Norton, 1979.

Crout, J. Richard. "Fixed-Combination Prescription Drugs: FDA Policy." In Louisa Lasagna, ed., *Combination Drugs: Their Use and Regulation*. New York: Stratton Intercontinental Medical Book Corporation, 1975.

Cuthbert, Maurice F., et al. "The United Kingdom." In William M. Wardell, ed., *Controlling the Use of Therapeutic Drugs: An International Comparison*. Washington, D.C.: American Enterprise Institute, 1978.

Cyert, Richard M., and James G. March. *A Behavioral Theory of the Firm*. Englewood Cliffs, N.J.: Prentice-Hall, 1963.

Davis, Karen, and Roger Reynolds. "The Impact of Medicare and Medicaid on Access to Medical Care." In Richard N. Rosett, ed., *The Role of Health Insurance in the Health Services Sector*. New York: National Bureau of Economic Research, 1976.

Davis, Lance E., and Douglass C. North. *Institutional Change and American Economic Growth*. Cambridge: Cambridge University Press, 1971.

Davis, Milton S. "Variations in Patients' Compliance with Doctors' Orders: Analysis of Congruence between Survey Responses and Results of Empirical Investigations." *Journal of Medical Education,* 41: 1037–48 (November 1966).

Diamond, Peter A., and Michael Rothschild, eds. *Uncertainty in Economics: Readings and Exercises*. New York: Academic Press, 1978.

"Digoxin Tablets." *The Medical Letter,* 15: 97–98 (November 23, 1973).

Doeringer, Peter, and Michael J. Piore. *Internal Labor Markets and Manpower Analysis*. Lexington, Mass.: D. C. Heath, 1971.

Dowling, Harry F. *Tetracycline*. New York: Medical Encyclopedia, 1955.

————. "The American Medical Association's Policy on Drugs in Recent Decades." In John B. Blake, ed., *Safeguarding the Public: Historical Aspects of Medicinal Drug Control*. Baltimore: Johns Hopkins University Press, 1970.

————. *Medicines for Man*. New York: Knopf, 1970.

Drug Topics Red Book. Oradell, N.J.: Medical Economics Co., 1897–.

Duesenberry, James S. *Income, Saving and the Theory of Consumer Behavior*. Cambridge, Mass.: Harvard University Press, 1949.

Dunbar, Paul B. "Memories of Early Days of Federal Food and Drug Law Enforcement." *Food, Drug and Cosmetic Law Journal,* 14: 87–139 (February 1959).

Dunn, Charles W. *Federal Food, Drug and Cosmetic Act: A Statement of its Legislative Record*. New York: G. E. Stechert, 1938.

————. "The Durham-Humphrey Bill." *Food, Drug and Cosmetic Law Journal,* 5: 854–865 (December 1950).

Dupree, A. Hunter. *Science in the Federal Government: A History of Policies and Activities to 1940.* Cambridge, Mass.: Harvard University Press, 1957.

Dworkin, Fay. "Impact of Disclosure of Safety and Efficacy Data on Expenditures for Pharmaceutical Research and Development." Paper delivered at the Seminar on the Economics of the Pharmaceutical Industry, Newark, N.J., October 14, 1978.

Dykstra, D. L. "Patent and Proprietary Medicines: Regulation Control Prior to 1906." Ph.D. dissertation, University of Wisconsin, 1951.

Earles, M. P. "Salversan and the Concept of Chemotherapy." *Pharmaceutical Journal,* 204: 400–402 (April 18, 1970).

Easterlin, Richard A. "Does Money Buy Happiness?" *The Public Interest,* 30: 3–10 (Winter 1973).

"Editorial." *New England Journal of Medicine,* 258: 97 (January 9, 1958).

Etzioni, Amitai. *A Comparative Analysis of Complex Organizations,* rev. ed. New York: Free Press, 1975.

Farrell, M. J. "The New Theories of the Consumption Function." *The Economic Journal,* 69: 678–696 (December 1959).

Feinstein, Alvin. "Clinical Biostatistics IX: How Do We Measure 'Safety' and 'Efficacy'?" *Clinical Pharmacy and Therapeutics,* 12: 544–558 (May-June 1971).

Ferber, Robert, and Hugh G. Wales. "The Effectiveness of Pharmaceutical Advertising: A Case Study." *Journal of Marketing,* 22: 395–407 (1958).

————. *The Effectiveness of Pharmaceutical Promotion.* Urbana: University of Illinois Press, 1958.

Fine, Sidney. *Laissez-Faire and General Welfare State.* Ann Arbor: University of Michigan Press, 1956.

Finland, Maxwell. "Antibiotic Blood Level Enhancement: Editorial." *Antibiotic Medicine and Clinical Therapeutics,* 5: 359–363 (June 1958).

Firestone, John M. *Trends in Prescription Drug Prices.* Washington, D.C.: American Enterprise Institute, 1970.

Fishbein, Morris. *A History of the American Medical Association, 1847–1947.* Philadelphia: Saunders, 1947.

Food Law Institute. *Federal Food, Drug and Cosmetic Law: Administrative Reports, 1907–1949.* Chicago: Commerce Clearing House, 1951.

Frank, P. F., et al. "Protection of a Military Population from Rheumatic Fever." *Journal of the American Medical Association,* 193: 775–783 (September 6, 1965).

Freedman, Daniel X. "Discussion." In Joseph D. Cooper, ed., *Decision Making on the Efficacy and Safety of Drugs.* Vol. 1 of *Philosophy and Technology of Drug Assessment.* Washington, D.C.: Interdisciplinary Communication Associates, 1971.

Freidson, Eliot. *Doctoring Together: A Study of Professional Social Control.* New York: Elsevier, 1975.

Friedman, Lawrence. "Freedom of Contract and Occupational Licensing, 1890–1910: A Legal and Social Study." *California Law Review,* 53: 487–534 (1965).

Friedman, Milton. *A Theory of the Consumption Function.* Princeton: Princeton University Press, 1957.

———. *Capitalism and Freedom.* Chicago: University of Chicago Press, 1962.

Fuchs, Victor R. *Who Shall Live? Health, Economics, and Social Choice.* New York: Basic Books, 1974.

Fulda, Thomas K. *Prescription Drug Data Summary, 1974.* Department of Health, Education and Welfare publication no. SSA-76-11928. Washington, D.C.: Government Printing Office, 1976.

——— and Paul F. Dickens III. "Controlling the Cost of Drugs: The Canadian Experience." *Health Care Financing Review,* 1, no. 2: 55–64 (Fall 1979).

Gaffin, Ben, and Associates. *Report on a Study of Advertising and the American Physician.* Chicago: American Medical Association, 1953.

———. *A Study of Medical Advertising and the American Physician, Part II: The Physician's Viewpoint.* Chicago: American Medical Association, 1953. Reprinted in U.S. Congress, Senate, *Drug Industry Antitrust Act* (S. 1552), Hearings before the Subcommittee on Antitrust and Monopoly of the Committee on the Judiciary, 87th Congress, 1st session, pts. 1–7, 1961–62.

———. *The Fond du Lac Study: An Intensive Study of the Marketing of Five New Ethical Pharmaceutical Products in a Single Market, Resulting in Some Theory of Scientific Marketing and Service Programs for Action.* Chicago: American Medical Association, 1956.

Galdson, Iago. *Progress in Medicine: A Critical Review of the Last Hundred Years.* New York: Knopf, 1940.

Gaps in Technology: Pharmaceuticals. Paris: Organization for Economic Cooperation and Development, 1969.

Gellhorn, Walter. *Individual Freedom and Governmental Restraints.* Baton Rouge: Louisiana State University Press, 1956.

Gerth, Hans H., and C. Wright Mills. *From Max Weber: Essays in Sociology.* New York: Oxford University Press, 1946.

Gibson, Robert W. "National Health Expenditures, 1978." *Health Care Financing Review,* 1: 1–36 (Summer 1979).

Goodman, Louis S. "The Problem of Drug Efficacy: An Exercise in Dissection." In Paul Talalay, ed., *Drugs in Our Society.* Baltimore: Johns Hopkins University Press, 1964.

——— and Alfred Gilman. *The Pharmacological Basis of Therapeutics,* 5th ed. New York: Macmillan, 1975.

Gouldner, A. W. "The Norm of Reciprocity: A Preliminary Statement." *American Sociological Review,* 25: 161–178 (1960).

Grabowski, Henry. *Drug Regulation and Innovation: Empirical Evidence and Policy Options.* Washington, D.C.: American Enterprise Institute, 1976.

——— and Dennis G. Mueller. "Industrial Research and Development, Intangible Capital Stocks, and Firm Profit Rates." *Bell Journal of Economics,* 9: 328–343 (Autumn 1978).

Grabowski, Henry G.; John M. Vernon; and Lucy Glenn Thomas. "The Effects of Regulatory Policy on the Incentives to Innovate: An International Comparative Analysis." In Samuel A. Mitchell and Emery A. Link, eds., *Impact of Public Policy on Drug Innovation and Pricing.* Washington, D.C.: American University, 1976.

————. "Estimating the Effects of Regulation on Innovation: An International Comparative Analysis of the Pharmaceutical Industry." *Journal of Law and Economics,* 21: 133–164 (April 1978).

Grant, R. L. "The How and Why of the Certification of Insulin." In Henry Welch and Felix Marti-Ibañez, eds., *The Impact of the FDA on Our Society.* New York: MD Publications, 1956.

Grier, James. *A History of Pharmacy.* London: Pharmaceutical Press, 1937.

Grove, Donald C. "Certification of Antibiotics." In Henry Welch and Felix Marti-Ibañez, eds., *The Impact of the FDA on our Society.* New York: MD Publications, 1956.

Gruenfeld, Leopold W., and Ann E. MacEachron. "A Cross-National Study of Cognitive Style among Managers and Technicians." *International Journal of Psychology,* 10: 27–55 (1975).

Handler, Milton. "The Control of False Advertising under the Wheeler-Lea Act," *Law and Contemporary Problems,* 6: 91–110 (Winter 1939).

Hansen, Ronald W. "The Pharmaceutical Development Process: Estimates of Development Costs and Times and the Effects of Proposed Regulatory Changes." In Robert I. Chien, ed., *Issues in Pharmaceutical Economics.* Lexington, Mass.: D. C. Heath, Lexington Books, 1979.

Harris, Richard. *The Real Voice.* New York: Macmillan, 1964.

Hastings, G. B., and R. Kunnes. "Predicting Prescription Prices." *New England Journal of Medicine,* 277: 625–627 (September 21, 1967).

Hayes, Lauffer T., and Frank J. Ruff. "The Administration of the Federal Food and Drugs Act." *Law and Contemporary Problems,* 1:16–35 (December 1933).

Hayes, Samuel P. *The Response to Industrialism, 1885–1914.* Chicago: University of Chicago Press, 1957.

Hechtlinger, Adelaide. *The Great Patent Medicine Era.* New York: Grosset & Dunlap, 1970.

Helms, Robert B., ed. *Drug Development and Marketing.* Washington, D.C.: American Enterprise Institute, 1975.

Hicks, John. *A Theory of Economic History.* Oxford: Oxford University Press, 1969.

Hirsch, Fred. *Social Limits to Growth.* Cambridge, Mass.: Harvard University Press, 1976.

Hofstadter, Richard. *The Age of Reform.* New York: Random House, 1955.

Holmstedt, Bo, and Goren Liljestrand, eds. *Readings in Pharmacology.* New York: Macmillan 1963.

Holvey, David N., ed. *The Merck Manual of Diagnosis and Therapy,* 12th ed. Rahway, N.J.: Merck Sharp & Dohme, 1972.

Homans, George. "Social Behavior As Exchange." *American Journal of Sociology,* 63: 597–606 (1958).

Hopkins, Richard J. "Medical Prescriptions and the Law: A Study of the Enactment of the Durham-Humphrey Amendment to the FDC Act." M. A. thesis, Emory University, 1965.

Horvitz, Richard A., et al. "Savings from Generic Prescriptions: A Study of 33 Pharmacies in Rochester, New York." *Annals of Internal Medicine,* 82: 601–607 (May 1975).

Houston, W. R. "The Doctor Himself As a Therapeutic Agent." *Annals of Internal Medicine,* 11: 1416–25 (February 1938).

"How Pharmacists' Generic Preferences Have Changed." *American Druggist,* May 15, 1974, pp. 25–36.

Hutt, Peter Barton. "Regulation of the Practice of Medicine under the Pure Food and Drug Laws." *Association of Food and Drug Officials of the United States,* 33: 3–22 (January 1969).

———. "Balanced Government Regulation of Consumer Products." *Food Technology,* 31: 58–63 (January 1977).

Idsøe, O., et al. "Nature and Extent of Penicillin Side-reactions, with Particular Reference to Fatalities from Anaphylactic Shock." *Bulletin of World Health Organizations,* 38: 159–188 (1968).

Ingelfinger, Franz J. "Medicine: Meritorious or Meretricious." *Science,* 200: 942–946 (May 26, 1978).

International Pharmacy Abstracts, Abstracts on Drug Equivalence: Bioavailability and Drug Equivalence. Vol. 7 (1970) to vol. 12, nos. 1–12 (January–June 1975). Washington, D.C.: American Society of Hospital Pharmacists, 1975.

Israel, Jerry, ed. *Building the Organization Society.* New York: Free Press, 1972.

Jackson, Charles O. *Food and Drug Legislation in the New Deal.* Princeton: Princeton University Press, 1970.

James, Barrie G. *The Future of the Multinational Pharmaceutical Industry to 1990.* New York: Wiley, 1977.

Jenkins, Reese V. *Images and Enterprises: Technology and the American Photographic Industry, 1839–1925.* Baltimore: Johns Hopkins University Press, 1975.

Jervey, J. W. "Common Law Rights and the Physician's Prescription." *New York Medical Journal,* 74: 110–112 (July 20, 1901.).

Johnson, B. F. "Biological Availability of Digoxin from Lanoxin Produced in the United Kingdom." *British Medical Journal,* 4: 323–326 (November 10, 1973).

Juhl, Erik, et al. "The Epidemiology of the Gastrointestinal Randomized Clinical Trial." *New England Journal of Medicine,* 296: 20–22 (January 6, 1977).

Kefauver, Estes. *In a Few Hands: Monopoly Power in America.* New York: Pantheon Books, 1965.

Keller, Morton. *Affairs of State: Public Life in Late Nineteenth Century America.* Cambridge, Mass.: Harvard University Press, 1977.

Kennedy, Donald. "Generic Drugs." Address to the Annual Convention, House of Delgates, New York Medical Society, October 23, 1978.

Kett, Joseph F. *Formation of the American Medical Profession, 1780–1860.* New Haven: Yale University Press, 1968.

Khandekar, Janardan. "Studies of Amygdalin (Laetrile) Toxicity in Rodents." *Journal of the American Medical Association,* 242: 169–171 (July 13, 1979).

King, Donald C. *Marketing Prescription Drugs.* Michigan Business Reports, no. 56. Ann Arbor: Bureau of Business Research, Graduate School of Business Administration, University of Michigan, 1968.

Kitch, Edmund W. "The Patent System and the New Drug Application: An

Evaluation of the Incentive for Private Investment in New Drug Research and Marketing." In R. L. Landau, ed., *Regulating New Drugs.* Chicago: Center for Policy Study, University of Chicago, 1973.

Kleinfield, Vincent A. "Commentary." In John B. Blake, ed., *Safeguarding the Public: Historical Aspects of Medicinal Drug Control.* Baltimore: Johns Hopkins University Press, 1970.

Koch-Weser, J. "Bioavailability of Drugs, Parts I and II." *New England Journal of Medicine,* 291: 233–237, 503–506 (August 1 and September 5, 1974).

Krantz, John C., Jr., ed. *Fighting Disease with Drugs.* Baltimore: National Council of Pharmaceutical Research, 1931.

Kremers, Edward, and George Urdang. *History of Pharmacy: A Guide and Survey.* Rev. by Glenn Sonnedecker. Philadelphia: Lippincott, 1976.

Kunin, Calvin M., et al. "Enhancement of Tetracycline Blood Levels." *New England Journal of Medicine,* 259: 147–156 (July 24, 1958).

Kunreuther, Howard. *Disaster Insurance Protection: Public Policy Lessons.* New York: Wiley, 1978.

Kurihara, K. K., ed. *Post-Keynesian Economics.* New Brunswick, N.J.: Rutgers University Press, 1954.

Lall, Sanjaya. *Major Issues in the Transfer of Technology to Developing Countries: A Case Study of the Pharmaceutical Industry.* New York: United Nations Conference on Trade and Development, 1975.

Lamb, Ruth deForest. *American Chamber of Horrors: The Truth about Food and Drugs.* New York: Farrar and Rinehart, 1936.

Landau, R. L., ed. *Regulating New Drugs.* Chicago: Center for Policy Study, University of Chicago, 1973.

Lasagna, Louis. "Discussion." In Joseph D. Cooper, ed., *The Philosophy of Evidence.* Vol. 3 of *Philosophy and Technology of Drug Assessment.* Washington, D.C.: Interdisciplinary Communication Associates, 1972.

———. "Research, Regulation and Development of New Pharmaceuticals: Past, Present and Future, Parts I and II." *American Journal of Medical Science,* 263: 8–18, 66–78 (January and February, 1972).

———, ed. *Combination Drugs: Their Use and Regulation.* New York: Stratton Intercontinental Medical Book Corp., 1975.

"Laws Regulating the Practice of Medicine in the Various States and Territories of the United States." *Journal of the American Medical Association,* 37: 1304–18 (November 16, 1901).

Leikin, S. L., et al. "Aplastic Anemia Due to Chloramphenicol." *Clinical Proceedings of the Children's Hospital of Washington,* 17: 171–181 (July 1961).

Lewis, C. L., et al. "Chloramphenicol (Chloromycetin) in Relation to Blood Dyscrasias with Observations on Other Drugs." *Antibiotics and Chemotherapy,* 2: 601–609 (December 1952).

Ley, Herbert L. "Discussion." In Joseph D. Cooper, ed., *The Quality of Advice.* Vol. 2 of *Philosophy and Technology of Drug Assessment.* Washington, D.C.: Interdisciplinary Communication Associates, 1971.

Linten, Fred B. "Leaders in Food and Drug Law, Part Five." *Food, Drug and Cosmetic Law Journal,* 5: 771–787 (November 1950).

Lowy, D. R.; L. Lowy; and R. S. Warner. "A Survey of Physicians' Awareness of Drug Costs." *Journal of Medical Education,* 47: 349–351 (May 1972).

Lyons, Richard. "Demoralized F.D.A. Struggles to Cope." *New York Times,* March 14, 1977, pp. 1, 49.

MacNeil, Ian. "The Two Futures of Contracts." *Southern California Law Review,* 47: 691–816 (1974).

Mahoney, Tom. *The Merchants of Life.* New York: Harper & Bros., 1959.

Marmor, Theodore. *The Politics of Medicare.* Chicago: Aldine, 1973.

Maronde, R. F., et al. "A Study of Prescribing Patterns." *Medical Care,* 9: 383–395 (September-October, 1971).

Marquardt, Martha. *Paul Ehrlich.* New York: Henry Schuman, 1951.

Marston, M. V. "Compliance with Medical Regimens: A Review of the Literature." *Nursing Research,* 19: 312–323 (July-August, 1970).

Massengill, Samuel Evans. *A Sketch of Medicine and Pharmacy.* Bristol, Tenn.: S. E. Massengill Co., 1943.

May, Charles D. "Gilded Antibiotics" [Editorial]. *Pediatrics,* 22: 415 (September 1958).

———. "Selling Drugs by 'Educating' Physicians." *The Journal of Medical Education,* 36: 1–23 (January 1961).

McAuliffe, William E. "Measuring The Quality of Medical Care: Process versus Outcome." *Milbank Memorial Fund Quarterly/Health and Society,* 57: 118–152 (Winter 1979).

McGuire, Thomas, et al. " 'An Evaluation of Consumer Protection Legislation: The 1962 Drug Amendments': A Comment." *Journal of Political Economy,* 83: 655–661 (May-June 1975).

McKeown, Thomas. *The Modern Rise of Population.* London: Edward Arnold, 1976.

McMahon, F. Gilbert. "Europeanization of American Drug Research" [Editorial]. *Clinical Pharmacy and Therapeutics,* 18: 375–376 (October 1975).

Meade, T. W. "Prescribing of Chloramphenicol in General Practice." *British Medical Journal,* 1: 671–674 (March 18, 1967).

Measday, Walter S. "The Pharmaceutical Industry." In Walter Adams, ed., *The Structure of American Industry,* 5th ed. New York: Macmillan, 1977.

Mellinkoff, Sherman M. "Chemical Intervention." *Scientific American,* 229: 102–112 (September 1973).

Menzel, Herbert, and Elihu Katz. "Comment on Charles Winick, 'The Diffusion . . .' " *Sociometry,* 26: 125–127 (May 1963).

Merck & Co. *Stock Application.* New York Stock Exchange no. A–12333 (March 21, 1946).

Merrill, Richard A. "Compensation for Prescription Drug Injuries." *Virginia Law Review,* 59: 1–120 (January 1973).

Miller, Russell R. "Prescribing Habits of Physicians: A Review of Studies on Prescribing of Drugs, Parts I–VIII." *Drug Intelligence and Clinical Pharmacy,* 7: 492–500, 557–564; 8: 81–91 (November 1973–February 1974). Reprinted in U.S. Congress, Senate, *Examination of the Pharmaceutical Industry,* Hearings before the Subcommittee on Health of the Committee on Labor and Public Welfare, 93rd Congress, 1st and 2nd session, pt. 4, 1973–1974, pp. 1369–96.

Mintz, Morton. " 'Heroine' of FDA Keeps Bad Drug Off Market." *Washington Post,* July 15, 1962, p. A1.

————. *By Prescription Only.* Rev. ed. of *The Therapeutic Nightmare* (1965). Boston: Beacon Press, 1967.

Mischel, Walter. *Personality and Assessment.* New York: Wiley, 1968.

Mitchell, Samuel A., and Emery A. Link, eds. *Impact of Public Policy on Drug Innovation and Pricing.* Washington, D.C.: American University, 1976.

Modell, Walter, ed. *Drugs of Choice, 1976-1977.* St. Louis: C. V. Mosby, 1976.

Modigliani, Franco, and R. E. Brumberg. "Utility Analysis and the Consumption Function: An Interpretation of Cross-Section Data." In K. K. Kurihara, ed., *Post-Keynesian Economics.* New Brunswick, N.J.: Rutgers University Press, 1954.

Motor Vehicle Facts and Figures, 1977. Detroit: Motor Vehicle Manufacturers' Association, 1977.

Muller, Charlotte. "Medical Review of Prescribing." *Journal of Chronic Disease,* 18: 689–696 (July 1965).

Munch, James C., and James C. Munch, Jr. "Notices of Judgment: The First Thousand." *Food, Drug and Cosmetic Law Journal,* 10: 219–242 (April 1955).

————. "Notices of Judgment: Numbers 1,001 to 5,000." *Food, Drug and Cosmetic Law Journal,* 11: 17–34 (January 1956).

————. "Notices of Judgment: 5,001 to 15,000." *Food, Drug and Cosmetic Law Journal,* 11: 196–211 (April 1956).

Mundy, Gregory R., et al. "Current Medical Practice and the Food and Drug Administration." *Journal of the American Medical Association,* 229: 1744–48 (September 23, 1974).

National Research Council, Division of Medical Science. *Drug Efficacy Study; Final Report to the Commissioner of Food and Drugs, FDA.* Washington, D.C.: National Academy of Sciences, 1969.

Nelson, Richard R., and Sidney G. Winter. "Toward an Evolutionary Theory of Economic Capabilities." *American Economic Review, Papers and Proceedings,* 63: 440–449 (May 1973).

————. "Factor Price Changes and Factor Substitution in an Evolutionary Model." *Bell Journal of Economics,* 6: 466–486 (Autumn 1975).

New Product Survey. New York: Paul de Haen, 1977–1979.

Nisbett, Richard E., and T. D. Wilson. "Telling More Than We Can Know: Verbal Reports on Mental Processes." *Psychological Review,* 84: 231–259 (May 1977).

Noble, David. *The Progressive Mind, 1890-1917.* Chicago: Rand-McNally, 1970.

Nonproprietary Name Index. New York: Paul de Haen, 1974.

Okun, Arthur M. "Inflation: Its Mechanics and Welfare Costs." *Brookings Papers on Economic Activity,* 2: 351–390 (1975).

Parsons, Talcott. *The Social System.* Glencoe, Ill.: Free Press, 1951.

Pauls, Lynne M., and Baldwin E. Kloer. *FDA Enforcement Activities within the Pharmaceutical Industry: Analysis of Relative Incidence.* Indianapolis: Eli Lilly, 1958.

Pease, Otis. *The Responsibilities of American Advertising: Private Control and Public Influence, 1920-1940.* New Haven: Yale University Press, 1958.

Peltzman, Sam. "An Evaluation of Consumer Protection Legislation: The 1962

Drug Amendments." *Journal of Political Economy,* 81: 1046–91 (September 1973).

———. " 'An Evaluation of Consumer Protection Legislation: The 1962 Drug Amendments': A Reply." *Journal of Political Economy,* 83: 663–667 (May-June, 1975).

———. "Toward a More General Theory of Regulation." *Journal of Law and Economics,* 19: 211–240 (August 1976).

Pettingill, Julian. "Trends in Hospital Use by the Aged." *Social Security Bulletin,* 35, no. 7: 3–14 (July 1972).

Physicians' Desk Reference. Oradell, N.J.: Medical Economics Co., 1947–.

Prescription Drug Industry Fact Book. Washington, D.C.: Pharmaceutical Manufacturers' Association, 1973.

The Propaganda for Reform in Proprietary Medicines. Chicago: American Medical Association, 1905–.

"Proprietary vs. Non-Proprietary." *Journal of the American Medical Association,* 97: 1226 (illustration) (October 24, 1931).

Radner, Roy. "A Behavioral Model of Cost Reduction." *Bell Journal of Economics,* 6: 196–215 (Spring 1975).

——— and Michael Rothschild. "Notes on the Allocation of Effort." *Journal of Economic Theory,* 10: 358–376 (June 1975).

Reekie, W. Duncan. "Price and Quality Competition in the United States Drug Industry." *Journal of Industrial Economics,* 26: 223–237 (March 1978).

Rehder, Robert Richard. "The Role of the Detail Man in the Diffusion and Adoption of an Ethical Pharmaceutical Innovation Within a Single Medical Community." Ph.D. dissertation, Stanford University, 1961.

Rheingold, Paul D. "The MER/29 Story: An Instance of Successful Mass Disaster Litigation." *California Law Review,* 56: 116–148 (January 1968).

Richards, Dickinson W. "A Clinician's View of Advances in Therapeutics." In Paul Talalay, ed., *Drugs in Our Society.* Baltimore: Johns Hopkins University Press, 1964.

Ries-Arndt, Von E. "Neue Pharmazeutische Wirkstoffe." *Pharmazeutische Industrie,* 37: 4 (1975).

Riesman, David. *The Lonely Crowd: A Study of the Changing American Character.* New Haven: Yale University Press, 1950.

Rorem, C. Rufus, and Robert P. Fischelis. *The Costs of Medicines.* Publication no. 14 of the Committee on the Cost of Medical Care. Chicago: University of Chicago Press, 1932.

Rosett, Richard N., ed. *The Role of Health Insurance in the Health Services Sector.* New York: National Bureau of Economic Research, 1976.

Rudolph, Andrew H., and Eleanor V. Price. "Penicillin Reactions among Patients in Venereal Disease Clinics: A National Survey." *Journal of the American Medical Association,* 223: 499–501 (January 29, 1973).

Samuelson, Paul A. *Economics,* 11th ed. New York: McGraw Hill, 1980.

Scherer, Fred M. "Discussion." In Joseph D. Cooper, ed., *The Economics of Drug Innovation.* Washington, D.C.: American University Center for Study of Private Enterprise, 1970.

Schmalensee, Richard. *The Economics of Advertising.* Amsterdam: North Holland Publishing, 1972.

Schneider, Harold K. *Economic Man: The Anthropology of Economics.* New York: Free Press, 1974.

Schwartzman, David. *Innovation in the Pharmaceutical Industry.* Baltimore: Johns Hopkins University Press, 1976.

Shryock, Richard H. *Medical Licensing in America.* Baltimore: Johns Hopkins University Press, 1967.

Silverman, Milton. *The Drugging of the Americas.* Berkeley and Los Angeles: University of California Press, 1976.

—— and Philip R. Lee. *Pills, Profits, and Politics.* Berkeley and Los Angeles: University of California Press, 1975.

Simmons, Henry E. "Assuring Total Drug Quality." *Journal of the American Pharmaceutical Association,* New Series 13: 96–98 (February 1973).

Simon, Herbert A. *Models of Man.* New York: Wiley, 1957.

——. "Theories of Decision-Making in Economics and Behavioral Science." *American Economic Review,* 49: 253–283 (June 1959).

Sinclair, Upton. *The Jungle.* New York: Doubleday, Page, 1906.

Smick, K. M., et al. "Fatal Aplastic Anemia: An Epidemiological Study of its Relationship to the Drug Chloramphenicol." *Journal of Chronic Disease,* 17: 899–914 (October 1964).

Smith, Austin, and Arthur D. Herrick, eds. *Drug Research and Development.* New York: Revere Publishing, 1948.

Smith, Mickey C. *Principles of Pharmaceutical Marketing.* Philadelphia: Lea & Febiger, 1968.

——. "Social Barriers to Rational Drug Therapy." *American Journal of Hospital Pharmacy,* 29: 121–127 (February 1972).

Sollmann, Torald. "The Pharmacopoeia as the Standard for Medical Prescribing." *Journal of the American Medical Association,* 51: 2013–18 (December 12, 1908).

Sonnedecker, Glenn. "Contribution of the Pharmaceutical Profession toward Controlling the Quality of Drugs in the Nineteenth Century." In John B. Blake, ed., *Safeguarding the Public: Historical Aspects of Medicinal Drug Control.* Baltimore: Johns Hopkins University Press, 1970.

Starr, Paul. *The Social Transformation of American Medicine.* New York: Basic Books, forthcoming.

Steele, Henry. "Monopoly and Competition in the Ethical Drugs Market." *Journal of Law and Economics,* 5: 131–164 (October 1962).

Stern, Bernhard J. *American Medical Practice in the Perspective of a Century.* New York: Commonwealth Fund, 1945.

Sternsher, Bernard. *Rexford Tugwell and the New Deal.* New Brunswick, N.J.: Rutgers University Press, 1964.

Stigler, George J. "The Economics of Information." *Journal of Political Economy,* 69: 213–225 (June 1961).

——. *Capital Rates of Return in Manuacturing Industries.* Princeton: Princeton University Press for the National Bureau of Economic Research, 1963.

——. "The Theory of Economic Regulation." *Bell Journal of Economics,* 2: 3–21 (Spring, 1971).

Stolley, Paul D., et al. "The Relationship between Physician Characteristics and Prescribing Appropriateness." *Medical Care,* 10: 17–28 (January-February 1972).

Swain, Henry L. "The Attitude of the Profession toward Patent Medicines and Appliances." *Yale Medical Journal,* 8: 169–176 (December 1901).

Swazey, Judith. *Chlorpromazine in Psychiatry: A Study of Therapeutic Innovation.* Cambridge, Mass.: M.I.T. Press, 1974.

Sweeney, Charles A. "Federal Trade Commission in Control of False Advertising of Foods, Drugs, and Cosmetics." *Food, Drug and Cosmetics Law Journal,* 12: 606–616 (September 1957).

Talalay, Paul, ed. *Drugs in Our Society.* Baltimore: Johns Hopkins University Press, 1964.

Taylor, Norman. *Plant Drugs That Changed the World.* New York: Dodd, Mead, 1965.

Telser, Lester G., et al. "The Theory of Supply with Applications to the Ethical Pharmaceutical Industry." *Journal of Law and Economics,* 18: 449–478 (October 1975).

Thrush, M. Clayton. "The U.S. Pharmacopoeia and the National Formulary." *Journal of the American Medical Association,* 54: 437–441 (February 5, 1910).

Tishler, Max. "Role of the Drug House in Biological and Medical Research." *Bulletin of the New York Academy of Medicine,* 35: 590–600 (September 1959).

Traynor, Roger J. "The Ways and Meanings of Defective Products and Strict Liability." *Tennessee Law Review,* 32: 363–376 (Spring 1965).

Tugwell, Rexford. *The Democratic Roosevelt.* Garden City, N.J.: Doubleday, 1957.

Turner, James S. *The Chemical Feast.* New York: Grossman, 1970.

Tversky, Amos, and Daniel Kahneman. "Judgment under Uncertainty: Heuristics and Biases." *Science,* 185: 1124–31 (September 1974).

The U.S. Generic Drug Market. New York: Frost and Sullivan, 1976.

U.S., Bureau of the Census. *Thirteenth Census of the United States.* Vol. VIII, *Manufactures, 1909: General Report and Analysis.* Washington, D.C.: Government Printing Office, 1913.

——. *Census of Manufactures.* Vol. II, *Industry Statistics.* Washington, D.C.: Government Printing Office, 1947–1972.

——. *Census of Manufactures.* Special Report Series, *Concentration Ratios in Manufacturing.* Washington, D.C.: Government Printing Office, 1967–1972.

U.S., Congress, House. *Food, Drug, and Cosmetic Act.* House Report 2139, 75th Congress, 3rd session, 1938.

——. *A Bill to Amend Section 503(b) of the Federal Food, Drug, and Cosmetic Act* (H.R. 3298). Hearings before the Committee on Interstate and Foreign Commerce, 82nd Congress, 1st session, 1951.

——. *Amending Section 503 (b) of the Federal Food, Drug, and Cosmetic Act.* House Report 700, 82nd Congress, 1st session, 1951.

——. *Report to the Secretary of HEW* [by the] Citizens Advisory Committee on the Food and Drug Administration. House Document 227, 84th Congress, 1st session, 1955.

——. *Hearings on Drug Safety before the Subcommittee on Intergovernmental Relations of the Committee on Government Operations.* 88th Congress, 2nd session, 1964.

U.S., Congress, Senate. *Digest of the Pure Food and Drug Laws of the United States and Foreign Countries.* By William E. Mason. Senate Report 3, 57th Congress, 1st session, 1901.

————. *Food, Drug, and Cosmetic Act* (S. 1944). Hearings before a Subcommittee of the Committee on Commerce, 73rd Congress, 2nd session, 1934.

————. *Food, Drug, and Cosmetic Act* (S. 2800). Hearings before the Committee on Commerce, 73rd Congress, 2nd session, 1934.

————. *Amending Sections 303 (c) and 503 (b) of the Federal Food, Drug, and Cosmetic Act.* Senate Report 946, 82nd Congress, 1st session, 1951.

————. *Administered Prices in the Drug Industry.* Hearings before the Subcommittee on Antitrust and Monopoly of the Committee on the Judiciary, 86th Congress, 1st and 2nd sessions, 1960–1961.

————. *Administered Prices: Drugs.* Senate Report 448, 87th Congress, 1st session, 1961.

————. *Drug Industry Antitrust Act* (S. 1552). Hearings before the Subcommittee on Antitrust and Monopoly of the Committee on the Judiciary, 87th Congress, 1st and 2nd sessions, 1961–1962.

————. *Drug Industry Act of 1962.* Senate Report 1744, 87th Congress, 2nd session, 1962.

————. *Competitive Problems in the Drug Industry.* Hearings before the Subcommittee on Monopoly of the Select Committee on Small Business, 90th Congress, 1st session, to 94th Congress, 2nd session, 1967–1977.

————. *Advertising of Proprietary Medicines.* Hearings before the Subcommittee on Monopoly of the Select Committee on Small Business, 92nd Congress, 1st session, to 93rd Congress, 2nd session, 1971–1973.

————. *Examination of the Pharmaceutical Industry.* Hearings before the Subcommittee on Health of the Committee on Labor and Public Welfare, 93rd Congress, 1st and 2nd sessions, 1973–1974.

————. *Competitive Problems in the Drug Industry: Summary and Analysis.* Committe Print of the Subcommittee on Monopoly of the Select Committee on Small Business, 92nd Congress, 2nd session, 1972.

————. *Drug Regulation Reform Act of 1979* (S. 1075). 96th Congress, 1st session, 1979.

U.S., Department of Health, Education, and Welfare. *Task Force on Prescription Drugs: Report and Recommendations.* Committee Print of the Subcommittee on Monopoly of the Senate Select Committee on Small Business, 90th Congress, 2nd session, 1968.

————. "Limitations on Payment or Reimbursement For Drugs." 40 Federal Register 32284 (July 31, 1975).

————, Review Panel on New Drug Regulation. *Final Report.* Washington, D.C.: Department of Health, Education, and Welfare, May 1977.

U.S., Federal Trade Commission. *Economic Report on Antibiotics Manufacture.* Washington, D.C.: Government Printing Office, June 1958.

————, and Securities and Exchange Commission. *Rates of Return for Identical Companies in Selected Manufacturing Industries.* Washington, D.C.: Government Printing Office, 1947–1973.

U.S., Food and Drug Administration. "Promulgation of Regulations under the Federal Food, Drug and Cosmetic Act." 3 Federal Register 3168 (December 28, 1938).

————. *Annual Report.* Washington, D.C.: Government Printing Office, 1939.

————. "Regulations for the Enforcement of the Federal Food, Drug, and Cosmetic Act." 6 Federal Register 1920 (April 15, 1941).

————. "Over-the-Counter Drugs." 37 Federal Register 85 (January 5, 1968).

————. "Procedures for Classification of Over-the-Counter Drugs." 37 Federal Register 9464 (May 1, 1968).

————. "Hearing Regulations and Regulations Describing Scientific Content of Adequate and Well-Controlled Clinical Investigations." 35 Federal Register 7250 (May 8, 1970).

————. "Combination Drugs for Human Use." 36 Federal Register 3127 (February 18, 1971).

————. "Fixed-Combination Prescription Drugs for Humans." 36 Federal Register 20037 (October 15, 1971).

————. "Drug Efficacy Study Implementation Notices." 37 Federal Register 2969 (February 10, 1972).

————. "Legal Status of Approved Labelling for Prescription Drugs: Prescribing for Uses Unapproved by the FDA." 37 Federal Register 16503 (August 15, 1972).

————. "New Drugs." 37 Federal Register 23185 (October 31, 1972).

————, Drug Listing Branch, Bureau of Drugs. *National Drug Code Directory.* Washington, D.C.: Department of Health, Education, and Welfare, 1969–.

U.S., Internal Revenue Service. *Sourcebook of Statistics of Income.* Washington, D.C.: Internal Revenue Service, 1948–1973.

U.S., Office of Management and Budget. *The Budget of the U.S. Government, and Appendix.* Washington, D.C.: Government Printing Office, annual.

U.S., Office of Technology Assessment, Drug Bioequivalence Study Panel. *Drug Bioequivalence.* Washington, D.C.: Government Printing Office, 1974.

U.S., Patent Office. *Patent 2,446,102.* (July 27, 1948).

U.S. Pharmacopoeial Convention. *The Pharmacopoeia of the United States of America.* Philadelphia: P. Blakiston's Son, 1820–.

Waksman, Selman A. *My Life with the Microbes.* New York: Simon & Schuster, 1954.

Walker, Hugh D. *Market Power and Price Levels in the Ethical Drug Industry.* Bloomington: Indiana University Press, 1971.

Wallerstein, Ralph O., et al. "Statewide Study of Chloramphenicol Therapy and Fatal Aplastic Anemia." *Journal of the American Medical Association,* 208: 2045–50 (June 16, 1969).

Wardell, William M. "Introduction of New Therapeutic Drugs in the United States and Great Britain: An International Comparison." *Clinical Pharmacy and Therapeutics,* 14: 773–790 (September-October, 1973).

————. "Therapeutic Implications of the Drug Lag." *Clinical Pharmacy and Therapeutics,* 15: 73–96 (January 1974).

————. *Controlling the Use of Therapeutic Drugs; An International Comparison.* Washington, D.C.: American Enterprise Institute, 1978.

————. "Rx: More Regulation or Better Therapies?" *Regulation,* 3, no. 5: 25–33 (September-October 1979).

———— and Louis Lasagna. *Regulation and Drug Development.* Washington, D.C.: American Enterprise Institute, 1975.

Welch, Henry, et al. "Blood Dyscrasias: A Nationwide Survey." *Antibiotics and Chemotherapy,* 4: 607–623 (June 1954).

Welch, Henry, and Felix Marti-Ibañez, eds. *The Impact of the FDA on Our Society.* New York: MD Publications, 1956.

"What Companies Do Pharmacists Prefer When Dispensing These 12 Generic Rx's?" *Pharmacy Times,* 40: 60–66 (February 1974).

White, Morton. *Social Thought in America: The Revolt against Formalism.* Reprint of 1949 ed. London: Oxford University Press, 1976.

Wiebe, Robert H. *The Search for Order, 1877–1920.* New York: Hill and Wang, 1967.

Wiggins, Steven N. "Product Quality Regulation and Innovation in the Pharmaceutical Industry." Ph.D. dissertation, Massachusetts Institute of Technology, 1979.

Wiley, Harvey W. *The History of a Crime against the Food Law.* Washington, D.C.: Harvey Wiley, 1929.

Willcox, R. R. "Influence of Penicillin Allergic Reactions on V.D. Control Programmes." *British Journal of Venereal Disease,* 40: 200–209 (September 1964).

Williams, Edward B. "Exemption from the Requirement of Adequate Directions for Use in the Labelling of Drugs." *Food, Drug and Cosmetic Law Journal,* 2: 155–172 (June 1947).

Williamson, Oliver E. *Markets and Hierarchies: Analysis and Antitrust Implications.* New York: Free Press, 1975.

Wilson, Stephen. *Food and Drug Regulation.* Washington, D.C.: American Council on Public Affairs, 1942.

Winick, Charles. "The Diffusion of an Innovation among Physicians in a Large City." *Sociometry,* 24: 384–396 (December 1961).

Witkin, H. A., et al. *Psychological Differentiation.* New York: Wiley, 1962.

Wolfram, Charles W. "The Antibiotics Class Actions." *American Bar Foundation Research Journal,* 1976, no. 1: 253–363 (1976).

Wood, H. C. "Nostrums." *Journal of the American Medical Association,* 32: 908–911 (April 29, 1899).

Worthington, Nancy L. "National Health Expenditures, 1929–1974." *Social Security Bulletin,* 38, no. 2: 3–20 (February 1975).

Young, James H. *The Toadstool Millionaires: A Social History of Patent Medicines in America before Federal Regulation.* Princeton: Princeton University Press, 1961.

———. *The Medical Messiahs.* Princeton: Princeton University Press, 1967.

Statutes Cited

Agricultural Department Appropriations, 34 Stat. 669 (1906).

Appropriations for Sundry Civil Expenses, 31 Stat. 1133 (1901).

Controlled Substances Act; 84 Stat. 1242 (1970).

Drug Amendments of 1962, 76 Stat. 780 (1962).

Federal Food, Drug, and Cosmetic Act, 52 Stat. 1040 (1938).

Federal Food, Drug, and Cosmetic Act, Humphrey-Durham Amendment, 65 Stat. 648 (1951).

Federal Food, Drug, and Cosmetic Act, Miller Amendment, 62 Stat. 582 (1948).

Federal Trade Commission Act, Wheeler-Lea Amendment, 52 Stat. 111 (1938).

Harrison Anti-Narcotics Law, 38 Stat. 785 (1914).

Pure Food Act, 34 Stat. 768 (1906).

Pure Food Act, Sherley Amendment, 37 Stat. 416 (1912).

Title 35, U.S. Code: Patents, 66 Stat. 792 (1952).

Court Cases Cited

Alpha v. *Mathews,* 530 F.2d 1054 (1976).

American School of Magnetic Healing v. *McAnnulty,* 187 U.S. 94 (1902).

Ciba Corporation v. *Weinberger,* 412 U.S. 640 (1973).

Dent v. *West Virginia,* 129 U.S. 114 (1888).

Federal Trade Commission v. *Raladam Co.,* 283 U.S. 643 (1931).

Hoffman–La Roche v. *Califano,* Civil no. 78–0467, U.S. District Court for the District of Columbia (pending).

Upjohn Co. v. *Finch,* 422 F.2d 944 (1970).

U.S. v. *Charles Pfizer and Co. et al.,* 426 F.2d 32 (1970).

U.S. v. *Johnson,* 221 U.S. 488 (1911).

U.S. v. *Storer Broadcasting Co.,* 351 U.S. 192 (1956).

U.S. v. *Sullivan,* 332 U.S. 689 (1948).

USV Phamaceuticals Corp. v. *Weinberger,* 412 U.S. 655 (1973).

Weinberger v. *Bentex Pharmaceuticals et al.,* 412 U.S. 695 (1973).

Weinberger v. *Hynson, Wescott and Dunning,* 412 U.S. 609 (1973).

Index